GENDER RITUALS

GENDER RITUALS

Female Initiation in Melanesia

Edited by
Nancy C. Lutkehaus
and
Paul B. Roscoe

Routledge
New York and London

Published in 1995 by
Routledge
29 West 35th Street
New York, NY 10001

Published in Great Britain by
Routledge
11 New Fetter Lane
London EC4P 4EE

Copyright © 1995 by Routledge

Printed in the United States of America on acid-free paper.

Library of Congress Cataloging-in-Publication Data

Gender rituals : female initiation in Melanesia / edited by Nancy C. Lutkehaus &
   Paul B. Roscoe.
     p. cm.
   Includes bibliographical references and index.
   ISBN 0-415-91106-0 (cl.) — ISBN 0-415-91107-9 (pbk.)
    1. Initiation rites—Melanesia.   2. Puberty rites—Papua New Guinea.
  3. Women—Papua New Guinea—Rites and ceremonies.   4. Women—Papua
New Guinea—Social conditions.   I. Lutkehaus, Nancy C.   II. Roscoe, Paul B.
GN671.N5G46   1995
392'.14—dc20   94-39869
                                             CIP

CONTENTS

PART I

INTRODUCTION

PART II

DEFINING WOMEN:
GENDER IMAGES IN FEMALE INITIATION RITES

PART III

ACHIEVING WOMANHOOD:
THE LIFE CYCLE AS CULTURAL PERFORMANCE

ILLUSTRATIONS AND TABLES

PLATES

FIGURES

MAPS

TABLES

Acknowledgments

The idea for this book was first broached, a long time ago, in the car park of the Ark Royal pub in Wells-next-Sea, England. Since then it has evolved through informal sessions at the 1985 and 1986 annual meetings of the Association for Social Anthropology in Oceania, a working session at the 1987 meetings, and a formal symposium in 1988.

In the course of this protracted history, we have incurred many debts. We should like to acknowledge those who contributed to our various ASAO sessions, in particular scholars who presented papers that do not appear in this volume: John Barker, Terence Hays, Janet Hoskins, Marilyn Strathern, Anne Marie Tietjen, Valerio Valeri, and Margaret Williamson. We are also deeply indebted to Terence Hays for acting as discussant at the 1987 session and for his subsequent assistance; and to Paula Brown and Gilbert Herdt for serving as codiscussants to the 1988 symposium.

We thank Priscilla Benoit for her work in transferring the collection to computer disk, Steve Bicknell for assistance with the artwork, and Susan Coopersmith for proofing help.

We are much obliged to the University of Wisconsin Press, Madison, Wisconsin, for permission to reprint chapter 6 in shortened form from Thomas Maschio's book, *To Remember the Faces of the Dead* (1994).

Finally, much appreciation is due Marlie Wasserman, originally of Rutgers University Press, now of Routledge, who first encouraged us to publish this collection and, with the good humor and forbearance of a saint, subsequently shepherded it to completion.

CONTRIBUTORS

KATHLEEN BARLOW is an Assistant Professor of Anthropology at the University of Minnesota. She specializes in psychological anthropology and the anthropology of gender and has conducted fieldwork among the Murik of Papua New Guinea. She is cocurator of "Canoe and Basket: Plural Voices and Potential Meanings in Murik Art" at the Fowler Museum of Cultural History, University of California, Los Angeles.

DEANE FERGIE is Lecturer in Anthropology at the University of Adelaide. She has conducted field research among the Mekeo and (pseudonymous) Babae of Papua New Guinea and in the Marree-Birdsville Track District of Australia. Her book, *Australian Interiors: Exploring the Outback as Cultural Terrain*, is due out soon.

BRIGITTA HAUSER-SCHÄUBLIN is Professor of Anthropology at the University of Göttingen. She specializes in gender studies and the anthropology of space, and has conducted extensive fieldwork in Bali and among the Abelam and Iatmul of Papua New Guinea. She is author of *Frauen in Kararau* (Ethnologisches Seminar der Universität und Museum für Völkerkunde, Basel, 1977) and of *Kulthäuser in Nordneuguinea* (Akademie Verlag, Berlin, 1989).

NANCY C. LUTKEHAUS is Associate Professor of Anthropology at the University of Southern California, where she is affiliated with the Program for the Study of Women and Men in Society. She conducted fieldwork among the Manam and Enga of Papua New Guinea and has recently completed a book about Manam Island society and the ethnography of the British anthropologist, Camilla Wedgwood.

THOMAS MASCHIO is an independent scholar who lives and works in New York City. He carried out nineteen months of fieldwork with the Rauto of Papua New Guinea and is author of *To Remember the Faces of the Dead: The Plenitude of Memory in Southwestern New Britain* (University of Wisconsin Press, 1994).

x

PAUL B. ROSCOE is Associate Professor of Anthropology at the University of Maine. He has conducted twenty-five months of fieldwork among the Yangoru Boiken of Papua New Guinea. His publications have appeared in *American Anthropologist, American Ethnologist, Current Anthropology, Journal of the Royal Anthropological Institute,* and *Man.*

LORRAINE SEXTON is employed with Medical Marketing Group of Blue Bell, Pennsylvania. She conducted fieldwork among the Daulo people of Papua New Guinea and is author of *Mothers of Money, Daughters of Coffee: The Wok Meri Movement* (UMI Research Press, 1986).

PATRICIA K. TOWNSEND is Faculty Associate at the University of Buffalo and is currently working with refugees from several countries resettled in western New York. She conducted research among the Saniyo-Hiyowe of Papua New Guinea. Her textbook, *Medical Anthropology,* co-authored with Ann McElroy, is widely used.

PREFACE

From Alice Walker and Pratibha Parmar's film, *Warrior Marks* (see also Walker and Parmar 1993) to the pages of *Ms. Magazine,* female initiation has been much in the news lately, a consequence of the attention Western feminists have attracted to the issue of "female genital mutilation." As part of ritual procedures embedded in cultural notions about cleanliness, pollution, and what it is to be a woman, girls in many parts of Africa, the Middle East, and Southeast Asia undergo clitoridectomy, labial excision, and/or vaginal infibulation. These practices have been widely condemned in the West, especially by feminists. Their prohibition was discussed at the UN's Cairo population conference, and there are movements to have the practice added to the UN's codifications of human-rights abuses.

Female genital "mutilation" presents anthropologists with an ethical dilemma. On the one hand, the practice is abhorrent to the Western tradition from which our discipline has sprung. On the other, anthropology's pretensions to cultural relativity and its frequent assertion of the moral equality of cultural orders dispose it to defend non-Western traditions from Western ethnocentrism. In the name of the Lord or public health and order, missionaries and colonial authorities roundly condemned and attempted to prohibit as offensive to Western mores practices like infanticide, subincision, clitoridectomy, and cicatrization, but traditionally the anthropologist turned a culturally blind eye. In a context in which a long-neglected sensitivity to women is now urged, however, female genital "mutilation" presents the dilemma of trying to support the rights of women while showing respect for those females who continue to find their dignity through traditions of initiation (see Gordon 1991 and accompanying dialogues).

Perhaps one of the few uncontroversial issues in this controversial area is that anthropologists have generally failed to satisfy the public's interest in the matter. It is not just that, with few exceptions (e.g., Boddy 1982, 1989; Talle 1993), we have failed to provide grounded studies of female circumcision, clitoridectomy, and infibulation in their cultural and normative contexts; we have also signally failed to examine female initiation as a whole.

Thirty years ago, Brown (1963:837) characterized Richards's (1956) monograph on Bemba female initiation as still "the most complete and detailed description of a girl's initiation ceremony." The sad fact, as La Fontaine (1985:162) has noted, is that the observation remains as true today as it was then. When attention is paid to female initiation, moreover, that attention is all too often an analytical afterthought—as though female initiation were merely an appendage to, or imitation of, male initiation.

This neglect is perplexing. La Fontaine (1985:162) attributes it to the relative rarity of female initiation, but this assertion can be sustained only by accepting her stricture that initiation is a rite involving *groups* of initiands: male initiation then occurs in around 30 percent of societies compared to only about 10 percent for female initiation (Cohen 1964:71–99; Schlegel and Barry 1979:201). If, as in other definitions, this restriction is relaxed to include rites focused on individuals, a different picture emerges. Hays's (n.d.:10–11) survey of cross-cultural initiation studies indicates that around 50 to 60 percent of societies then emerge as initiating females compared to just 30 to 40 percent for males (see also Brown 1963:845–847; Frayser 1985:482–483; Paige and Paige 1981:286–288; Schlegel and Barry 1980:698; Whyte 1978:86; Young 1965:14).

Some scholars (e.g., Bettelheim 1962[1954]:145; Schlegel and Barry 1980:698) have argued that because male initiation typically involves many more participants than female initiation, it has been more visible to ethnographic attention. Certainly, initiation rites for females are generally smaller in scale than those for males: Schlegel and Barry (1979:201) found them almost twice as likely to be small-scale affairs, focused on an individual, than more elaborate affairs centered on a group. But what female initiation lacks in scale it makes up for in frequency. Because they focus more often on individuals than groups, female initiations necessarily occur more frequently than male initiations. Consequently, ethnographers have to be lucky if they want to observe group-centered male initiations, which take place only every few years, but they are unlikely to miss individual-centered female initiations, which take place several times a year.

Scale may explain the ethnographic attention afforded male initiation but probably not because of the visibility it confers. Rather, ethnographers may have taken scale to index *importance,* as did structural functionalists, who attributed analytical significance to large-scale, group-based ritual rather than small-scale, individual rites. Interpretivists may have fallen into the same trap, assuming scale signifies *indigenous* perceptions of significance— an assumption that may be valid for some communities but, as the chapters in this volume demonstrate, cannot be assumed a priori for all. Given the

dynamics of academia, large-scale ritual may also have attracted more analytical attention because of the publication-generating possibilities and
resources it provides.

As has often been observed (Bettelheim 1962[1954]:145; Frayser
1985:137; Jacobs 1989:76), the historical preponderance of male ethnographers is surely a further, persuasive reason for the imbalance of attention to
male rather than female initiation. Under the sway of male-oriented, Euro-
centric prejudices, many ethnographers may have presumed that indigenes
see male rather than female ritual knowledge as the more important to life
and welfare, or that male rather than female ritual affairs are more central
to understanding sociopolitical structure and organization (e.g., Elkin
1964[1938]:189–194). Those male ethnographers who do research female-
centered institutions also encounter significant pragmatic difficulties which,
though they can be used too glibly to excuse the neglect of female realms
(Gregory 1984; Weiner 1976:12), are real nonetheless and help explain our
threadbare information on female gender rituals.

Whatever the cause of anthropology's neglect of female initiation, these
rites clearly warrant much greater attention. Toward redress, this volume
draws together detailed descriptions and analyses of female initiation in
eight communities in the Pacific nation of Papua New Guinea (Map 1.1).[1]
Located in the Western Pacific region often referred to as Melanesia,[2]
carved by colonial rule from the eastern half of the great island of New
Guinea, Papua New Guinea's population numbers only 3.5 million, less
than one-tenth of 1 percent of current global population. Nonetheless, its
people speak a staggering 600 to 800 languages, approaching a quarter of the
world's total. Cultures are equally dense and diverse. Subsistence modes
range from hunting and gathering, through fishing and horticulture, to
intensive agriculture. Social forms run the gamut from small-scale, semino-
madic, egalitarian kin groupings, through sedentary, big-men communities,
to hierarchically structured chiefdoms. Ritual and artistic production ranges
from the humble to the flamboyant, from the unelaborated to an exaggera-
tion that sometimes seems to border on self-parody.

Rites of initiation are among the most common and prominent of these
symbolic productions, occurring in communities of all sizes, subsistence
bases, and social types. If anything, female initiation is even more prevalent
here than elsewhere in the world: Hays's (n.d.:14) inspection of three cross-
cultural surveys finds some form of female initiation rite practiced in 83
percent of New Guinean societies. Yet here, too, if we are to judge from
publications devoted primarily or exclusively to initiation, anthropological
attention has focused overwhelmingly on male rather than female rites.

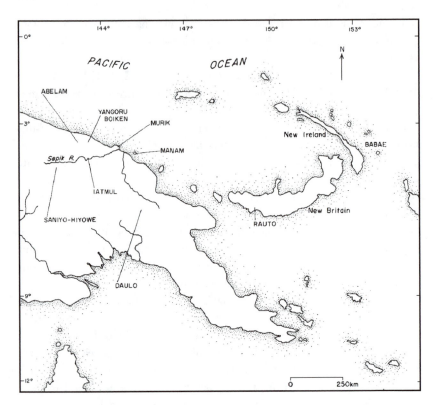

MAP I . I   Papua New Guinea.

Whereas literally scores of such publications have focused on male initiation, we have discovered only a handful devoted to female initiation (Camp 1979; Nilles 1939; Ross 1965; Wedgwood 1933; Whiteman 1965), three of them on the same group—Chimbu—and all but Wedgwood's by nonanthropologists. In a few further instances, female initiation has been afforded significant analytical attention alongside its male counterpart (Godelier 1986:chapter 3; Hays and Hays 1982; Vorman 1915).

However modest its other intentions, this volume greatly expands the anthropological literature on female initiation in Papua New Guinea. Following Nancy Lutkehaus's introduction, Brigitta Hauser-Schäublin and Paul Roscoe examine the sociocultural ramifications of gender images in female initiation. Comparing the Ndu-speaking Abelam and Iatmul of the Sepik Basin, Hauser-Schäublin argues that the existence of puberty rites among the horticultural Abelam and their absence among the riverine Iatmul is related to the existence among the Abelam of perceptions that the physiological reproductive powers of women are paralleled by male procreative powers centered on the long-yam cult. Adding the Ndu-speaking Yangoru Boiken to the Abelam/Iatmul comparison, Roscoe argues that initiation in these societies focuses on the politico-ritual empowerment of individuals, and that variations in the elaboration of female initiation and of the articulation of female with male initiation are a consequence of variations in the degree to which women are perceived as integral to the formal politico-ritual life of the community.

The chapters by Kathleen Barlow, Deane Fergie, and Thomas Maschio show how female initiation rites are related to cultural conceptions of the person, and how the performance of these rites acts as a part of the process of achieving full personhood. Analyzing female cult-initiation rites among the Murik of the Sepik delta, Barlow shows how key metaphors are deployed to express women's potential to achieve influence and prestige and shape actions that reproduce Murik society. From an analysis of the pseudonymous Babae of Island Melanesia, Fergie makes a crucial point, echoed by several other contributors, that our understanding of initiation is impoverished if we fail to attend to the wider corpus of ritual in which it is embedded. On Babae, the rituals of this broader corpus are not only rites of passage in themselves, they are also integrated into a total corpus that constitutes life as itself a rite of passage essential to the reproduction of the Babae cosmos. In his contribution, Maschio notes a common tendency to interpret Melanesian male and female initiation rites as means through which men invoke ideas that advance their social control of women and youths. Among the Rauto of New Britain, however, we become aware that the rites women perform to mark menarche are means by which they—as opposed to men—become creators and elaborators of their culture's worldview and "disseminators" of aspects of its moral tone, as well as its aesthetic style and mood.

Patricia Townsend, Nancy Lutkehaus, and Lorraine Sexton focus on how the female body, as the locus of puberty and other life-cycle rites, functions as a metaphor for aspects of the social body. Townsend describes how, among the Saniyo-Hiyowe of the Sepik, menarche is a ritual occasion when relationships centered on the person of a young woman are "opened up" in preparation for her marriage. When she is widowed, these relationships are "closed up" again in a series of observances that deconstruct the marriageable woman constructed at puberty. Using her own field data and notes made by Wedgwood fifty years ago, Lutkehaus argues that the menarche rites practiced on the Schouten island of Manam are concerned not solely with the expression and perpetuation of dominance in this "chiefdom" society, as Allen (1967) contended, but also with the use of menstruation, human reproduction, and growth to control fertility and social reproduction. Like Townsend and several other contributors, Sexton finds that menarche rites among the Daulo of the Eastern Highlands are part of a ritual sequence that transforms a girl into a married woman. Recently, these rites have become a leitmotif in initiation into women's *wok-meri* savings associations, a rite that recapitulates the female life cycle, thereby calling attention to the importance of women in physical and social reproduction.

Notwithstanding our best efforts to diversify the volume's ethnographic coverage, a glance at Map 1.1 reveals limitations that tend to reflect areal variations in contemporary New Guinean ritual production. The Sepik and Island Melanesia, long recognized as areas of elaborate art and ritual, are well represented in contrast to areas like the Highlands, which have often been characterized as lacking a developed artistic tradition and having a more "pragmatic" than "spiritual" outlook on the cosmos (e.g., Lawrence and Meggitt 1965; Newton 1972). The common problem we encountered was that ethnographers from other areas felt unable to contribute because they had gathered only limited data on female initiation, the communities in which they had lived had no such rites, or the rites had long ago disappeared.

Although an important impetus for this project was ethnographic, casting the analytical spotlight directly on female initiation also helps illuminate gender and feminist issues and comparative anthropology. Just as the analyses in this collection have been influenced by feminist theory, so, Lutkehaus argues in her introduction, the study of gender in Melanesia in general, and in female initiation in particular, has much to offer feminist scholarship and the anthropology of gender. In his conclusion, Roscoe notes that theories of initiation have been shaped not only by attention to male rather than female rites but also, to a degree exceeded by few other human institutions, by comparative analysis. He explores the implications, for the study and theory of initiation, of shifting the focus of attention to female initiation.

NOTES

1. The fact that this volume does not include a broader variety of female initiation cases from other parts of the Pacific is a result of happenstance and does not reflect the ethnographic distribution of female rites in the Pacific generally or Melanesia in particular. The case studies we present represent the response we received to several solicitations of participants through the channels of the Association for Social Anthropology in Oceania.

2. Despite the contested status of the term "Melanesia" as misleading and anachronistic (Terrell 1986, Thomas 1989), we use it to refer to the area that includes present-day Irian Jaya, Papua New Guinea, Vanuatu, the Solomon Islands, New Caledonia, and Fiji. We have done so, moreover, despite the volume's concentration on Papua New Guinea because the general reading public is often more familiar with the region traditionally known as Melanesia than with the contemporary nation-state of Papua New Guinea. Many of the statements made about female initiation in Papua New Guinea, and its relationship to male initiation, appear to apply to other Melanesian societies as well. For references to male and female rites in some of these societies, see Allen (1967); van Baal (1966); Deacon (1925, 1934); Jolly (1991); Layard (1942); and Rodman (1981).

Part I

INTRODUCTION

1

FEMINIST ANTHROPOLOGY AND FEMALE INITIATION IN MELANESIA

Nancy C. Lutkehaus

One of the primary insights to emerge from the anthropological study of initiation in Papua New Guinea, and Melanesia in general, over the past decade or so has been an awareness of the complex, multidimensional nature of these rites (e.g. Keesing 1982; Strathern 1988; Whitehead 1986), and the comprehension that a single initiatory rite or set of rites may "do" several things at once (see Roscoe's conclusion to this volume).[1] As a result, the analysis of initiation in Melanesia has yielded new insights into the multidimensional relationships among the individual, gender identity, life-cycle rituals, and other aspects of society.

Several intellectual forces have contributed to this understanding, but none has had a stronger impact recently than the development of a feminist anthropology.[2] With the wave of feminist activism that developed in the United States and Europe during the 1960s and 1970s, gender began to be recognized as a fundamental element in individual and group identity. At the same time, the study of gender in Melanesia, often elaborated within the context of the analysis of initiation, has influenced the feminist study of gender.

From the beginning there was an affinity between anthropology and feminist scholarship because of their interest in similar issues. Both feminist scholars and feminist anthropologists sought to place women at the center of their analyses (Hermann and Stewart 1994). Prominent among the issues they addressed were the origins of sexual inequality and the question of whether male dominance was a human universal.[3] Feminists looked to anthropology for explanations of sexism and its origins and for alternative models of male-female relations. Feminism's initial influence was on the anthropological study of "sex roles" and the "status" of women. This led to cross-cultural analyses of male-female relations, of women's social positions vis-à-vis men's, and of variation in culturally appropriate masculine and feminine behavior (Reiter 1975a; Rubin 1975).

A corollary project was to restore women's voices by focusing on their behavior and statements. But, as important as this "additive" approach has been in placing women as the central focus of research, this was not the primary contribution of feminist studies to anthropology, or vice versa. Lurking within the enterprise of feminist scholarship has always been the feminist political goal of social change (Collier and Yanagisako 1987; Harding 1987; Ortner 1974).

Feminist anthropologists also contributed to the development of our understanding of gender as a culturally and historically specific category (MacCormack and Strathern 1980; Ortner 1974; Ortner and Whitehead 1981). The concept of the cultural construction of gender has opened new ways of thinking about the broad functions of the categories *male, female,* and *reproduction* in different societies. Post-1970s developments by anthropologists interested in the study of male initiation in Melanesia reflected the influence of feminist theory and practice within anthropology. Symbolically oriented studies of male initiation expanded their focus to include the affective and cognitive effects of initiation rituals on individual male identity and behavior (Herdt 1981). Not surprisingly, these and other studies of male initiation have revealed that initiation rituals constitute a powerful locus for the reproduction of cultural beliefs and practices concerned with gender roles and sexuality (Godelier 1986; Herdt 1982a, 1982b, 1989; Schmid and Kocher-Schmid 1992), while gradually the notion of the cultural construction of gender has been extended to include male (Herdt 1984) and female (Herdt and Stoller 1990) sexuality as well.

Moreover, developments in feminist theory—especially in the realm of kinship and gender (Collier and Rosaldo 1981; Collier and Yanagisako 1987, 1989)—have led to a new understanding of the broader articulation of initiation rites with other aspects of society such as economic and political organization (Lindenbaum 1987; Strathern 1988; Whitehead 1986, 1987). What is surprising is that so few of these insights have been applied to the analysis of female initiation, in Melanesia or elsewhere. To a great extent, this is due to the narrow definition of initiation as pertaining to groups rather than individuals and the less elaborate nature of female puberty ceremonies compared to large-scale male initiation rites (see Roscoe's conclusion to this volume). The tendency to see female rites as pale imitations of male initiation rites has also meant a failure to seriously consider female rites on their own terms. Ironically, the emphasis that has been placed on the study of male initiation in Papua New Guinea has obscured important insights to be gained from the study of female initiation.

Feminist scholarship has also given impetus to a new anthropological focus on women's bodies and reproductive experiences as sources of power as well as subordination. Significantly, ethnographic studies from New Guinea are singled out as providing cases in which "nurturance and reproduction are broadly defined and a high value is placed on the roles of both men and women in 'growing up' the next generation" (Ginsburg and Rapp 1991:328). Although these studies have brought to scholarly attention cultural notions of male fertility, menstruating men, and paternal nurture, it is ironic that *female* initiation in Papua New Guinea and its relationship to broader notions of cultural reproduction has yet to receive the same critical attention. The papers in this volume directly address different aspects of this relationship.

A discussion of the relevance of feminist theory for the study of female initiation in Melanesia, or the significance of the chapters in this volume to the study of gender, must first consider briefly the history of the dialectical relationship between anthropological sex-and-gender study in Melanesia, and feminist scholarship and anthropology. As the following discussion attempts to show, there are at least five areas in which Melanesian ethnography has had an impact on feminist scholarship and the anthropological study of gender. These include the cultural construction of human sexuality, fertility and reproduction, personhood, and the relationship between personhood and gender identity.

As the essays in this volume show, to varying degrees all five of these concepts represent important idioms in female initiation and puberty rituals. Taken as a whole, these interrelated notions have challenged the Eurocentrism of the analytic categories feminists initially used in their analyses of gender.

THE STUDY OF GENDER IN MELANESIA AND FEMINIST ANTHROPOLOGY

Since the early twentieth century, when Malinowski published *Sex and Repression in Savage Society* (1927) and *The Sexual Life of Savages* (1929), anthropologists working in Melanesia have focused on aspects of male-female relations and sexuality.[4] However, as Marilyn Strathern (1987a:11) has pointed out, Malinowski's study of the sexual life of the Trobriand Islanders was not about gender in the modern sense of the term. Rather, "attention was paid to relations between the sexes invariably as an adjunct of institutional life. The early ethnographers (such as Rivers, Layard, Wedgwood, Fortune) were concerned with the formal properties of marriage systems, with cult activity or with domestic and familial relations. . . . But what was meant by 'male' and 'female' was largely unproblematic." Thus, for example, Camilla Wedgwood's (1937) research about Manam Island women had more to do with the study of sex roles and the "status" of women in Manam society than with the meaning of what masculinity and femininity meant to the Manam (Lutkehaus 1982, 1995).

These structural-functionalist studies tended to describe social systems as dichotomies composed of a "public" versus a "private" or "domestic" sphere of activities. Concomitantly, the development of kinship theory was predicated on a similar analytic distinction between the politico-jural domain and the domestic (Fortes 1969). Moreover, the distinction between public and domestic spheres seemed to correlate with male dominance over women and male solidarity as the main principle of social integration. Male initiation and male cults were thought to reproduce and perpetuate these status differences between the sexes (Langness 1967). Accordingly, the discussion of women's roles was relegated to chapters on kinship, marriage, and the family.

Although early feminist anthropologists also sought to explain women's subordinate status in terms of their relegation to the domestic sphere (Rosaldo 1974), later work amended this argument by demonstrating the complexity of women's activities and status, vis-à-vis men, in their multiple roles as wives, sisters, and mothers (Sacks 1979; Rosaldo 1980).

Feminist scholars have also criticized the structural-functionalist perspective as biased for evaluating men's activities as consummately social—concerned with the collectivity and social integration—and women's as inherently domestic—fulfilling biological rather than social needs (Collier and Yanagisako 1989; Edholm, et al. 1977; Ginsburg and Rapp 1991). They have questioned the main premises of kinship theory by challenging the distinction between the politico-jural and domestic domains, and thus the validity of politico-jural relations as the basis of male authority. As a result, they have demonstrated that it is impossible to understand interaction within "domestic" spheres without simultaneously understanding the organization of the political and economic relations that provide goals and resources for both sexes. Ultimately, through their demonstration of the interpenetration of the two domains, they have established that the distinction between gender and kinship as two separate analytic domains is irrelevant (Collier and Yanagisako 1987, 1989).

In a similar vein, a feminist perspective has led anthropologists to criticize the focus in Melanesian anthropology on public collective life, with its predominantly male participants and its disregard for the manner in which women promote their own interests (Feil 1978; Lederman 1986). This has led to a simplistic model of men and women as separate and opposed interest groups, each with their own visions of society (McDowell 1984; Strathern 1984, 1987a). They have also criticized a male bias among anthropologists who ignore the complexity of women's roles in Melanesian societies. Faithorn (1976) points out the significance of factors other than gender, such as age and social context, in the determination of women's roles. She also notes the importance of the social distinction between women as sisters and women as wives in determining their relationships with men (see also Ortner 1981; Shore 1981). Implicit in her observations is the notion that women cannot be studied in isolation from men (Brown and Buchbinder 1976).

As the essays in this collection demonstrate, there are important implications in these premises for the study of rites of passage in general and initiation rituals in particular. First of all, they challenge the distinction some anthropologists make between collective male initiation ceremonies and individual female puberty rites (Allen 1967; La Fontaine 1985), a distinction that replicates the Durkheimian division between the sacred (social/group) domain and the profane (biological/individual) (see Roscoe's conclusion). This distinction perpetuates the bias toward collective activities being considered of greater significance to society than events that focus on only one individual at a time. Not only does this tendency disregard the fact that individual rites can be used metonymically to refer to groups and social processes and that the organization and performance of individual rites can have wider significance for a social whole; it also overlooks the relationship of these individual rites to other life-cycle rituals, either male or female (cf. Barlow, Fergie, Roscoe, Townsend, this volume), or to large-scale collective rituals (cf. Hauser-Schäublin, Lutkehaus, this volume). As Maschio and Barlow demonstrate, the male:public realm and female:domestic realm dichotomy simply does not hold. Different phases of the Rauto female puberty rites celebrate a woman's role within the domestic realm and her political and economic role within the public realm. Not only do Rauto women participate in both realms, but their participation in them is inextricably interconnected. Among the Murik, a woman's initiation into the female *sambaan* cult heralds her growing authority among her kinsmen and kinswomen to organize important exchange activities on behalf of her descent group as a whole.

THE CULTURAL CONSTRUCTION
OF GENDER AND SEXUALITY

The concept of gender, as distinct from the biological notion of sex, became prevalent only relatively recently within feminist discourse, and even later within general academic discourse. Feminist anthropologists did not take the categories, *male* and *female*, at face value, as biological givens, but regarded their definitions both as cultural constructions and, therefore, as part of the power positioning of the sexes in relation to each other. Following Ortner's (1974) and Ortner and Whitehead's (1981) lead, feminist anthropologists now understand gender, sexuality, and reproduction to be culturally and historically specific notions invested with meaning by particular societies.

Margaret Mead's description of the plasticity and cultural variation in normative male and female behavior elaborated in *Sex and Temperament in Three Primitive Societies* (1935) is one of the earliest—if not *the* earliest—ethnographic contribution to the feminist notion of the cultural construction of gender. This comparative study of men's and women's behavior in three Papua New Guinea societies challenged the then prevalent orthodoxy of Western science and society concerning the innate nature of male and female behavior.[5] More recently, feminist scholars, male as well as female, have begun to analyze the cultural construction of masculinity in Melanesia (Herdt 1981, 1987) and other non-Western and Western societies, as well as the existence in some societies of a cultural role for a third gender.[6] Despite Mead's prescience, her studies were constrained by her interest in social norms and their impact on gender stereotypes and behavior, and were flawed by her ethnocentric notions of the *person* (Gewertz 1984; Errington and Gewertz 1987).

Ironically, despite the presence of the term *sex* in the titles of their work, Malinowski's and Mead's early studies of men and women did not deal primarily with sex per se, much less with what has come to be considered the cultural construction of sexuality (Caplan 1987; Snitow, et al. 1983; Vance 1984). Largely due to the personal nature of the information and, thus, the "micropolitics" of obtaining such data, the anthropological study of sexuality (or, at least, its publication) has lagged behind the study of the cultural construction of gender. Early on, feminist scholars were aware of the power relations inherent in the collection of information about women and gender and the biases such power relationships might have on the nature of the questions a researcher asks and the responses she/he receives (Harding 1987; Harding and Hintikka 1983).[7]

Herdt's groundbreaking study (1981) of male sexuality and Sambia male initiation, as well as studies of ritualized homosexuality in New Guinea in general (Herdt 1984), are major contributions to our understanding of the impact of culture on the development and malleability of sexual behavior. Lindenbaum's (1984:338) observation of the absence of parallel data on female homosexuality remains true about information on female sexuality in general. Barlow (this volume) provides an antidote through her interviews with Murik women concerning female sexuality in the context of male and female initiation. Interestingly, however, she points out that it was only upon her subsequent return to the Murik, after having given birth herself, that women told her about the secret sexual aspects of the cult.

Barlow's Murik data also remind us that the same culture may have various, even contradictory, concepts of femininity, each associated with different female roles and social contexts. Prominent among these are the contrast between women as mothers (nurturers/givers) versus women as sexual beings (dangerous and powerful/takers). Female initiation may deal primarily with one or the other of these dimensions of femininity, or some combination thereof. Thus, female sexuality is the dominant metaphor in the Murik female initiation cult, while maternal nurturance is the main trope in the Daulo women's wok-meri movement (Sexton, this volume). Most frequently, however, female sexuality and reproduction are celebrated as two interrelated dimensions of female fertility and power. As such, they provide major themes in female initiation ceremonies. For example, while the Babae *vevene* sequence (Fergie, this volume) ostensibly celebrates female procreation—it is held in honor of a primipara—the budding sexuality of adolescent girls is a secondary focus. And while the Rauto acknowledge that sexuality can have both positive and negative value, in the context of the female initiation, the positive qualities of a girl's incipient sexuality are celebrated through the symbol of the areca nut (Maschio, this volume).

Although sexual symbolism was understood initially to refer literally to men and women or male-female relations, gradually we have come to understand its function as ideology and metaphor (Ortner and Whitehead 1981; Strathern 1978, 1988). Thus, as useful as the notions of the cultural construction of gender and sexuality have been for feminist scholarship, Marilyn Strathern (1988) argues that they are insufficient for the analysis of the pervasive "genderization" of the social and material world that we find in Melanesia and other societies. Once the meaning of these categories is questioned, one realizes that the meanings of other social categories must be questioned as well. The analysis of gender and sexual symbolism involves relating these symbols to other cultural symbols and meanings and to other aspects of social life and experience. Thus, Barlow (1988) tells us that the Murik consider the domestic house not only to be a woman, but to be a mother; whoever comes inside the dwelling must be fed, for all women are associated with maternal nurturance and generosity. As several of the chapters in this volume demonstrate, the notion of power itself is conceived of in gendered forms. In cultures such as the Rauto, initiation rites become the venue in which women are seen to have the capacity to express or manifest both "masculine" and "feminine" forms of power while, among the Daulo, women have created an indigenous discourse that represents women's new economic autonomy from men with metaphors of marriage and female procreation.

Increasingly, anthropologists working in non-Western societies and other historical periods have shown us that we need to stop thinking about gender as simply a question of the relations between male and female (Comaroff 1985; Stoler 1989). More broadly construed, gender as metaphor contains the notion that relations between the sexes and notions of gender difference are images that express ideas about other aspects of culture, about life-forces or general values, relationships of power and authority between individuals and groups, or the creation and maintenance of racial and/or national boundaries and identities (Jolly and Macintyre 1989; MacCormack and Strathern 1980; Ortner 1974; Stoler 1991; Strathern 1987a; Weiner 1980). Thus, although female initiation deals at the level of the individual with the cultural construction of femininity, at another level these rites may be symbolic of the reproduction of society as a whole. They may also express not just cultural notions of femininity, but, more fundamentally, what it means to be human.

SEX ANTAGONISM VERSUS
GENDER COMPLEMENTARITY

Impressed by the rigid segregation between the sexes in sleeping arrangements, eating, and daily activities, post–World War II male ethnographers working in the Papua New Guinea highlands characterized male-female relations as "antagonistic" (Langness 1967; Meggitt 1964; Read 1952). They also considered the purpose of male initiation to be the separation of boys from their mothers and the development of male solidarity in opposition to women (Langness 1974). More recently, the limits of the notion of "sex antagonism" have been demonstrated, in terms of understanding both the tenor of relations between men and women in Melanesia, and the cultural logics that underlie concepts of gender (Herdt and Poole 1982; Strathern 1988). Due largely to the impact of feminist scholarship, anthropologists have become aware of issues such as gender as metaphor (Meigs 1976; Strathern 1978) and the study of power and hierarchy in relationship to gender (Josephides 1985; Kelly 1993; Lepowsky 1993; Strathern 1987a,

1988), and generally have rethought women's roles in Melanesian societies (Brown and Buchbinder 1976; O'Brien and Tiffany 1984).

The essays in this volume demonstrate that the relationship between the sexes in Papua New Guinea is more complex than the notion of sex antagonism allows. As Fergie points out for the Babae, in many lowland and island societies in particular the ritualized "antagonism" between the sexes expressed in certain ceremonies is counterbalanced by the concept of sexual complementarity as necessary to the reproduction of individuals and the cosmos. Roscoe, too, stresses the symbolic and sociological interarticulation of men and women among the Yangoru Boiken. As Yangoru big men readily admit, their own political success depends critically on the activities of their wives. Similarly, Barlow argues that although Murik conceptions of male and female emphasize the differences between the sexes, they are seen as complementary rather than oppositional, and both are viewed as essential to the continuity of the social whole. Hauser-Schäublin argues that both the Abelam male yam cult and female initiation rites celebrate the respective procreative powers of men and women, their mutual dependency, and the exchange between them of male and female powers and products necessary to the physical and cosmological reproduction of Abelam society (see also Losche 1982). On the other hand, Rauto female initiation celebrates women's access to both "male" and "female" forms of power.

A consideration of the range of life-cycle rituals a society celebrates for both males and females, along with a comparison of the similarities, differences, and complementarities among these gender-specific rites, reveals broader, sometimes contradictory, cultural conceptions, as well as interrelationships, between men and women in Melanesian societies. In both Rauto and Abelam female ceremonies women take possession of the men's ceremonial house or grounds for the duration of their rites, a symbolic statement that their ritual activities deserve as important and as central a stage as the ritual activities of men.

Far from denying the existence of sexual antagonism, we suggest that the range of variation among and within individual Melanesian societies is far more complex than the notion of "sex antagonism" implies (Lutkehaus 1982). Moreover, in many Papua New Guinean societies, especially in the Sepik region (Lutkehaus and Roscoe 1987), the underlying ideology seems to be one of complementarity between the sexes, the necessity of sexual difference, and the combination of both "male" and "female" powers for the successful reproduction not only of individuals, but of whole societies and cosmologies.

SOCIALIZATION, CHILD DEVELOPMENT, AND INITIATION RITES

Anthropological research in the Pacific, and in Papua New Guinea in particular, has been the catalyst for some of the earliest cross-cultural work on childhood, child development, and socialization. Thus Malinowski (1927, 1929) sought to challenge some of Freud's statements such as the universality of the Oedipal complex (cf. Spiro 1982), and Mead (1930), in addition to her work on sex and temperament, had earlier investigated the relationship between animism and imagination in Manus children. Part of the appeal of New Guinea (and neighboring Australia) to various researchers interested in socialization has been the elaborate initiation ceremonies characteristic of many of these societies (Bettelheim 1962[1954]; Lidz 1989; Whiting 1941). As Roscoe discusses in his conclusion, social explanations of initiation rites have long considered the primary function of the rites to be the socialization of the individual. Their conceptual appeal may stem from the fact that in the context of initiation rituals the body presents a vivid image of "construction": "We appear to be literally witnessing the formation of the cultural or social person, and the passage from childhood to adulthood becomes a metonym for all the processes by which persons are so moulded" (Strathern 1992:67).

There is no doubt that aspects of female initiation ceremonies concern the shaping of culturally appropriate emotions and behavior. Thus, Fergie's attention to the performative dimensions of the vevene ritual sequence among the Babae (this volume) presents us with a detailed description of how such events evoke shame, laughter, and "intoxication" among pubescent girls. She analyzes these emotions as related to a pubescent girl's growing awareness of her own sexuality and women's need to control this nubile sexuality. Expressed metaphorically as the "domestication of a pig," Babae women's concern for establishing control over female sexuality represents a theme prevalent in many initiation rituals: the adult exercise of authority over younger members of their society. This seems to be especially true of sexuality, linked as it is with female fertility and reproduction. Given the social ends to which Babae women wish to put a pubescent girl's sexuality, it is not surprising that this demonstration of control, while apparently peripheral to the main focus of the event, occurs in the context of a ritual whose ostensible purpose is to celebrate the birth of a woman's first child. Rauto women, too, through their ribald laughter and clowning, appear to ridicule the shy embarrassment of the young initiate when her body is rubbed with oil (Maschio 1988). The implication of their behavior, Maschio suggests, is that the girl is being taught not to be ashamed of her body and its incipient sexuality, but to value it and the power it affords her.

While aspects of female initiation ceremonies are undoubtedly concerned with the inculcation of skills and attitudes necessary for performing given social roles, the essays in this volume challenge this narrow definition of the function of female initiation. As Roscoe argues in his conclusion, they also question the validity of the related idea that the purpose of female initiation is to formally acknowledge that the initiates have come into a completely new stage of social being—that they have crossed the threshold that separates childhood or adolescence from adulthood. Rather than single threshold events, these essays suggest that female initiation rites are part of lengthier temporal processes concerned with the transformation of females. The Murik, for example, celebrate a number of different rituals to mark the first achievements of children. Female initiation is but one in a series of events that individuals can participate in during their lifetime that contribute toward their achievement of not simply adulthood, but "full personhood" in Murik society.

In Rauto, Manam, and Murik, as well as other Melanesian societies (Deacon 1934; Jolly 1991) women's participation in female initiation rituals, while theoretically available to all women, create differences in status among women, as well as between women and men. Thus, initiation does not simply mark the transition from adolescence to adulthood for these women, but contributes to their potential to become particular kinds of adults. To consider female initiation in isolation from its larger cultural and temporal contexts is to obscure the role these rites often play in social processes that intimately connect the creation of personhood and gender identity to the political economy and cosmology of society as a whole.

This point bears on another issue these essays raise: these ceremonies do not focus on initiates alone. Among the Yangoru Boiken, Saniyo-Hiyowe, and Manam, although a single young woman may be the sole focus of the puberty rites, the initiate's sponsors acquire prestige and status for having organized the event. While the issue of sponsorship as a source of prestige has been noted for male initiation, it is worth stressing vis-à-vis female initiation, as it underscores the integral role these ceremonies play in larger social and political processes despite their performance for a single initiate.

PERSONHOOD AND FEMALE INITIATION

Although Strathern (1986a, 1988) has argued that the concept of the cultural construction of gender has run its course, it was pivotal in liberating us from essentialist notions of "male" and "female," and from ethnocentric notions of personhood and the individual. Strathern's work on Hagen gender constructs (1978, 1980, 1981) was in the forefront of studies that helped to make feminist scholars aware of the ethnocentric biases of the categories they used in their analyses of gender (Strathern 1984; see also Gewertz 1984). Feminist anthropologists working outside Melanesia have been particularly interested in the cultural notions of personhood and gender that are characteristic of many Melanesian societies (Leonardo 1991:29). Despite variability in specific Melanesian cultural logics, comparative research has shown that they are broadly similar in the differences they exhibit from the Western notion of personhood and the individual (Linnekin and Poyer 1990).[8]

A major theme to emerge from the literature on Melanesian personhood is the primacy that substances—in particular, sexual substances such as semen and breast milk, bodily substances such as blood and bones, and food—play in the determination of individual identity and kinship. Exchange theory initially introduced the idea that items circulating between persons are symbols of the relations between them. Ethnographic data from Melanesia reveals that the substances bestowed in intercourse and nurture are analogous to objects given in gift exchange (Clay 1977; Herdt 1982b; Meigs 1984). According to the symbolic logic of gift exchange, the converse of this is also true: objects are conceived of as being the products of relationships between persons. In many Pacific societies, children are symbolically analogous to wealth objects and, hence, are important products and symbols of social relations. More directly, things (food, sexual substances) transform a person's identity. Thus, the act of nurturing is commonly interpreted as transmitting and creating identity, since persons are thought to take on the (social) identity of the substances they ingest (LiPuma 1988; Meigs 1984).

Unlike the Western concept of a child as the exclusive biological product of two opposite-sexed individuals, in Melanesia a child is considered the product of multiple relationships, what Strathern (1988) refers to as the notion of the "multiple person." Rather than a biological given, an individual's kinship identity is considered to be the result of numerous individuals' contributions to a person's physical growth. Thus, a person's identity is an aggregate of social relations, the links he or she has to other individuals. These connections are the result of the contribution of substances, including paternal and maternal sexual substances, but also food given by relatives during childhood. The ramifications of this premise are manifold, encompassing cultural theories of conception, nurturance, sexuality, death, and the afterlife.[9]

The essays in this volume contribute to this discourse on Melanesian personhood in several ways. We see evidence of nurturance and gift-giving as a means of conferring identity and insuring affiliation in Murik and Babae notions of gender and group affiliation. The concept of a "multiple person" and the importance of nurturance also explains the Manam emphasis on feeding a girl during her *imoaziri* rites; those women who feed the initiate both contribute to her transformation into an adult woman and lay claim to her help in the future. Fergie's point that Babae notions of sociality and ties of kinship are based more on the shared substances of nurturance than on sexual substances is yet another instance of the Melanesian model just described. As Fergie notes, competition for an individual's identity continues through death, as ancestors are also subject to the competitive claims of the living.

To varying degrees, the Murik, Abelam, Manam, and Yangoru Boiken all demonstrate one of the most prevalent themes noted for initiation rites: the acknowledgment or creation of gender difference. The message conveyed in these societies is of the social necessity of both "male" and "female" powers and potentialities, to the creation of which initiation ceremonies contribute. This concept resonates with Strathern's notion that Melanesian initiation ceremonies serve to make individuals "incomplete."

"MAKING INCOMPLETE":
SAME-SEX VERSUS CROSS-SEX INDIVIDUALS

Strathern (1992:66) argues that Western notions of socialization are inadequate to explain the cultural meaning of Melanesian initiation rites. In contrast to socialization as the "social construction" of the individual, Melanesian initiation is preoccupied with the need to *decompose* or *dismantle* aspects of an individual. A new child is initially a "cross-sex" (male/female) or androgynous entity, composed of both male and female elements, which in order to sexually reproduce must be put into a "same-sex" (single-sex) state (i.e., either "masculinized" or "feminized") (Strathern 1988).

The aim of Melanesian initiation, Strathern argues, is to make individuals "incomplete" in order that they may become reproductive members of society. Previously androgynous or cross-sex adolescents must be culturally "deconstructed" through the transformative process of ritual into same-sex males and females. Thus, she asserts, "central to many male initiation ceremonies is the transformation of the initiate not from a 'female' [or feminized] to a 'male' state, but from a cross-sex to a same-sex one. . . . Male ritual does not produce 'males' out of 'females,' but potential 'fathers' out of 'persons.' What is produced is a sexually activated person, a potential reproducer, an incomplete person whose identity must be completed in relation with another" (1988:26–27; see also Mosko 1983).

In a similar vein, Townsend, in her discussion of Saniyo-Hiyowe puberty and widowhood rituals, describes these female-focused rites as reciprocal cultural processes that involve the production and re-production of women whose identities are incomplete, waiting to be completed not only in relation to a spouse, but to an entire group of affines.

Strathern's theory subsumes many of the disparate details and redundant themes found in male and female initiation throughout Melanesia, as well as important elements of a variety of theories other scholars have offered as explanations for aspects of these rites. For example, Mead (1949:98) suggests that "the initiatory cult of New Guinea is a structure which assumes that men can become men only by men's ritualizing birth and taking over—as a collective group—the functions that women perform naturally." Mead's insight into male initiation as men's symbolic control over the rebirth of boys, making them into men, is compatible with Strathern's statement about the necessity in Melanesian societies to transform a cross-sex individual (with male initiation, the androgynous boy) into a same-sex individual—an adult man. This transformation, Strathern suggests, is symbolized by the imagery of rebirth.

FEMALE INITIATION AS
TRANSFORMATION AND PERFORMANCE

Any analysis of gender and initiation in Melanesia has to focus on social action and performance. It is human agency—in the form of exchange and the performance of rituals such as initiation—that effects the transformation of one gender state into another. This emphasis on human agency and social action reminds us of an easily forgotten aspect of initiation rites: that they are social performances. Even when these rites are held in seclusion, they are performances complete with actors and audience.

Several of the essays in this volume discuss people's beliefs in the efficacy of initiation rituals as activities that precipitate specific changes. Maschio, for example, refers to the process of "the ritual construction of gender," the way in which the words, actions, and aesthetic dimensions of ritual performances affect and transform the initiates. The objects presented to initiates, while symbols of cultural memory, are also externalizations of the self and aspects of their new identity.

RITUAL TRANSVESTISM:
CLOTHES AS SYMBOLIC GENITALIA

The performative dimension of Babae women's rituals that Fergie mentions in particular consists of clowning and transvestism. She sees these as evidence of the pleasure women take in playing with form in the ritual context.

Transvestism involves manipulation of the body as well as gender form. In initiation rituals clothes function as symbolic genitalia. Transvestism thus becomes a form of aesthetic communication that uses the body as the medium for its message. But why, in the context of rituals that supposedly celebrate specific gendered dimensions of the human body and the differences between the sexes, do we find transvestism? Some form of transvestism is prevalent in most of the female initiation rituals described in this volume (see Barlow, Hauser-Schäublin, Maschio, and Roscoe) and in many male initiation rituals in New Guinea.

Bateson (1958[1936]) considered transvestism, a prominent feature of both male and female Iatmul *naven* ceremonies, to be a means of marking difference. It signaled the unusual circumstances the performers found themselves in during the ritual and highlighted their behavior as different from their quotidian life because it appropriated the culturally expected behavior of the opposite sex. In the context of female initiation, when women don male attire it signals awareness of their unusual behavior, thus also sanctioning this behavior as permissible and appropriate within the frame of the ritual performance. For example, when Murik women attack female initiates in the course of female initiation, they are dressed in men's fighting attire. The contrast between their male clothing and their female sex is analogous to the contrast between their aggressive ritual behavior and their usual, maternal, nurturing gender role (Barlow, this volume).

THE BODY AND FEMALE INITIATION

"The Personal is Political," the rallying cry of feminist activism in the 1960s and 1970s, centered on the struggle for women's control over their bodies (Snitow, et al. 1983). Born of this struggle, feminist scholars and anthropologists readily agreed with Foucault's (1978, 1979) identification of the body as *the* site of contestation between individuals and the state over autonomy and power.[10] Many feminist theorists see the female body in particular as the locus par excellence for the inscription of relations of dominance in Western patriarchy. Given this assumption, feminists have focused on the female body and reproduction as key tropes in various Western discourses— from scientific to colonial, to mass media and popular culture (Diamond and Quinby 1988; Jacobus, et al. 1990; Jaggar and Bordo 1989). This interest stems in part from their awareness that discourse does not simply reflect but, more powerfully, also shapes people's ideas about women and the female body. Moreover, the potency of gender symbolism and sexuality lies in the fact that sexual relations have material and practical consequences that concern power relations between men and women and between different classes and races (Stoler 1991). Ginsburg and Rapp (1991:331) suggest that the study of sexuality and reproduction should be at the center of contemporary anthropological theory. They argue that the "politics of reproduction," the social relations, practices, and ideology that surround the organization and control of reproduction at specific historical moments, intersect in important ways with social hierarchies and other aspects of political economy (Miller 1993). These various theories share a conviction of the intimate relationship between production and reproduction, between gender, culture, and political economy (Leonardo 1991).

Anthropologists have also analyzed the use of the female body and reproduction as key symbols for the social body and cultural reproduction in Melanesia (Strathern 1987a:8; Weiner 1978, 1979), and the relationship between Melanesian concepts of personhood and sociality based on the symbolic elaboration of the body (Battaglia 1990; Clay 1986). But the rhetorical and symbolic role the female body plays in much Melanesian discourse is different from the role it often plays in Western patriarchal society.

THE RITUAL MANIPULATION OF THE BODY

In discussions of both male and female initiation rites, analytic attention frequently focuses on the physical manipulation of the initiates' bodies—the performance of ordeals, scarification, circumcision, infibulation—and the emotional and symbolic significance of these often painful and traumatic acts (Bettelheim 1962[1954]; La Fontaine 1985; Lincoln 1981; Richards 1956). The usual explanation is that these acts test the initiates' preparation for adulthood. The scars, tattoos, and other forms of bodily "mutilation" are permanent signs of the initiates' change of status and ability to endure the pain associated with acquiring them.[11]

Recent interpretations of male initiation in Papua New Guinea contrast male rites with female ceremonies by noting that although boys and girls may be subjected to the same forms of physical "mutilation" (e.g., nosebleeding in the Eastern Highlands; cf. Hays and Hays 1982), quite different cultural meanings underlie these manipulations. Boys, it is said, must be "made" into men (Newman and Boyd 1982) whereas girls are simply "prepared" for marriage, the implication being that it takes a complex cultural process to transform boys into men, while girls become women "naturally."

The essays in this volume suggest that there is a further dimension to the emphasis on the body in initiation ceremonies, one related more specifically to cultural notions of sexuality, beauty, and power that many Papua New Guinea cultures associate with male and female initiation. Thus, Maschio (this volume, 1994) believes that the Rauto practice of beautifying and painting the skin represents a ritual attempt to cultivate outward physical signs of the development of the self and social identity.

MENSTRUATION AND "RITES OF MATURITY"

Because they are commonly believed to mark an individual's transition from adolescence to adulthood, initiation rites are frequently referred to as "rituals of maturity." Menarche, which signals a girl's "coming of age" or sexual maturity in many cultures, seems to be the great divide that separates scholarly definitions of "rites of maturity" into opposing camps. Some scholars consider menarcheal rituals, because they are closely linked to a physiological event and thus usually performed only for one individual, to be "puberty rites." They reserve the term *initiation* for those rites that do not coincide with or focus on menarche (and thus usually include a group of initiates) (Allen 1967; La Fontaine 1985:14; Richards 1956). Others, such as Brown (1963), include rites of first menstruation as a type of female initiation, regardless of whether one or several initiates are involved (however, such rites cannot include marriage). As Roscoe notes in his conclusion, most authors in this volume take a third position. They feel that to distinguish between female puberty ceremonies and initiation is premature if not irrelevant. The more important issue is how either of these events relate to other life-cycle rituals and to a society's political and economic organization. Rather than seeing rites of maturity as a once-in-a-lifetime occurrence, both types of rituals, whether they occur singly, serially, or in conjunction with marriage, are but one in a series of life-cycle events that a society celebrates as part of the cultural process through which an individual achieves personhood. Thus, for many societies, the achievement of full personhood is not a one-time event but a process that continues throughout an individual's lifetime (cf. Barlow, Lutkehaus, Roscoe, Townsend, this volume; Hoskins 1989).

More important than definitions that include or exclude menarche is an understanding of the cultural significance of the preoccupation of "rites of maturity" with ideas of menstruation, sexuality, and procreation. Any discussion of female rites, be they puberty or initiation, must analyze how their concern with the body and its physiological functions is also a preoccupation with broader social concerns of morality, politics, and the regeneration of society.

Certain actions and tropes that relate to beliefs and practices concerning menstruation, such as washing the body of the initiate, appear in several of the rituals described in this volume. Among the Saniyo-Hiyowe, a girl who has completed the puberty ritual is said metonymically to have "washed." It is very common cross-culturally for notions of pollution and taboo to be associated with menstruation, for menstrual blood is frequently considered to be an especially powerful substance (Buckley and Gottlieb 1988; Douglas 1966, 1970). Thus, bathing and washing are activities frequently performed in female puberty rituals to protect the initiate and cleanse her of bodily pollution (Lutkehaus, this volume).

Notions of menstrual pollution are commonly not isolated beliefs but influence a set of cultural practices concerning bodily care. The body must be protected from sickness and death due to a range of potentially danger-ous or polluting substances and situations. The precautions taken for a pubescent girl may be a specific case of more general cultural practices per-formed whenever someone, male or female, is in a vulnerable state.

Menarche may be marked symbolically by giving the initiates new skirts to wear (Rauto, Manam) or, as among the Yangoru Boiken, by giving them skirts for the first time (Roscoe 1988). In the context of female initiation, red is also often associated with menstrual blood. The Rauto, for example, condense a set of ideas about sexuality and power associated with menstrual blood into the symbol of fire. However, as Maschio points out, a focus only on the symbolism of menstruation would ignore the broader message of Rauto puberty ritual that is concerned more generally with fertility, power, and social regeneration.

IMAGES OF POWER:
SEXUALITY, BEAUTY, AND GROWTH

The sexual attractiveness and health of initiates are key themes in female initiation ceremonies. Not exclusive to female ceremonies, they are also prevalent in male initiation. This is further evidence of the androgynous or equivalent nature of male and female powers and of the relationship of physical beauty and sexuality to larger cultural themes of potency, fertility, and generativity.

The attention given to the care of the body in many of the rituals is not simply for prophylactic purposes but, more positively, to enhance the beauty and sexual attractiveness of the initiate or to ensure her healthy development. Rauto puberty rites are distinguished from other types of achievement ceremonies by their cultivation of the physical attractiveness of adolescents (Maschio, this volume). Some informants even characterize the ceremonies as a form of "love magic" since one of their primary aims is to make the initiates attractive to members of the opposite sex. The reasons for this particular emphasis on the body may seem obvious—after all, "coming of age" refers to the onset of physiological changes that signal adult sexual-ity. This attention, however, needs to be accounted for in cultural terms.

The prevalence of the use of the color red in female initiation rites is not associated only with menstrual blood. In Manam, it also expresses ideas of health, growth, and personal attraction and is associated with the beauty and sexual desirability of both women and men. The week-long imoaziri rites culminate with the public presentation of the initiate at a feast held in her honor. Her body, glistening with coconut oil and red paint, is bedecked in new grass skirts, fragrant herbs and flowers are tucked into newly woven armbands, and she is adorned with her family's finest dog's-teeth and shell ornaments. This attention to physical appearance exemplifies a cultural theory of the relationship between beauty and power. Physical attractiveness implies forms of power such as seduction—both of other humans and of valuable objects—and fertility, as manifest in procreation and the ability to accumulate wealth.

Other female initiation rituals focus attention on controlling or channeling female sexuality in specific directions. During the Babae vevene ceremony, older women say they must "domesticate the pig," i.e., exert control over the budding sexuality of pubescent girls in an attempt to channel it in the socially acceptable direction of marriage. Similar control forms the central focus of the Murik sambaan or female initiation ceremony, where women are ritually empowered to engage in sexual intercourse with their husband's ceremonial partners. However, sexuality is usually linked to the idea of reproduction. Even with the ritual intercourse of the Murik sambaan there is the belief that a child born of such a union is special and highly valued.

CONCEPTION AND PROCREATION:
THE THEME OF RENEWAL

Ever since Malinowski (1922) noted the Trobriand Islanders' denial of the father's role in the conception of his child, anthropologists have been intrigued with Melanesian theories of conception, in part because these theories were so often found to be different from Western biological explanations of "the facts of life" (Jorgensen 1983). But anthropologists also understand that indigenous conception theories represent cultural ideologies or schemas that provide clues to important realms of behavior and belief such as personhood, kinship, and gender. Studies from Papua New Guinea show a high value placed on the roles of both men and women in "growing up" the next generation, in ritual contexts as well as in daily life. Although Western ideas lead us to assume ethnocentrically that procreation must refer to a gendered discourse about processes of the female body, evidence from a variety of Melanesian societies shows that notions of menstruation, procreation, and nurturance need not be associated exclusively with women. There is evidence of male pregnancy in the Highlands (Meigs 1976) and male procreation of yams as symbolic children (Hauser-Schäublin, this volume, 1989a). Not only is maternal nurturance an important social value, as Barlow demonstrates for the Murik, but paternal nurture is also seen to be essential to the continuity of kin groups (Battaglia 1985).

The themes of birth, rebirth, and fertility have long been recognized as key tropes in Melanesian male initiation and initiation rituals in general (Eliade 1958; Keesing 1982; La Fontaine 1985; Lincoln 1981; Whitehead 1986; Van Gennep 1960[1908]). Interpretations of the significance of this symbolism range from the common explanation of birth as a metaphor of the initiates' "rebirth" into a new social status, to psychoanalytic and psychological interpretations that see male initiation practices as reflecting men's envy of female reproductive capacities (Bettelheim 1962[1954]; Mead 1949) or their desire to appropriate or control them (Langness 1967; Lattas 1989). Whitehead (1986), following Van Gennep, sees male initiation as a type of fertility cult in which men celebrate and ritually reproduce their control over fertility—the fertility of crops and of hunting; the fertility that allows them to transform boys into men and to create kin group solidarity; the potency to create and control exchange valuables and thus to create social bonds; and the power of aggression and violence. Men's control over fertility is thus identified as the source of male dominance over women (ibid.).[12] If anything, the literature on male initiation in New Guinea has provoked feminists to think more broadly about fertility as a male principle.[13]

Again, the importance of considering female rites along with male rites must be emphasized. Contrary to what Whitehead (1986:285) and others (Forge 1966; Rubel and Rosman 1978; Tuzin 1972) have said, Hauser-Schäublin (this volume) demonstrates that the yams to which Abelam men ritually give birth are not thought of as exclusively "male"; they are both "male" and "female." More importantly, without a consideration of Abelam female initiation rites, these other scholars have ignored the fact that, in the context of female puberty rites, the Abelam celebrate female fertility and procreation as well. Moreover, she argues that when we analyze both male and female life-cycle rituals, we see that the Abelam have a notion of complementary forms of male and female procreation, both of which are necessary for the reproduction of society.

Unfortunately, anthropologists themselves have tended to reproduce the biases of their predecessors where female ceremonies are concerned. Not only have they ignored female puberty ceremonies because of the tendency in these ceremonies to focus on only one individual, they may also have been guilty of slighting them because of their literal focus on fertility and reproduction rather than the more "exotic" and surprising imagery that male fertility and procreation presents. To ignore the role ascribed to women and female fertility is to devalue physiological reproduction, an attitude that is not the case in Melanesian cultures. It is also to misrepresent the complexity and significance of fertility, power, and reproduction in Melanesia.

MARRIAGE: THE NEXUS OF PRODUCTION AND REPRODUCTION

Marriage does not receive extensive cultural elaboration in many Papua New Guinea cultures. In others, such as Manam, the boundaries that distinguish female puberty ceremonies from marriage are blurred, as the latter ideally should immediately follow the former. When the two ceremonies are separated in time, the rituals themselves are very similar, with marriage mirroring the final public stage of the puberty rites. It is frequently the case that marriage or female puberty ceremonies, in and of themselves, do not confer adult female status on a woman. Rather, among the Manam as well as the Murik, Babae, and Yangoru Boiken, a woman's achievement of adult status is dependent upon her giving birth or adopting a child (see also Hoskins 1989). This is perhaps most explicit in Babae society where the vevene ceremony, which is held specifically to honor a primipara, overshadows or encompasses marriage and puberty celebrations.

The Daulo (Sexton, this volume) provide an intriguing example of the analogies women make between internal physiological processes, marriage—traditionally the culturally appropriate context in which to enact procreation—and new arenas of production and exchange women find they have access to since the advent of coffee as a cash crop in the highlands. Sexton's analysis of the wok-meri movement has relevance beyond the narrow purview of the anthropology of Melanesia. The use Daulo women make of the tropes of female puberty and marriage ceremonies in their discourse and practice surrounding their establishment of an all-women's savings and credit organization underscores the point that if we want to fully understand the indigenous meaning of new social movements and economic developments, and the dynamic role that women play in them, we must first understand the cultural meanings associated with traditional practices such as female puberty ceremonies, marriage, and other rites of passage.

The wok-meri movement is also interesting because it demonstrates that modernity and money are not always "practically mediated by and symbolically associated with men" in Melanesia (Jolly 1992:39). We cannot simply assume that women, in Melanesia or elsewhere, are always associated with tradition and the traditional, even though they may choose to symbolize their own participation and success in modern activities, such as money-making ventures, in traditionally gendered terms. For one could argue that changes in the political economy in highland New Guinea that the wok meri movement represents also signal a change in the rhetorical value of the female body and reproduction for the Daulo women (Sexton 1982).

WIDOWHOOD AND "SYMBOLIC MENOPAUSE"

From birth to death in many Melanesian societies the life cycle of the individual (or groups, see Mosko 1989) represents in microcosm the regeneration of society (Fergie, this volume). Symbolized metonymically by the body—whose processes of growth, procreation, and maturation provide logical links with social regeneration—life-cycle events present heightened moments for the reenactment and reproduction of key social values and the emotions that underlie them.

Townsend's analysis of Saniyo-Hiyowe rituals of puberty and widowhood reveals a complementary opposition between two such rites, with a widow's actions ritually "undoing" what was symbolically done to her body at puberty. After concluding her puberty rites, a young woman is said to have "washed"—a metaphor that socially acknowledges her adherence to the cultural rules for personal hygiene that accompany her new physical condition as a menstruating woman. It also marks her as ready for marriage. In contrast, a widow is prohibited not only from washing during widowhood; Townsend argues that the effect of widowhood itself is to reverse the nubility and sexuality of the pubescent girl. Interestingly, the Saniyo-Hiyowe say that both widows and married women do not menstruate, implying perhaps that husbands control their sexuality and fertility. Slowly over several years a widow's feminine (sexual) identity is gradually rebuilt, culminating, like the pubescent girl, with her washing and freedom to remarry. This period of symbolic menopause allows the widow to separate socially and emotionally from her deceased husband's group in preparation for her alliance with new affines. In this sense, widowhood also symbolically unties the social and sexual relations in which a woman formerly was enmeshed and frees her to engage in a new set of affinal relations, eventually restoring her sexuality as well.

GENDER AND POWER IN FEMALE INITIATION

I have argued that, in addition to expressing cultural notions of femininity, images of the female body and procreation found in Papua New Guinea initiation rituals are also key metaphors for the expression of cultural ideologies of power and agency. More specifically, power itself is often conceived of as gendered. This is revealed most clearly in different notions of male and female fertility, expressed either in terms of productivity—gardens, exchange networks, valuables—or reproduction—children, ceremonial yams. Since men and women are often believed to be powerful and procreative in different ways, differences in gendered forms of power can be the basis for unequal relations of authority and male dominance.

As many of the essays in this volume reveal, however, differences in male and female power are also the basis for gender complementarity. Hauser-Schäublin notes the necessity of the exchange of gender-specific products and powers in Abelam ideology. Female powers are not only seen as complementary to male powers (Losch 1982), but both are deemed necessary to the regeneration of society. When we look carefully at the cultural meanings of gender, the multiple and sometimes contradictory nature of femininity and, hence, of female power becomes apparent. Sexuality and maternal nurturance are both valued dimensions of female identity, and both aspects of female identity are sources of female power. We also find that women have the potential to manifest both "male" and "female" forms of power (see Barlow, Maschio, this volume, in particular). In different contexts, both men and women manifest aggressive as well as procreative powers.

Interpretations of male initiation in Papua New Guinea have emphasized that the ritual segregation of males from females functions to form bonds of male solidarity predicated on sex antagonism and the avoidance of women (Langness 1974; Herdt 1982a), or, at the very least, that it replicates a social hierarchy in which men are higher than women (Godelier 1986). In contrast, the development of an analytic focus on the body has led feminist anthropologists to frame questions about male initiation in terms of the relationship between the body and power—for example, Lindenbaum's comparative work on the mystification of female labors (1987) and ritualized homosexuality (1984), and Whitehead's (1986) on varieties of male fertility cults in New Guinea.

Missing from these analyses has been adequate attention to the meaning of female rites in comparison to male initiation. More than simply a matter of "adding" women or giving them a voice, a focus on female initiation illuminates the cultural dynamics of power and social reproduction that studies of male initiation alone have tended to mask. For example, the analysis of female initiation among the Yangoru Boiken, Rauto, Murik, and Manam reveals that these female rites also play a role in the creation and perpetuation of social hierarchy. They can reproduce inequality among women, as well as between women and men. The ability of sponsors to organize and finance the rites serves to differentiate female initiates from other women and provides them with the potential to become big women (Rauto) or leaders within their respective clan group (Murik) or village community (Yangoru Boiken, Manam). Among the Murik and Yangoru Boiken these initiates also help their husbands achieve higher status as well.

EXCHANGE AND FEMALE INITIATION

A focus on the dynamics of culture, gender, and political economy character-izes the most sophisticated work by feminist anthropologists (Leonardo 1991). Such an approach recognizes the embedded nature of gender, both as lived social relations and as ideology, and how women's desires are shaped and con-strained by the social systems in which they live. It is through their under-standing of the political economy of exchange relations that feminist anthropologists have developed new ways of conceptualizing gender and rela-tions between the sexes in Melanesia (cf. Errington and Gewertz 1987; Jolly 1991; Josephides 1985; Lederman 1986, 1990; Strathern 1988; Weiner 1979). Strathern's *The Gender of the Gift* (1988) is the most ambitious synthetic analysis of the relationship among gender, initiation, and political economy in Melanesia to date. Ironically, Strathern argues, because of their status as "gift" rather than "commodity" economies, Melanesian societies are best viewed through anthropological rather than feminist categories, as the latter distance themselves from appropriate cultural categories (1986b, 1988:145).[14]

The essays in this volume provide insight into the role of exchange in female initiation and its articulation with other social and economic relations and values. Thus, in addition to their function as adornments that beautify a girl, the ornaments Manam and Saniyo-Hiyowe sponsors give an initiate also display the wealth of her parents or clan and can influence later bridewealth negotiations. The entire second phase of Rauto female puberty ceremonies concerns the presentation of shell money and curved boar's tusk valuables that signify the initiate's right to engage in their exchange. Another function of these rites is to "raise the name" or enhance the social reputation of the adolescent or kin group for whom they are performed. The Murik present a more unusual form of "gift" exchange in female initiation, as the initiates give themselves sexually to men who are a ritual grade above their husbands. This gift of sexuality promotes the ritual status of the woman's husband as well as her own social standing within her descent group.

Roscoe also argues that female initiation plays an important sociopolitical role among the Yangoru Boiken. In a vein similar to arguments that male initiation serves to forge group solidarity, but with a twist, he sees Yangoru Boiken female initiation as an attempt to forge an identity of interests among women as members of their husbands' kin segments. More specifi-cally, their participation in these rites reinforces their identity with their husbands' sociopolitical aspirations, to which they are major contributors through the raising of pigs and production of food and children. In fact, Roscoe attributes the greater elaboration of female initiation rites among the

Yangoru Boiken, in comparison to other Ndu-speaking groups, to the greater interdependence between men and women in establishing sociopolitical reputations at both individual and group levels.

CULTURAL REPRODUCTION:
FEMALE INITIATION AS METAPHOR AND PRAXIS

Reproduction is not only *not* devalued in Melanesian societies, it also carries a much broader set of meanings than in Western culture. Weiner's work on gender and exchange in the Trobriand Islands in particular has contributed a reevaluation of the model of exchange and reciprocity in Melanesia and a new appreciation of the dynamic relationship between conceptions of gender, exchange, and social reproduction (1976, 1978, 1979, 1980, 1992). Encompassing more than simply biological reproduction, yet different from the structural-functionalist (Fortes 1969) and Marxist-feminist (Moore 1988) notions of social reproduction, Weiner's concept of cultural reproduction focuses on the notions of value and social identity and the "regeneration" or "rebirth" of these identities and values through time.

As a cultural schema, reproduction refers to more than just the female body and biological procreation; rather, it incorporates ideas about social relations, the exchange of valuable resources, power, and cosmology. According to this schema, reproduction is a political and economic, as well as a biological, process. It also includes the notion of male fertility and reproduction. For if reproduction does not simply refer to the biological process of procreation, but more broadly to the regeneration of culturally valuable objects and social relations, then men too have a procreative role to play in the reproduction of society.

Interestingly, the Trobriand Islanders have neither male nor female initiation rituals. Instead, the exchange of male and female wealth items, such as banana-leaf bundles and *kula* shells, at important moments in the life cycle, especially at death, and the existence of men's and women's separate spheres of exchange, fulfill many of the functions that male and female initiation ceremonies serve elsewhere (Weiner 1988). Like Strathern, Weiner sees exchange —not just the exchange of material objects but of intangible substances as well—as fundamental to the determination of gender identity and the regeneration of society. Weiner's and Strathern's perspectives, which have often clashed (cf. Strathern 1981), converge on the importance of reproduction as a key form of sociality in Melanesian societies. For embedded in the symbolism and practices of these rituals are clues to a society's fundamental beliefs, not only about gender but also about personhood, power, and life itself.

Although it should now be apparent that a broad range of themes related to cultural reproduction are expressed in Papua New Guinean female initiation rituals, we do not wish to argue that these rites therefore form the privileged site for the investigation of cultural notions of reproduction. Rather than adopting a Maussian strategy of looking at female initiation as a "total social phenomenon" (Mauss 1967:1), a culturally strategic event upon which one can hinge all the "this and that" of ethnography, we see female initiation rites as important events or stages in larger social processes and cycles fundamental to the life of both individuals and whole societies.

Thus, we suggest the utility of looking at female initiation rites not only in relationship to male initiation, but, more importantly, as part of a larger corpus of rituals that celebrate not only the life cycle of a woman but the life cycle of the public groups or larger community in which they are embedded. The trope of the life cycle becomes the central organizing motif, both for the anthropologist's analytic framework and for the cultural schema of particular societies. Fergie offers the most explicit development of this point in her discussion of how the sequence of rituals associated with women, female sexuality, and childbirth are themselves but one sequence within a larger ritual corpus that includes rituals of birth and death and rebirth, of beginning and end and regeneration. In its entirety the corpus forms a rite of passage for the reproduction not only of Babae society but of their cosmos.

Lest this discussion of the cultural trope of reproduction seem mired in an ahistoricity that ignores the changes that have affected Papua New Guinea societies since the advent of colonialism, Sexton's analysis of Daulo idioms of marriage and reproduction in the context of wok meri, a new women's social movement, reminds us of the protean ability of basic cultural concepts to express new relationships and practices and of the creative minds of the women who have used them.

NOTES

1. I am grateful to Rena Lederman, David Lipset, Paul Roscoe, and Ann Stoler for comments on earlier drafts of this introduction. Paul Roscoe, in particular, was heroic in his efforts to help clarify and pare down my wordy prose.

2. Other forces shaping this development include advances in symbolic and structuralist anthropology.

3. See Leacock (1972, 1981) and Rosaldo and Lamphere (1974).

4. See Weiner's (1987) introduction to *The Sexual Life of Savages* for a discussion that places Malinowski's writings about Trobriand sexuality and male-female relations in historical context.

5. Mead's earlier study of the issue of "nature" versus "nurture" among adolescent females in Samoa (1928) paved the way for her more general statement about the effects of culture on male/female behavior in *Sex and Temperament*.

6. See Brandes 1981; Brod 1987; Gilmore 1990; Kimmel and Messner 1989 for social constructionist studies of masculinity. On the concept of a third gender, see Herdt 1994; Nanda 1990; Shore 1981; Whitehead 1981; and W. Williams 1987.

7. See Keesing (1985) on the "micropolitics" of a male ethnographer's attempt to collect data about women.

8. The classic work on personhood remains Leenhardt's *Do Kamo: Person and Myth in the Melanesian World* (1979[1947]). Recent additions to the extensive literature on gender, personhood, and identity in Melanesia include Battaglia 1991; Biersack 1982; Clay 1986; Errington and Gewertz 1987; Harrison 1985; Lepowsky 1993; Wagner 1991; White and Kirkpatrick 1985.

9. The Melanesian concept of the multiple person is distinct from, but related in interesting ways to, the notion of multiple identities current in discourse about personhood in Western culture (cf. Kolodny 1992; Strathern 1992).

10. Mary Douglas (1966, 1970) also provided anthropologists with an earlier focus on the body as a key symbol of society.

11. Fewer female initiation ceremonies involve bodily "mutilation" than male ceremonies (Brown 1963; La Fontaine 1985; Schlegel and Barry 1979). For discussions of female facial tattooing and ritual scarification in Papua New Guinea, see Barker and Tietjen (1990) and Williamson (1979, 1987). Significantly, the most celebrated form, that of female "circumcision" or clitoridectomy, is associated with insuring sexual purity rather than testing a young woman's maturity or strength.

12. Although Whitehead has presented the most extensive comparative analysis of this point, others have argued along similar lines (cf. Langness 1974; Keesing 1982).

13. Collier and Rosaldo (1981) were the first to develop a detailed discussion of male fertility as a dimension of male dominance in "simple," hunting-gathering societies.

14. For critiques of Strathern see Biersack (1991), Kirby (1989), and Thomas (1991).

Part II

Defining Women: Gender Images in Female Initiation Rites

2

PUBERTY RITES, WOMEN'S NAVEN, AND INITIATION

Women's Rituals of Transition in Abelam and Iatmul Culture

Brigitta Hauser-Schäublin

This essay is concerned with two Middle Sepik peoples in Papua New Guinea: the Abelam and the Iatmul. These two groups are said to be closely related linguistically (Laycock 1965:181) and culturally (Forge 1966:23), and to show traits of what Lutkehaus and Roscoe (1987:579) have called "Sepikness." If this "Sepikness" goes beyond superficial similarities and is an expression of a kind of underlying common structure, however, it casts into sharp relief the question of why the Abelam practice female puberty rites while the Iatmul do not.

In this essay, I suggest that there exists a fundamental difference in structure between Iatmul and Abelam culture based, on the one hand, on different modes of subsistence and social organization and, on the other, on gender relations. Although Abelam female puberty rites are all-women events, their structure and meaning are closely linked to the ceremonial growing of long yams, which is carried out exclusively by, and dominates the lives of, men. Both are concerned with procreation in general and controlling and increasing the power to generate life in particular. Both culminate, in essence, in an equation of the core secrets, the menarcheal girl and the yam stone crucial to the yam cult. Among the riverine Iatmul, by contrast, horticulture and especially male cultivation of long yams is only marginal, since they primarily subsist on fish and sago, which is provided almost exclusively by women. Here, we find instead that women's rituals— *naven* ceremonies and female initiations, at least those documented in colonial time[1]—clearly follow in outline and structure those of male naven ceremonies and male initiations.

THE ABELAM AND THE IATMUL

The Abelam and the Iatmul of the East Sepik Province belong to the Ndu-language family of the Sepik-Ramu Phylum (Laycock 1965). As Lutkehaus and Roscoe (1987:579) point out, the Middle Sepik can be characterized as an area of intense intercultural traffic, and many highly valued items have been regularly traded between the Abelam and Iatmul through intermediate villages in the Wosera (southern Abelam) and Sawos regions (Schindlbeck 1980). Despite their linguistic and cultural affinities, however, the Abelam and Iatmul live under quite different ecological conditions (Allen 1986). The Iatmul dwell on the very banks of the Sepik River, while the Abelam live well into the grassy hinterlands of the river and up into the southern foothills of the Prince Alexander Mountains.

Traditionally,[2] the Iatmul subsist mainly by sago gathering and fishing and so can be classified as hunters and gatherers. Because their own sago stands are insufficient for their needs, however, they also must barter fish for sago with villages in the bush to the south (Gewertz 1977) and the north (Hauser-Schäublin 1977:38–47; Schindlbeck 1980:154–215) of the Sepik River. The Abelam, by contrast, are horticulturalists who live mainly by the cultivation of yam and taro, and villages are largely self-sufficient for food. Among the Iatmul, women play a prominent role in the subsistence economy: they provide their families' daily supply of fish and sago, and the exchange of fish for sago is exclusively a women's affair, even though the barter sometimes takes place far from their home village. Among the Abelam, however, daily subsistence requirements come mainly from the gardens and are furnished about equally by both sexes.

Iatmul social organization and division of labor also differ from those of the Abelam. Relations between Iatmul men and women are much tenser than among the Abelam: they are not expressed in oppositions having to do with subsistence activities in their broadest sense, as is the case among the Abelam between the yam cult, on the one hand, and female fertility, on the other. Instead, gender relations are bound rather rigidly into patterns of kinship. Iatmul men's ritual life and its products are kept secret: they are detached from everyday life and never displayed publicly as are long yam tubers among the Abelam. Iatmul ritual life is more "homogenous" in the sense that its structure and contents cannot be separated into different "complexes" as Abelam ritual life can be separated into the long yam cult and male initiation.

In both cultures, men's life centers around elaborate, collective rituals from which women are excluded, and in both cultures these rituals are centered on men's houses of towering proportions. But here the similarities end. Among the Iatmul, men meet in everyday life inside the ceremonial house, and most of their ritual is conducted inside the house, hidden from the eyes of women and children, or on the vast ceremonial ground in front of it, which is temporarily fenced off for the occasion. Their ritual production centers around contacts with the world of spirits, represented by a large variety of masks and figures and by the sound of musical instruments; it also centers around elaborate male initiations and, in the past, it included the head-hunting complex. Among the Abelam, by contrast, the interior of the ceremonial house is used only during male initiations and for the storage of *sacra*. In their everyday life, men do not enter the ceremonial house but meet in the open space in front of it, where everyone can see what is going on. Here, too, yam growing rituals are held: their main ritual products, long tubers regarded as animate but mortal, humanlike beings, are beautifully decorated and then displayed openly in front of the ceremonial house.

Among the Iatmul, a man's ritual status is more structurally determined than among the Abelam, depending on his position within his lineage and/or clan, his position within the hierarchically graded initiatory system, and his esoteric knowledge of secret names, spells, and myths. Among the Abelam, it is also important for a man to proceed through the stages of initiation, but neither this nor his clan membership determines his social position. Instead, social recognition and even influence and power are attained by achievements in growing long yams, an ability that the Abelam always explain in terms of ritual knowledge. To keep influence and power, moreover, requires proving one's yam-growing ability continuously over the years.

FEMALE PUBERTY RITES AMONG THE ABELAM

Although first menstruation ceremonies are not practiced among the Iatmul, they are common in many parts of the Middle Sepik region, occurring among the southern neighbors of the Iatmul, among the Sawos (Schindlbeck

1981), among the Arapesh (Mead 1940), and among the Yangoru Boiken (Roscoe, this volume). They also are practiced by the Abelam at the time of a girl's first period, though they vary significantly from one place to another.[3]

For the Central Abelam village of Kalabu, Kaberry (1941:361) mentions a girl's seclusion and scarification. The day before she emerges from the menstruation hut, a feast is held. Her father contributes the greater part of the food, including long yams and coconuts. Soup is made and distributed among the women. The next day, the girl is bathed in a mixture of water and the pounded pith of a special cane, and afterwards shaved and decorated with shells.

For the Eastern Abelam, Forge (1970a:274) mentions an initiation ceremony at first menstruation involving seclusion, a series of exchanges, and displays of wealth by the girl's father and his exchange partner. The young woman is scarified at dawn by a senior woman who cuts patterns on her breasts, belly, and upper arms. On the ceremonial ground, the women then perform secret rites, from which men are banned, that include transvestite women who imitate their husbands and brothers and pantomime sexual intercourse. These rites continue for a whole day and end at nightfall with the ritual cleansing of the ceremonial ground. These rites have much in common with those I was told of in Kiniambu, nowadays a Boiken-speaking village in the southern grasslands. Schindlbeck (1981) also describes female transvestite behavior during puberty rites among the Sawos of Gaikorobi, and I am reminded also of rites performed among the Iatmul during women-only naven ceremonies at a marriage. Among the Central and Western Abelam (Losche, pers. comm.), however, transvestite behavior at puberty rites is unknown. Among the Western Abelam (Losche 1982:325), the girl is decorated with shell necklaces and beads, and brought to the ceremonial ground (*amei*) where she silently watches exchanges of food, accompanied by shell rings and money, between patri- and matrilateral relatives.[4]

My own data were collected in the Central Abelam village of Kalabu, where Phyllis Kaberry had worked forty years earlier.[5] Between 1978 and 1983, I witnessed four first menstruation ceremonies, called *wambusuge* after the *wambe* cane, the juice and pounded pith of which are used to wash a girl before she leaves the menstruation hut.[6] As soon as a girl starts menstruating for the first time, her mother sends her to the menstruation hut (*kalmbangga*) at the edge of the bush. The mother then informs her husband and hurries off to her brother's hamlet to tell him that blood—the bodily medium linking a girl with her mother's brother—has began to flow, and to discuss the preparations for the feast that must be held two days hence. The news of the girl who has become a woman then quickly spreads through the village.

2.1   Women take over the ceremonial ground for a *wambusuge*. Abelam; Kalabu
Village, 1980. Photo credit: Jörg Hauser

The first menstruation feast—and women consider this joyful event as
exclusively their feast—takes place when the girl is still in the menstruation
hut. In preparation, the mother, assisted by her sisters, her brother's wives,
her husband, and his relatives, starts to collect large amounts of firewood,
coconuts, tobacco, betelnut, *ka* yams, long *wapi* ceremonial yams, and other
food. Although the firewood and coconuts are provided mainly by women

on a rather casual basis, the big specimens of ka and wapi yam are often brought by men in a manner resembling formal presentations. Sometimes, women—mostly close relatives of the girl—will enter the men's yam store houses themselves and take out the specimens they want. Men may protest vaguely but they know the women would not heed them and might even invade their store houses collectively if they were denied what they considered adequate yams.

Early on the day of the feast, which is also called wambusuge, the mother, her sisters, and her brothers' wives gather in one section of the hamlet, while the father's sisters and his brothers' wives gather in another (see plate 2.1). Helped by women from the same locality, hamlet, or ceremonial ground, the two sets of relatives set about cooking banana, ka yam, and taro—for this occasion, boiling the tubers in their skin. They also start boiling ka soup, which is later emptied into coconut bowls and garnished with grated coconut. Later, the women provide food to all those people who helped in preparing the day's distributions and the exchanges.

Early in the afternoon, the women bring the long yams out from where they have been stored, away from the scorching sun. Normally, on pain of verbal abuse from the menfolk, women are not allowed to approach a ceremonial house but, instead, must follow a path that leads around the edge of the ceremonial ground. On this day, however, all such restrictions are lifted. The women carry the long yams onto the ceremonial piazza and lay them on the ground immediately in front of the plaited facade base of the ceremonial house, if there is one. While some of the girl's close male relatives start cutting up coconuts, the women inspect the tubers. The girl's brothers and her father then begin to slice the yams up with a bone dagger, laying one slice after the other so that the original shape of the tuber is retained (see plate 2.2). Their work completed, the men then withdraw from the ceremonial ground and disappear for the rest of the day.

At about 3:00 P.M., women from all over the village and from neighboring villages gather at the piazza, first sauntering over to examine the dissected tubers, casually commenting on the yam varieties used and the size and number of the tubers displayed. The guests then settle down around the ceremonial ground, chatting with each other and laughing, until the whole hamlet is crowded with women and small children. Their female hosts then give them tobacco and betelnut, distribute the boiled taro and ka yam, and finally present each guest with the most highly valued food gift, a slice of raw wapi yam and a piece of coconut.

Every woman present, guest or host, brings to the ceremony a bowl filled with yam soup topped with grated coconut. Having received their gifts of

2.2   Long yams are sliced up for distribution among the women. Abelam;
Kalabu Village, 1980. Photo credit: Jörg Hauser

food, they then exchange these bowls of soup. The exchanges follow no set
clan or moiety (*ara*) lines: all the women I questioned insisted that they
were "free" (i.e., unrestricted). Nevertheless, some women endeavor to
exchange their soup with women they particularly like; once a woman initiates such an exchange, the other has no alternative but to reciprocate. Male
exchanges, by contrast, are more clearly structured, occurring between specific partners (*sambera*) of opposed moieties and involving pronounced ideas
of indebtedness. Men keep a strict account of how many specimens of yam
or pig they have given and constantly demand an equivalent gift in return.
In women's wambusuge exchanges, however, the idea of indebtedness is
much less pronounced, and they are governed much more by individual
choice. The nearest they come to resembling male exchanges is in such
women's comments as: "We have already received food twice on this ceremonial ground. We shall have to wait until X [the oldest of our premen-
strual girls] becomes a *naramtagwa* [i.e., a menarcheal girl]. Then they will
receive food on our amei."

Once all the bowls have been exchanged, everyone returns home, the
empty bowls generally being returned the next day. Unlike men's ceremon-

ies, no speeches are delivered at these wambusuge events, and no claims of leadership are made.

What I have described so far constitutes the public aspects of the wambusuge ceremony. But there are other aspects of the ritual that are not open to the public and constitute women's secrets. They revolve around the girl in the menstruation hut. During the whole day of the wambusuge feast, nothing is seen of the girl: in the cases I witnessed, the entrance to her small house was shut, as though it were deserted. The next day, however, the girl emerges from her seclusion, and close female relatives ritually bathe her in the juice of the wambe cane, which grows near running water. Afterwards, her head is shaved, she is decorated with many different necklaces, shellbands are tied around her wrists, and she receives a new netbag made by her mother that contains ovula shells. In former times, the girl was supposed to wear these decorations until her next menstruation but nowadays she wears them for just a day or two. In these earlier days, too, she received a kind of grass skirt called *kwaare*, consisting of immature, white, sago-frond fibers.[7]

Until about 1955, Abelam girls were scarified at their first menstruation. The operation took place in the small menstruation hut, and because their blood was believed capable of cooling the ground and devastating plant life, especially tubers, the girls were positioned on wild taro leaves to protect the earth. As female elders held them steady, standardized patterns (*ramoni*) were cut on their breasts, bellies, and upper arms, an experience sufficiently arduous that some were said to have fainted. The operation was conducted with a splinter of *ulma*, a white stone (probably quartz) used to demarcate on an amei ground the length of tubers displayed there at yam festivals, and to cut the penis of a newlywed man to release polluted blood accumulated during his first intense period of sexual intercourse with his wife. The scarifications were performed by an old woman practiced in the art. The villages of Kalabu 1 and 2 each had their own specialist. One, who was highly respected for her ritual knowledge and skill, pointed out to me that while she was a well-known specialist in scarification, her brother was an artist celebrated for the quality of his carvings, an equivalence of men's and women's secret knowledge that several other people also pointed out.[8]

Because she is considered to be in an exceptionally powerful and dangerous condition during her seclusion, the naramtagwa is not allowed to touch the ground with her bare feet. If she needs to defecate, she must walk into the bush, one step after the other, over *pangal* sago spathe. During her seclusion, she is fed exclusively on "dry," "male" food: roasted yam, preferably of the wapi variety, but also ka yam. Meat, yam soup, and all vegetables, fruits,

coconuts, and even water are proscribed, as is betelnut and everything considered female—that is, everything grown and harvested by women or classified as female. When the girl eats, moreover, she must not touch her food:
instead, the women looking after her wrap it in a nettle leaf for her to hold.
These food proscriptions, which apparently are still observed, continue for
several weeks after the girl has left seclusion. They are lifted by a female ritual elder, usually the woman who performed the scarification, who gives the
girl a mixture of bush herbs together with a betelnut, after which she is
allowed gradually to start eating "female" food again.

THE YAM CULT AND
MEN'S ATTEMPTS TO GENERATE LIFE

To understand both the wambusuge rite and other dimensions of the
Abelam female puberty rite, we need to understand Abelam men's ritual
propagation of long wapi yams and the fact that they consider this activity a
kind of exclusively male procreation of a humanlike being. Long-yam growing is masterminded by older men who are considered ritually capable by
virtue of their advanced ritual knowledge and initiatory status. Assisted by
prepubescent boys and by men whose wives are nursing a baby and who
therefore are currently continent, they first plant different varieties of wapi
seedling in special yam gardens. For the next six months, under severe
dietary and sexual proscriptions and aided by beings from the other world—
stars and ancestral spirits (mainly *nggwalndu* and recently deceased relatives)—they labor intensively and continuously to grow the longest tubers
they can. During this period, they prefer to sleep in their gardens to stay in
close contact with the spirits and their yams. Following the harvest, the
largest specimens are then decorated and displayed at yam festivals before
being presented to exchange partners.

The anthropological literature (Forge 1966; Tuzin 1972; Harrison 1982)
emphasizes the phallic character of Sepik long yams, and certainly Abelam
yams are associated with male pride and aggressiveness. But, as I have tried
to show elsewhere (Hauser-Schäublin 1988), yam cultism is more than just
phallic. Linguistic evidence suggests that yam growing also involves procreative powers that are considered female in nature. The yam seedling from
which the tuber grows, for example, is called *tagui*, "placenta." Once the
yam has reached its full length, the shriveled seedling is then spoken of as a
"mother" who has given all her vitality to her baby. The white earth sprin-
kled on top of the yam mound following planting is called *munya*, "breast
milk," for it is supposed to feed the yam as a mother suckles her baby. The

yam grower's role in this propagation is that of a genitor. Just as a mother's (menstrual) blood is said to contribute to an embryo's growth so, by his careful tending of the long yam, the grower's "blood" is said to go into the yam making it his offspring.

Appropriately, the yam itself—the grower's "child"—is regarded as a humanlike being. Like a human, it possesses a kind of "soul" (*komunyan* or *nyambapmu*),[9] an agency that can move about freely in the shape of a pig, a huge snake, or a firefly buzzing through the night, but which always returns to the tuber—unless it is killed, in which case the tuber also dies. Once harvested, the different parts of the tuber are named after the limbs of the human body: one speaks of a long yam's "head," its "breast," its "upper arms," its "thighs," and so on. In preparing it for display, it is decorated like a male ceremonial dancer, and this analogy between yam and dancer is quite explicitly drawn: a yam is considered as much a humanlike body as a ceremonial dancer is considered a yam.

This duality of yam as both flesh-and-blood being and vegetative being is echoed in myths that tell of how a man died and turned into the first yam. What the myth reveals, however, is that the human aspect of the yam is modeled not on an ordinary mortal but on one who has died and lives in the other world. When a man grows a huge long yam, in other words, he is in a sense involved in resurrecting or incarnating a being from the spirit world, the realm of the dead. This conclusion is corroborated by the practice of naming a yam fit for festival display after such a being, usually an nggwal-ndu spirit or a male relative of a senior generation who died some time ago but still is remembered.

Similar analogies between vegetative and flesh-and-blood beings that straddle the spiritual and secular world also occur in other ritual practices (for a detailed discussion, see Hauser-Schäublin 1988). At the end of a male initiation, for example, when the initiates break through a fence onto the ceremonial ground to begin a nightlong dance, their decoration is that of a ceremonial yam. Their faces are completely painted, their eyes must remain closed throughout the night, and they wear plaited headdresses called *noute* after the dried vine that emerges from the "head" of the yam. They are referred to as "dead like nggwalndu spirits" (*nggwalndu nde kyak*) because, in returning from their initiation, they are thought to be returning from the realm of the dead, a world of bliss and beauty, which is why they are beautifully decorated.

For another example, the Abelam use the same expression for planting a yam seedling as they do for burying a corpse. This analogy is also pursued in mortuary ritual. When a death has occurred in the village, the body of the deceased is brought to the ceremonial ground for a wake. There, it is laid on banana leaves before the ceremonial house, and close relatives decorate it with all of the shell valuables the person owned in life: a man is decorated like a ceremonial dancer, a woman like a naramtagwa at first menstruation. The point is that, until about fifty years ago, decorated yams were displayed in just the same way, and among the Western Abelam they still are.[10]

To continue with the description of the long-yam cult: it is well known that Abelam yam growers never eat their own yams. In addition to other powerful substances, they have vested their own "blood" in their tubers, and even the mere idea of consuming them made my informants shudder. Instead, yam growers bring their decorated tubers to a yam festival and present them to their sambera, their exchange partners. Following hours of discussion and the feasting of their guests, and after a night of singing and dancing, the members of one ceremonial moiety in a village give their tubers, in a competitive and aggressive atmosphere, to members of the other. (Occasionally, an even more elaborate exchange, including many live pigs, takes place between villages rather than moieties.)

But what does the presentation of a long yam to an exchange partner mean? At an immediate level, it is an attempt to shame the partner by giving him longer and larger yams than he will be able to return. At a symbolic level, however, the analogy between yam and human being implies that long-yam givers are offering children who, though "dead," mute, and immobile, are nonetheless animate. And since the act of handing over the "hot" yam to the exchange partner cools it so that it may be consumed, the givers thereby are offering children for the receivers' consumption. We are thus transported into the dimensions of ritual cannibalism, which, as Marshall Sahlins (1983) has emphasized, always has a symbolic meaning even if the cannibalism involved is real. In the Abelam case, I suggest, men produce children that are vegetative incarnations of the spirit world by a kind of "androgenesis." And, just as men cannot marry their own daughters but must give them away to others, so they cannot eat these "children" themselves but must give them away to their exchange partners. By consuming these long yams, the exchange partner indulges a kind of communion with the yam grower's family or village, in the sense that he incorporates into himself a vegetable/spirit member of the giver's family. Thereby, he signals not so much aggressiveness (although this cannot be excluded completely) as a fundamental communion with the grower and ritual participation in his affairs.

THE PROCREATIVE POWERS
OF MEN AND WOMEN

If men's procreative powers manifest themselves in producing animated long yams, then how are women's procreative powers manifest? This question brings us back to the wambusuge ceremony. At first blush, it may seem that this ceremony comprises two aspects that are loosely related at best: on the one hand, there are the events of the wambusuge feast, when the women seize the ceremonial ground and the long yams and hold a feast; on the other, there is the girl in the menstruation hut—though her physical condition is the cause of the wambusuge ceremony, she does not become the actual focus of the women's activities on the ceremonial ground. In this section, I examine the former events; in the next section, I consider the girl herself. As I hope to demonstrate, these two ritual elements are closely related both sociologically and symbolically.

As I have noted, everything connected with women and femaleness is inimical to the cultivation of long yams. Thus, throughout the whole six months of the yam growing season, yam growers are supposed scrupulously to avoid sexual intercourse. The result—as Scaglion (1978) has shown for the Western Abelam village of Neligum—is a six-month birth season paralleling a six-month yam season, with the majority of births occurring from October to December, shortly after the planting season. It is because they eschew any contact with women and claim to generate life in their yams without women's participation or interference that I have described men's production of long yams as "androgenesis." The tribute women pay to this androgenetic procreation is their renunciation of the sexuality they are said to embody.

At the core of women's fundamental procreative power, a power that lies beyond men's control, are sexual development and maturation, this power is displayed in a girl's first menstruation. Unpredictable and thus uncontrollable, first menstruation signals the onset of sexual maturity. A girl has now become an adult woman, able to lead a sexually active life—and, indeed, she is likely to marry soon afterwards. She now must follow the rules of conduct toward men and long yams that befit a grown-up woman. Following her puberty ceremony, her cicatrization scars communicate her new status to everybody she meets.

Just as men insist on women's temporary renunciation of performed sexuality so that they can grow long yams, so, in the wambusuge, women claim men's vegetative products—long yams—as men's contribution to women's fertility and its generation. In a sense, men's vegetative children are needed as a sacrifice to a woman's sexual maturity. Moreover, it is the ritual killing of these yams, their dissection and division on the ceremonial ground, that is the condition for women's further fertility and procreation. These equivalences, I suggest, are the fundamental message of this part of the Abelam menarcheal ceremony, a message that only becomes apparent when the wambusuge is related to the yam cult. It also becomes apparent that concepts of gender are directly linked to the meaning of horticulture and indirectly to the products of subsistence: vegetative and human life and their generation by men's and women's procreative powers are conceived as mutually interrelated.

THE NARAMTAGWA AND THE YAM STONE

As the events of the wambusuge unfold on the ceremonial ground, the newly menstruating girl remains inside the menstruation hut. She is considered to be extremely "cold," as opposed to the desired "hotness" of men and tubers—the blood and flesh of the naramtagwa again seen as antithetical to vegetative life—and this "coldness" must be combated by her puberty rites in order to safeguard the village. Thus, she is fed with roasted yam (preferably wapi) to warm her up. She holds these tubers in nettles to shield them from the coldness of her hands—nettles also are used to beat people in initiations, to cleanse oneself after burying a corpse, and after first menstruation, because they are considered ritually powerful means of warming the skin and removing pollution. Finally, the girl is bled in scarification to reduce her ability to pollute, the coldness of the released blood being "killed" by the ritual hotness of the wild taro on which it is made to drip. Generally the precinct of men alone, wild taro is associated with physical aggression, killing, and enmity.

For men, however, the girl in the menarche hut does not just embody the "coldness" that is antithetical to them and their long yams. She also serves as a metaphor in ritual discussions about these yams. Most, if not all, Abelam men keep a few oddly shaped stones in their yam houses that are thought to promote the growth and fertility of the tubers and are sometimes buried in the yam gardens following planting. In addition to these individually owned stones, each village also possesses a few stones that are associated with the growth of the major tuber crops and are kept in a special hut to which only one or two men in the village have access. One of these, an upright stone, is associated with the wapi long yams and, I was told, has "marks" on its "skin" "like a Sepik/Iatmul man has on his back." Before the planting season starts, the guardian of the stone, usually an old man collectively chosen by the yam growers, is said to decorate this wapi stone "like a long yam" and "like a ceremonial dancer." Growers who hope to grow outstanding long yams send shell rings to the stone, which the guardian lays out on the ground before it so that they point in the direction of the owners' yam gardens. The guardian then calls the names of the ring givers, and the lines of rings are said to act as a "bridge" that carries the stone's power to the grower's garden to support his tuber-growing efforts. (My informants compared the stone in its small house to a "power station" from which electric power is led to every house.)

During men's yam-growing rituals on the amei, reference is often made to this secret stone but only through metaphor. And though its shape is distinctly phallic, at least to western observers, it is spoken of in these ritual metaphors as female.[11] When men sing *kanggu* songs at displays of the longest yams, moreover, women are excluded and the growers then sing about the yamstone as follows (these songs are published in their entirety in Hauser-Schäublin 1989b:194–229):

> This woman in [name of the hamlet with the yam-stone house] is decorated and she is happy.
> This woman belongs to me.
> She looks happily at her achievements,
> This naramtagwa who lives in [name of a naramtagwa's hamlet].

At another event, when the guardian of the Kalabu village yam stone had died, the stone was publicly alluded to in songs as "she who is menstruating." Furthermore, looking at the yam stone is compared to looking at a well-hidden vulva.

Although one may be surprised at first to find such metaphors used to describe an artifact that is the material center of the exclusively male yam cult, they reveal important structural equivalences within Abelam culture. I suggest that the yam stone, the symbol of men's procreative powers over vegetative life, is directly equated to the naramtagwa, the symbol of women's procreative powers. Both are secluded in special huts surrounded by gender-specific secrecy: the yam stone is surrounded by male secrecy, the naramtagwa by female secrecy. Both are ritually washed with the same mixture of herb and cane juice before their ceremonial decoration. The "marks" on the stone's "skin" are strikingly analogous to the scarification marks on the naramtagwa's skin. And while both are kept hidden and never brought to the ceremonial ground, feasts to honor both are held on this piazza. The colorful yam displays are thought to please the yam stone, while the women's seizure of the amei and their dissection of long yams in the wambusuge is done to honor the girl.

A fundamental complementarity in the meaning of men's and women's life thus emerges: the men's yam cult, its secret, sacred stone, and the men-

TABLE 2.1   THE PROCREATIVE POWERS OF ABELAM
MEN AND WOMEN

Men's Procreative Powers	Women's Procreative Powers
Produce vegetative children (yams)	Produce flesh-and-blood children
Source in the world of the dead	Source in women's body; innate
Involve successful cooperation with the spirits of the other world	Involve successful maturation of a girl (bodily change from girl to woman)
Long tubers publicly displayed on the ceremonial ground to celebrate successful procreation of long yams	Women gather publicly on the ceremonial ground to celebrate successful (innate) transformation of a girl into a woman
"Secret" is yam stone hidden in the yam-stone house	"Secret" is the menarcheal girl hidden in the menstruation hut
Yams "killed" to acknowledge women's procreative power	Sexuality renounced to acknowledge men's procreative power

arche rites for girls can only be understood together. Nevertheless, there is an asymmetry to this complementarity: although men ritually refer to the yam stone as female, as a beautiful girl during menarche, I never came across the reverse metaphor, of a naramtagwa referred to as a yam stone and thus as a male.

Judith Brown (1963) has concluded that female initiation rites occur in those societies where women make a significant contribution to subsistence activities. At a general level, this argument seems to be confirmed by the Abelam data, but one would have to ask if there is any society in which women do not contribute substantially to subsistence. The answer probably depends on the definition of what constitutes subsistence activities. Abelam women take part in gardening, they cultivate ka yams, and the growing of taro and aerial yams is almost exclusively their domain. But they are excluded from ceremonial long-yam cultivation, and in this I see one of the main "causes" of Abelam female "initiation" rites.[12] Female "initiation" is not about subsistence activities per se, as Brown suggests, but rather about the meanings and values attached to *modes* of subsistence, and culturally specific ideas about the different forms of procreative powers that men and women possess (see also Hauser-Schäublin 1989a). In the case of the Abelam, these modes of subsistence are horticulture in general and the growing of yams in particular, and these ideas involve men's androgenetic procreation of ceremonial yams as opposed to women's reproductive fertility—as summarized in table 2.1.

2.3   A *naven* during a Iatmul marriage ceremony. The woman mocks men's
        aggressive behavior toward women. Iatmul; Kararau Village, 1973.
        Photo credit: Jörg Hauser

THE IATMUL NAVEN: RITES OF ACHIEVEMENT

Having analyzed female puberty rites among the Abelam and their meaning in
relation to men's preoccupations with growing long yams, I now want to turn
to the Iatmul, the Abelam's neighbors to the south. If both cultures are
indeed closely related, then one would expect to find female puberty rites

among the Iatmul that are similar to those of the Abelam. But we do not. The reason for this substantial cultural difference thus deserves some attention.

Among the Iatmul, we find a completely different subsistence economy. Here, women's subsistence contributions are even greater than among the Abelam: a woman is almost solely responsible for providing her family daily with its food (Gewertz 1977, 1983; Hauser-Schäublin 1977). Men are occupied rather with ritual production, through which they claim control over women's subsistence production. They produce nothing comparable, though, to the long yams that Abelam men procreate, grow, and finally present as a "mature," animated being. If, as I have argued for the Abelam, female puberty rites are linked to ideas about complementary gender-specific, procreative qualities, activities, and products of fertility, then this would explain why puberty celebrations are absent among the Iatmul.

What we do find among the Iatmul are naven ceremonies. As Bateson (1958[1936]) brilliantly demonstrated, the Iatmul perform these ceremonies whenever a male or female child performs a gender-specific task for the first time. Some of these ceremonies are exclusively all-women affairs—as, for example, the ceremonies staged for a marriage at the bride's father's home and then, following the marriage payment, in the husband's house (plate 2.3).[13]

Despite surface appearances, however, these all-women naven cannot be equated to Abelam menarcheal ceremonies. To begin with, to the best of my knowledge, they are performed neither at first menstruation nor at a woman's first birth. Second, whereas Abelam menarcheal rites celebrate the successful, innate psychophysical maturation of a girl, naven rites celebrate instead sociocultural achievements. Third, these all-women naven, like all naven ceremonies, are not simply gender-oriented rituals but also rituals to do with kinship. To be sure, their transvestite aspects involve women structurally identifying with their husbands, but they do so in mockery of proud and aggressive male behavior. The fact remains that naven participants perform first and foremost in their role as specific kin to the person for whom the ritual is held, not simply as a person of a specific gender. Finally, Iatmul women never seize men's ritual products for their own purposes as Abelam women seize men's long yams; indeed, among the Iatmul, male ritual products are always hidden and never publicly displayed. And women never seize the ceremonial ground as Abelam women seize the amei for the wambusuge feast. If a ritual occurs inside a dwelling house, then the Iatmul do ignore the structure's usual separation into male and female compartments. But, in keeping with the kinship nature of these rituals, this seizure involves kin groups privately taking over male space, not gender groups collectively and publicly seizing male space.

IATMUL WOMEN AND MALE INITIATION

In former times, Iatmul fringe villages apparently practiced female initiation, but its character was very different from Abelam puberty rites, not least in the fact that it was not compulsory. An old woman in the village of Aibom, for example, told me (Hauser-Schäublin 1977:176) she had been initiated with two companions at the urging of her brothers and over the protests of her mother. The ritual took place in a part of her dwelling house that had been fenced off for the purpose. The three girls were scarified by men around the nipples. Afterwards, they remained secluded for quite a long time. They were fed by their mothers and spent the time producing netbags and learning to play the Jew's harp. After "a year" they then should have been sent to the men's house to be scarified on the back like men and to undergo at least parts of male initiation. But then the big crocodile (i.e., the bull roarers) cried from the men's house, everybody was scared, and so they never did complete their initiation.[14]

The reason for this practice seems to be the importance Iatmul initiation has in reinforcing a person's descent group status by binding him or her into a socioreligious system that revolves around initiatory classes and their solidarity. Consequently, a woman's "value" seems to have been augmented by her initiation, as indicated in the case above by the insistence of the girl's brothers, over the objections of her mother, that she be initiated. Through her initiation, a girl's social status as a member of her natal, patrilineal clan was highlighted, becoming almost as significant as that of her brothers. As the woman in the case above herself pointed out, her scarifications prevented her from being taken by force or collectively raped—as was often done to make a girl marry a man she had no wish for—because she would have been revenged by the whole patriclan and members of the initiation system. Only if she later married according to traditional marriage rules (preferably of the *iai* type) would she relinquish this status. The Abelam place much less emphasis than the Iatmul on descent: unlike the Iatmul, they have no developed genealogies and no myths explaining and legitimating the origin of individual clans. Consequently, it is not surprising that I never heard of such an initiation practice among them; indeed, the idea of sending a daughter instead of a son to undergo male initiation seemed never to have occurred to my informants.

Among the Eastern Iatmul, I met two women in the village of Angerman, whose father had sent them to be initiated with the boys (Hauser-Schäublin 1977:170–172). Their father had held an important position within his clan, and his main motive, it seems, was to have one of them inherit his esoteric knowledge since he had no male heir. He had sent both rather than just one to the initiation house so that each would have the company of the other. They took part in all of the male rites except the subsequent head-hunting party.[15] By their initiation, these two women assumed a kind of double status, being women and yet, at the same time, persons with access to male ritual life. They married according to the traditional rules of iai marriage (father's father's sister's son's son) and led the life of women and mothers. But they were entitled to join the men at ceremonies and allowed to enter the men's house at their pleasure. Like men, moreover, they were prohibited on pain of death from divulging what they had seen and learned to other women—though, as it happened, only the senior of the two inherited their father's esoteric knowledge. To what extent the pair actually took advantage of their "male" status is uncertain, however; shortly after their initiation, the Second World War broke out and, once it was over, they became members of the SDA mission.

In the Central Iatmul village of Palimbei, I met another woman who had undergone male initiation, but for very different reasons. As a young, prepubescent girl, she was visiting her mother's village, Tigowi, and one day climbed a Malay apple tree to get some fruit. At that moment, unfortunately, two men started blowing long flutes in a fenced-off enclosure nearby. The two men noticed her in the tree and, although no men's house ceremony was in progress and nobody had warned her that the flutes would be sounded, they dragged her into the men's house, where she was gang raped. She then was scarified and underwent a shortened version of male initiation, learning the secrets of the men's house and viewing the men's sacred musical instruments. When, finally, she was allowed to leave the fenced off ceremonial ground, she was given only a tiny loin covering, not the long grass skirt with which initiated women normally were honored. Her mother cried at her daughter's state when she returned and immediately brought her back to Palimbei.

Although she had gained what was considered culturally important ritual knowledge, the woman nonetheless felt degraded, dishonored, derided, and incredibly shamed. Thereafter, she led a rather disorganized life, and the way she related her story to me, many decades after, mirrored the feelings she must have experienced and a suffering from which she never really had recovered. I recorded a similar instance in Aibom village. In both cases, the initiation was meant, and experienced, as a severe punishment and stigmatization. By retrospectively legitimating the discovery of male secrets, moreover, the practice seems to have been intended also to protect them. Were the girls not initiated, they would have passed what they had discovered on to others. Initiation, however, ensured that they would never do so.

CONCLUSION

Beyond the rather broad generalization that, among the Abelam and the Iatmul, female rituals of transition, initiations, and naven have to do with different stages in a woman's life, these rites are so different in the two societies that they hardly can be compared. Notwithstanding their linguistic relatedness, the common "Sepikness" of these two peoples obviously does not go beyond the analogy or similarity of a few external "traits"; there is no homology, similarity, or even identity in structure. Rather, I have argued, the ceremonies in these two cultures reflect different cultural orientations in modes of subsistence, social organization, and ideas about men's and women's qualities, activities, and the products of their different procreative powers. In sum, to subsume the content, function, and meaning of these ceremonies under a single label, "initiation," is simply wrong. Or, to put the matter the other way round, to talk of "initiation" in Abelam and Iatmul society is to pretend a cultural similarity and comparability where, in fact, there is almost none.

NOTES

1. Weiss (1994) argues that in precolonial times there existed elaborate female initiation rituals independent from those of men.

2. I hesitate to refer to "traditional" Iatmul and Abelam culture because, since my first fieldwork almost twenty years ago, substantial cultural change has taken place. But, since the purpose of this paper is not to give a description of the present day situation but an analysis of specific aspects of these cultures, I shall leave the phrasing unchanged.

3. MacLennan (n.d.) has made a study of menstruation, pregnancy, and childbirth among the Western Abelam, but it contains no additional information on menarche ceremonies.

4. These valuables are presented to the girl's mother's brother and are sometimes regarded as a kind of delayed brideprice for her mother. In other villages, menarche rituals are followed shortly afterwards by marriage ceremonies.

5. Fieldwork among the Iatmul took place in 1972–73 and among the Abelam between 1978 and 1983. Research was sponsored by the Swiss National Research Funds, Berne.

6. As I have described and discussed these wambusuge in detail elsewhere (Hauser-Schäublin 1987, 1989b:148–151), only a general outline is given here.

7. In everyday traditional life, no pubic aprons or "skirts" were worn: people went completely naked. Thus, the skirts worn during ceremonies by men and women must have had a greater significance than merely hiding the genitals. Unfortunately, these meanings have yet to be fully explored.

8. These ritual skills evidently were traditions within a family or clan, for the parents of these specialists also had been ritual experts.

9. The Abelam differentiate two transcendental aspects of a human being. One can be translated as a "soul" related to blood, the other as a "soul" related to bone (see Hauser-Schäublin 1983).

10. At one first menstruation ceremony, I saw a man carry a long yam tied to a pole onto the amei, just as nowadays is done at a yam festival. There, he loosened the ropes and laid the tuber carefully on the ground. (Kalabu and other mamu-speaking Abelam took over the practice of tying the tubers to poles from the Arapesh.)

11. Eric Schwimmer (pers. comm.) pointed out to me that the Orokaiva also speak of male things as if they were female because they are destined to be given to women. If I understand him correctly, the Abelam would use the feminine gender to express the close ritual association of the male speaker and "his" stone (forming something like a couple).

12. "Initiation" rites are sometimes defined as involving instruction of an initiate in tasks and meanings appropriate to their gender. Among the Abelam, at least, however, the wambusuge involves no instruction whatsoever.

13. For a detailed account of individual women's naven I witnessed in Kararau in 1972–73, see Hauser-Schäublin 1977:83–95.

14. Although her story was fragmentary, my informant also hinted at some kind of puberty ceremonies performed among the southern neighbors of the Aibom. Perhaps, therefore, the female initiation she described should be analyzed in relation to them also.

15. Bateson (1958[1936]:10) notes that only a very few women were initiated and that the ceremony was a simplified version of boys' initiation. Schmid and Kocher-Schmid (1991:171–173) mention briefly a former female initiation which obviously followed the pattern of men's rituals.

3

In the Shadow of the Tambaran

Female Initiation Among the Ndu of the Sepik Basin

Paul B. Roscoe

For some time there has been a sentiment in anthropology that if cross-cultural comparison is to bear fruit then it must be successful at the regional level before it can be contemplated at the holocultural—or global—level (Eggan 1954; Evans-Pritchard 1965; Holy 1987a; Schapera 1953).[1] In recent years, as a result, comparative analyses increasingly have limited themselves to the local or regional level (e.g., Fardon 1984–1985; de Heusch 1982[1972], 1985; Kuper 1982; Riviére 1984), a trend reflected also in Melanesian anthropology (e.g., Feil 1987; Knauft 1993; Modjeska 1982).

   The Ndu-speaking Abelam, Iatmul, and Yangoru Boiken—three of the more populous societies of the Sepik Basin—are excellent candidates for this sort of fine-grained, local comparison. The Abelam and Iatmul have been the subjects of many rich ethnographic accounts, while the Yangoru Boiken were the subject of my own fieldwork in 1979–81, 1987, and 1991. The three groups live in close geographical proximity: the Boiken and Iatmul live immediately west and south respectively of the Abelam, and they are separated from one another only by the Ndu-speaking Sawos peoples.[2] Moreover, current evidence suggests that the three are closely related historically. Many hundreds of years ago, it appears, early Ndu speakers lived in modern-day Sawos territory, on the shores of a vast saltwater embayment. When this inland sea subsequently began to recede, some of these ancestors moved northwards, assimilating or displacing an already resident, Torricelli-speaking population, to become the Boiken and Abelam. Later still, some western Sawos speakers moved southwards, spreading along the banks of the Sepik River to become the Iatmul (Roscoe 1989, 1994).

As one might expect of such closely related groups, male initiation among the Abelam, Iatmul, and Yangoru Boiken share many similarities (Bateson 1958[1936]:129–137, 244–246; Forge 1970a:275–279; Gesch 1985:255–257; Hauser-Schäublin 1989b:237–298; Roscoe 1990a). What is surprising, though, are the differences in the scale of their female initiation rites. When Europeans began significantly to influence their cultures in the 1920s and 1930s, the Iatmul apparently lacked any female initiation rites, the Abelam celebrated a single-stage puberty rite, while the Yangoru Boiken mounted elaborate, three-stage sequences that were closely articulated with their male initiation. This paper attempts to account for these striking variations. I argue that a primary motivation for initiation among these peoples was politico-ritual, the production of individuals equipped to achieve renown in formal politico-ritual arenas. Since males were seen as the central players in these arenas, each society was concerned to empower its sons through elaborate initiation ceremonies. The three groups differed, however, in the politico-ritual importance attached to women. Among the Iatmul, women were largely excluded from formal politico-ritual life; among the Abelam, they were peripherally included; while among the Yangoru Boiken, they were centrally implicated. Consequently, the stress each group placed on the initiatory empowerment of women differed proportionately.

THE YANGORU BOIKEN

In developing this argument, I shall base my analysis on a close study of Yangoru Boiken female "initiation." Speakers of the Yangoru dialect of the Boiken language, the Yangoru Boiken numbered in 1980 some fourteen thousand slash-and-burn cultivators living in the southern foothills below Mount Hurun in the Prince Alexander Range (for ethnographic overviews, see Gesch 1985; Roscoe 1991). The mainstays of their diet are yam, taro, and sago, supplemented with banana, pork, and a variety of bush and trade-store foods. Social life is territorially constituted by residence in seminucle-ated villages and socially constituted by membership in ideologically agnatic kin groups known as *tuahrung*, a term that can be roughly glossed as *subclan* and *clan*. These tuahrung, in turn, aggregate along the territorially defined axes of a moiety-based system of competitive pig exchange, which is the most important arena for evaluating the reputations of the big men around whom political activities swirl. In earlier days, the limits of effective political activity were roughly defined by war confederacies of some five to ten villages that, ideally at least, supported one another in offense and defense. Nowadays, these confederacies are little more than memories, and the area has become incorporated into subdistrict, provincial, and national political realms that greatly transcend the old borders.

By New Guinean standards, the Yangoru Boiken have a long history of contact with the European world. The first whites to enter their territory were missionaries of the Divine Word, who appeared in October 1912, on what was to be the first of many evangelizing tours before a permanent mission presence was established in 1948. By the 1930s, labor recruiters and administrative patrols had begun to appear. Often dramatic and frequently traumatic, these contacts had significant effects on Yangoru ritual life. By the 1950s, both male and the later stages of female initiation had been abandoned. Consequently, when I began fieldwork in 1979, only the first stage of female initiation was still practiced. Nonetheless, there were still a sufficient number of knowledgeable informants alive to piece together a fairly clear picture of the entire male initiatory sequence and all but the final stage of the female sequence as these were practiced in the villages of Sima, Hambeli, and Kworabre.

MALE AND FEMALE INITIATION
AMONG THE YANGORU BOIKEN

In Yangoru belief, male and female initiation imbued initiates with virtues that, in their complementary performance, elevated the politico-ritual eminence of spousal pairs and their kin groups.[3] In this intensely competitive society, reputation is judged by the degree to which men and women manifest their gender ideal—the degree to which they become "strong." For a man, this "strength" must be displayed in the community's formal theaters of politico-ritual action. In precontact days, he had to display willingness and ability in defending his kin group on the battlefield. Then, as now, he also had to shower pigs on his exchange partner, generously acquit his wealth obligations to maternal and affinal kin, and demonstrate an ability to persuade others to his cause through superior oratory.

As both men and women point out, success in these endeavors depends upon the activities of wives. To begin with, a wife is vitally important in bearing, rearing, and protecting a man's children. Her sons are important to her husband's "strength" because they are "his army": in bygone days, they were warriors, and even now their strapping presence at moots is silent testimony to the force of arms upon which he and his kin group can call. Daughters are important because their marriages and subsequent birthings are crucial conduits through which their father obtains wealth. Tales are told of would-be big men whose ambitions were thwarted by a lack of daughters—and hence wealth—and of "rubbish men" who later came to prominence on the wealth they received once their many daughters married and began to have children.

Equally important to a husband's renown is a wife's commitment to those tasks crucial in generating political valuables. Wives rear pigs for their menfolk, which can be sold for hefty sums, and they are crucial in garnering wealth from kinfolk. On the one hand, they help their husbands in the tedious task of trawling these kinfolk when wealth is needed. On the other, the wealth these kinfolk offer depends critically on how handsomely a man has met his reciprocal obligations in food, for which in turn he depends on his wife. A wife whose "cooking fire never goes out" is the most esteemed of women, and exemplary tales are always to hand of how one wife's energy was instrumental in the prominence of a big man, while another's laziness helped destroy her husband's ambitions.

As a man gains eminence by manifesting masculine ability, so a woman gains status for her abilities in tasks that contribute to his success. The crucial truth in Yangoru Boiken life, however, is that the full eminence of each can only be achieved if both manifest their gender-specific abilities together. A "strong" husband married to a "bad" wife likely will achieve some renown, as will a "strong" wife married to a "destitute" of a husband. But only a "strong" husband and a "strong" wife acting together can hope to gain full eminence for themselves and their kin group.

The political destinies of husband and wife are thus intimately entwined, and to advance these destinies male and female initiation aimed to imbue initiates with the virtues appropriate to their gender. Male initiation was believed to confer motivation and ability in battle, oratory, the pursuit and manipulation of shell wealth and pigs, and those aspects of food production, such as hunting, gardening, and sago processing, that were "men's work." Female initiation motivated women to bear and rear children, and conferred on them the full-bodied figure esteemed as the prerequisite for bearing and suckling many offspring. It furnished motivation and ability for long, arduous work in the fields and prodigious culinary production, and it inspired them to "settle down" in marriage with the best interests of their husbands and husbands' kin groups at heart.

For the Yangoru Boiken, in sum, the ideological justification for their initiation sequences lay in the interlinked politico-ritual fortunes of husband and wife. This ideology furnishes the most profitable avenue for making analytical sense of their female initiation rites—but at a cost, for the rites that conferred male and female "strength" were not limited to those conventionally labeled *initiation rites*. They included also rites accompanying first intercourse, the birth of a first child, and the initiation of a pair's daughters. Consequently, until European influence started their decline, Yangoru's initiation rites were as elaborate as any in New Guinea. Each sex progressed through six stages. The male sequence began around thirteen to fifteen years of age, with a communal induction into the *sumbwi* grade. Female initiation began at first menstruation, which in the 1980s occurred at an average age of sixteen, plus or minus three years. The second and third grades comprised the rites of first intercourse and first birth, respectively, which husband and wife underwent together. Following the birth of their first child, they were then initiated contemporaneously but separately into the *kwuli* (or *pana*) grade and, fifteen years later, ideally with the initiation of their first son, into the *suwero* grade. Finally, they were deemed fully initiated following the first-menstruation rites of their youngest daughter.

THE NARANDAUWA RITES

The decline of Yangoru initiation in the late 1940s and early 1950s left the first stage of female initiation, the *narandauwa* rites, as the most visible vestige of the traditional complex.[4] It commences with a girl's first menstruation, an event believed to come with the dawn. Because the girl's flow is believed to pollute both her and her parents, her mother's brothers are immediately summoned to build a small, conical seclusion hut (*tanguka*) on her hamlet piazza and a rudimentary lean-to for her parents (see plate 3.1). A third lean-to is sometimes constructed for a young ritual caretaker, usually an unmarried brother. Before the girl enters seclusion, her head may be shaved—though this custom is observed less commonly now than it once was—and she is ceremonially whipped by her agnates. Hoisted on the back of a young agnate, ideally a true brother, with another holding her legs, she is carried back and forth through a gauntlet that belabors her back with switches. Next, she is bidden to urinate and defecate, and, after being washed by her mother, she enters her seclusion hut. Here she will stay for the next four days with neither food nor water, tobacco nor betelnut, emerging only to be washed by her mother in the mornings and to participate in the ceremonial rites of her initiation. For their part, her parents enter the seclusion of their lean-to, where they remain for the next five days.

3.1   Parental shelter (left) and *tanguka* (right). Yangoru Boiken; Hambeli Village, 1987. Photo credit: Paul Roscoe

In ancestral times, the second morning was set aside for scarification of the girl's breasts and belly, but nowadays this custom is honored more in the breach than the observance. If her marriage has been arranged, her suitor's father will announce the betrothal by placing a small ring or, nowadays, more usually, a small sum of cash, at the entrance of her tanguka. The rest of the morning is given over to celebratory songs (*telekrie*) and to proclamations on the slit gongs of her newly menstrual status. That night more telekries are sung. Nothing of note then happens until the evening of the fourth day when, in a small rite known as *pa pwak* (heating the stones), the girl is brought out in the gathering dusk to be bathed in scented steam and honored by the first of many rounds of telekries that continue through to dawn.

In bygone days, the girl often would be brought around midnight of this fourth night to dance before a representation of her tuahrung's *wala* spirit—or, as it is known in Tok Pisin, her Tambaran. In many cases, the wala took the form of a *malingatcha* carving, a rather fearsome, decorated, humanoid statue some three to six feet tall, with a large head, arms akimbo, and legs apart (see Aufenanger n.d.:plate 9). In other instances, the spirit appeared as an ornamented, conical mask some two meters high, worn by a male dancer. In the most prestigious of these displays, though, both forms of the wala—

statue and mask—appeared. By the light of flaring firebrands, a decorated malingatcha was set up on the hamlet piazza before a bed of white *menja* leaves enclosed by dry sago-frond stems ornamented with feathers and hibiscus blossoms. Supported by their kin groups, the initiate's father and his mother's brothers then indulged in a mock-competitive display of shell rings, each group lining their wealth from the base of the statue out over the menja leaves. As each line fell short, its sponsors burst into telekrie songs to summon more wealth. By convention, however, the "competition" ended in a draw. Two masked wala spirits then emerged from the bush to dance briefly with the initiate in front of the malingatcha display before disappearing again.

Nowadays, malingatcha carvings and competitive wealth displays have disappeared in the face of missionary opposition and the decline of the shell-wealth economy. On the rare occasions when the wala is still "brought out," it appears only as a masked dancing figure. Whatever its form, however, it was and is imbued with potent magic, and on this account the girl falls under a wide set of proscriptions to protect her from its noxious influence. For many months henceforth, on pain of skin disease or arthritic degeneration, she can eat only from the cooking fires of her immediate family, and she must avoid meat, certain greens, cold water, coconut milk, tobacco, and betelnut.

The fifth day of seclusion constitutes the ceremonial highlight of the first initiatory stage, the day when the young woman is formally decorated as a narandauwa, a "woman whom people come and look at." Summoned by the slit gongs, her agnates and their sororal affines first ceremonially amass her *winjengi*, the "blood payments" that will be made to her maternal kin (see figure 3.1). The girl is then brought out of her seclusion hut, seated on a palm-flower sheath, and decorated with ornamental shell finery contributed by her kin group and its relatives. A ritually pure and preferably prestigious female relative seats herself before the girl and places in each of her hands a small sum of wealth—formerly, a couple of shell rings; nowadays about K20–40 in banknotes. The initiator wipes the palm of her hand in the sweat of her armpit, presses it to the girl's breast, and proffers it for her to lick (see plate 3.2). Next, she gives her charge a knot of *ningi* vine and a twist of cooking-fire ash to chew. Finally, she retrieves the wealth from the initiate's hands and passes it four or five times around the girl's head. This act signifies to the girl's maternal ancestral shades that her winjengi has been assembled and is ready to be conferred on their descendants.

The wealth is then disbursed: the largest payments are made first, to the girl's real and classificatory mother's brothers, followed by smaller ones to her parent's maternal kin (figure 3.1). Small sums are also paid to the cre-

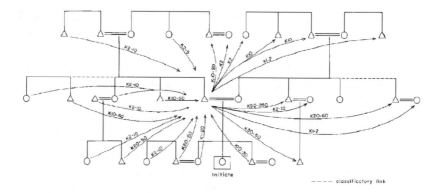

3 . 1   Typical contributions and disbursements at the *winjengi* (in 1980 PNG kina)

ators of the wala, to those who fed and cared for her parents during their seclusion, and so on. When all is done, the girl is given a morsel of cooked taro, which she passes from palm to palm to signify the reduction her winjengi have effected in her menstrual pollution, and then she formally breaks her fast by sipping a coconut soup proffered by her initiator.

When the crowd has left, the girl eats more substantially. Later, toward dusk, she is taken to the river to wash and, on her return, given a four-section length of *pitpit* cane, one section of which she is bidden to scrape off on each of the following nights. The next evening, she and her parents go down to the riverside, where they soften the leaves of certain magical shrubs and wild pitpit shoots over heated stones and rub the pulpy masses over their bodies.

On the evening when the girl's pitpit cane has been scraped bare, she emerges from seclusion for the last time. She dismantles her tanguka and burns it along with her initiation skirts. As the flames die down, she leaves with a gaggle of youngsters and young adults for the river. In ancestral days, what happened next depended on whether she had danced with the wala on the fourth night of her seclusion. If she had not, she might now be taken to a *yinanka* (rough/temporary house), a shoulder-high structure with sago-thatch roofing, fronded, sago-leaf walls, and a small entrance wadded with brambles and stinging nettles. Pushing her way through this scratching, stinging portal, she came upon the *pawalye* or "wala spirit of the water," a tableau formed by two painted and decorated women. If the initiate had previously danced with a wala, however, the pawalye was not staged; instead, she was made to crawl through another type of yinanka, a low tun-

3.2 Tambwi licks her initiator's armpit-sweat from her hand. Yangoru Boiken;
Hambeli Village, 1980. Photo credit: Paul Roscoe

nel of brambles and stinging nettles that purified her of the wala's power. Whatever the yinanka, the initiate emerged to encounter a gauntlet of young men, ideally her preferential marriage partners or "enemies" (Roscoe 1994:59–60), armed with whips and stinging nettles. Through this enfilade she was supposed to walk with unhurried pace, then jump into the river to join her young companions already splashing and frolicking in the water amid bundles of greenery torn from the bush. Nowadays, yinanka are rare, constructed only to purify those few initiates who have danced with the wala. More usually, initiates simply go down to the river to frolic in the water with their companions.

The events at the river mark the end of a girl's seclusion, though she must remain near her hamlet until her second period occurs. At this point, she is again tabooed food and water, but only for the first day. The following morning, she is taken down to the river, where she is instructed to rub the charred bark of the *meng* tree over her skin and prepare and consume a soup made with the bark of the *tuarepolyahe* tree. She then returns to the hamlet and breaks her fast.

The final rites take place a week to a month later. In some cases, they begin with a little ceremony at the river. The girl's father stands in the water with some ginger root placed in the aperture of a shell ring between his feet, and she dives through his legs, takes up the ginger in her mouth, and consumes it. After, or instead of, this rite, she bakes some fish in her hamlet, and distributes it to whichever small children are present. Next, she addresses Mount Hurun in his guise as the culture-hero, Walarurun, informing him that he must now assume the remainder of her taboos. Finally, she consumes a morsel of meat and a twist of ningi plant and, by this act, is free to eat whatever and wherever she pleases.

NUBILITY, POLLUTION, AND THE NARANDAUWA

The Yangoru Boiken recognize several purposes to the narandauwa rites. By celebrating the initiate's new fertility, they mark her nubility, a fact broadcast far and wide by the slit gongs and telekrie songs sung and sounded in her honor. Other events increase her desirability as a bride. In the past, her scarifications testified to her fortitude, the signs of a "good" woman. The pa pwak ritual and the meng and tuarepolyahe rites are said to "fatten" her so she will bear many children and have ample breast milk to nourish them. Yet other rites inspired in her the virtues of a good wife. In the past, the most important of these were the various wala tableaus, the significance of which I shall consider later. Nowadays, wifely virtues are mainly instilled at the girl's winjengi, when she ingests ningi vine, fire ash, and her initiator's armpit sweat. The latter implants the elder's virtues in the girl, the former "breaks open" (i.e., molds) her thinking toward the hard work required for food production and assisting her husband in gathering wealth.

The transferences of wealth at the winjengi ceremony play both secular and spiritual roles. In a secular vein, they facilitate the wealth transactions that attend the initiate's future marriage and childbirths. At the heart of wealth circulation in Yangoru is a belief that a woman's natal tuahrung must be compensated for the contributions of substance and character that she makes to her children. Her son's obligations to thus "pay for his skin/body" endure until his death: at life-cycle rituals and whenever his mother's brothers are in need, he—or his agnates on his behalf—must help them with wealth. In the case of her daughter, however, similar lifelong obligations would pose a problem: at her marriage, the daughter's bridewealth is sup-posed to transfer primary claims on her person from her natal kin group to her husband's. But for her natal group to be able to dispose of her in this way, they must first terminate her mother's brothers claims on her. It is this that the winjengi payments accomplish.

In addition to their transactional intent, winjengi payments also play a spiritual role, one grounded in a complex nexus of ideas about age- and gender-related pollution (sara). A girl's first menstruation is considered a profoundly polluting event; consequently, many practices associated with menarche are said to contain its dangers. The girl is confined to a seclusion hut so that she cannot pollute the community and the land. During seclu-sion, she is tabooed food lest her sara contaminate it, causing her to become blind or arthritic. At the end of her seclusion, everything that has come into contact with her—her clothing, netbag, and shelter—is burned so that the pollution adhering to it cannot harm others.

While these rites contain the girl's sara, her winjengi payments help lift it. This process is conceptualized in a quite literal sense: her pollution is believed to adhere to her winjengi payments and be carried away with them. Indeed, her maternal kin are careful to wash the shell wealth they receive to remove the sara enveloping it. In addition, it is believed, the whippings administered at the beginning and end of the girl's seclusion, the taro-han-dling rite at her winjengi, and the ablutions with shrubs and shoots two days later also remove sara from her person.

These measures notwithstanding, the narandauwa rites do not leave a girl completely free of pollution. Because she is now menstruous, she will re-main contaminated for much of the rest of her life. This more enduring pol-lution, which I shall refer to as "age-related" pollution, can only be lifted by a series of subsequent ritual actions, among the most important of which are the rites attending her first intercourse and the birth of her first child.

RITES OF FIRST INTERCOURSE AND FIRST BIRTH

Nowadays, rites of first intercourse are observed rather less frequently and rigorously than they were before. They begin immediately after a marriage's consummation, which usually occurs from several months to a year or more after payment of the brideprice. Commonly, first intercourse takes place in the gardens or on the grassy periphery of an all-night festival. The partners return to their home hamlet, where they sit together in quiet embarrassment outside the bride's house. Since the pair have hitherto been obliged to avoid one another's company, this simple act signals clearly to others what has taken place.

By their first intercourse, the couple place themselves in a dangerously polluted state and must therefore enter seclusion. After the groom's mother has removed the bride's belongings and utensils to avoid their contamination, the couple enter the bride's house, where they remain for five days. The first is spent without food and water, a fast that is broken the following morning with a little ceremony outside the house, presided over by a highly esteemed male or female elder. First, the couple chew the sap from a ningi shrub. Next, their initiator premasticates two betelnut wads, giving one to the wife and the other, wrapped in another species of ningi, to the husband. The pair chew these wads, ingesting the elder's saliva as they do, and afterwards are bidden to go and wash in the river. They are then free to eat and drink although, because they are still polluted, their food is prepared by female in-laws and eaten using leaves and chopsticks to avoid contamination by their hands.

Except for evening washes at the river, the couple remain in or near their house for the next three days. On the afternoon of the fifth day, they again wash, and small amounts of wealth are conferred on their maternal relatives. With these transferences, the pair are freed from their seclusion and can once again eat normally. Finally, on the seventh day, they remove what remains of their pollution by rubbing the bark of the *meng tigia* sapling over their skin and washing with the sap and bark of the *nangele tigia* tree.

As with first intercourse rites, birth rites are practiced less conscientiously nowadays than they were before. Like first intercourse, birthing is also considered highly polluting, and parents are therefore secluded with their newborn in a small bivouac at the edge of their hamlet's ceremonial ground. In theory, they should remain here without food or water for five days; in practice, they are want to shorten their stay as they become more seasoned parents. For a first birth, though, seclusion is rigorously observed. It ends with a special set of rites that begin at dawn on the fifth day. An esteemed clan elder takes the father down to the river and bids him to consume ginger and several mouthfuls of water. That afternoon, relatives gather for the payment of child wealth by the baby's agnates to its maternal relatives. In earlier days, maternal relatives received one or two large shell rings; nowadays, they can expect K200–300 (much smaller amounts are paid at later births). Small sums of wealth are also given to the parents' maternal relatives. The old man who earlier attended the father has the pair chew the sap from a ningi shrub, followed by premasticated betelnut wads, the husband's wrapped with another variety of ningi. These rites free the pair from their seclusion, though for the next three weeks they must remain in or around their hamlet, and the mother must retire at night to another temporary structure, the *yukerayukera yendayendaka* (half-good, half-bad house).

With the exception of the childwealth payments, the aims of first inter-course and birthing rites were precisely those of the initiation enclosures and menarcheal huts. The ritual items consumed by the couple imbued them with the strengths and motivations appropriate to their gender. The ginger and ningi shrubs heated the husband's blood, respectively confer-ring on him oratorical flair and the motivation and ability to procure pigs and shell rings. And the saliva of his initiators, ingested from their premas-ticated betel wads, imbued him with their virtues. Likewise, the ningi shrubs consumed by his wife motivated her to pursue wealth on her hus-band's behalf, and the saliva she ingested from her initiator's betel wads motivated her to "follow the old person's talk"—to perform the tasks a woman should.

The seclusions, food taboos, and wealth paid at first-intercourse and first-birth rites remove the pollution arising from these events and lift some of the parents' age-related pollution. First-birth rites are especially impor-tant in this regard: in fact, one educated informant, inclined to quantifica-tion, ventured that they reduced age-related pollution "by about a half." With the first-birth rites, parents also become fully recognized as adults. In contrast to common anthropological assumption, therefore, puberty and ini-tiation rites do not mark the transition to adulthood in Yangoru. Rather, to the extent that Yangoru notions of adulthood can be translated into Western terms, this transition is marked by the rites of first birth.

THE KWULIRAUWA OR PANARAUWA RITES

By every account, there are significant variations in stagings of the naran-dauwa, first-intercourse, and first-birth rites. Consequently, the foregoing descriptions must be considered representative rather than definitive. Even in traditional times, some initiates never saw the wala in any of its forms, usually because their fathers could not afford the expense. On the other hand, the daughters of wealthy men were shown especially lavish versions. There were also significant differences from one village to another. In the Ambukanja area, directly to the east of Sima and Kworabre, for example, there was no tradition of wala displays, and the initiate was secluded for three weeks rather than just nine or ten days.

Because different kin groups had title to somewhat different sets of rites, the *kwulirauwa* (kwuli woman) or *panarauwa* (pana woman) rites attending the next stage of female initiation exhibited even more variety, posing obvious problems for describing a definitive panarauwa sequence. In what follows, therefore, I describe those experienced by my main female informant, commenting on the more significant differences described by two others.[5]

Panarauwa initiates were typically primipara who, in this virilocal society, had left their natal homes and tuahrung to join their husbands' group. In theory, similarly aged cowives of a subclan were initiated together, separately from the wives of other subclans; in practice, clans frequently combined the initiations of their wives. The initiators were older cowives of the suwero ritual grade, assisted by relatives from allied kin groups and by the wives of their husbands' exchange partners.

A woman's initiation into the panarauwa grade began once her husband had been taken off to the men's *hworumbo,* the great palisaded, male-initiation enclosure. For my main informant, the first rite was the *panahlu.* After donning new banana-leaf skirts, the initiates were taken to a clearing where each was paired off with an initiator. Holding their initiator's hands, they were instructed in the panahlu, an energetic, leaping dance that they then had to perform for several hours. Toward dusk, they were sent home only to encounter, en route, the first of several wala displays: a decorated woman, half-hidden by an arbor of tree boughs and palm fronds, holding aloft a *hwala* shell ring on a stick. After dancing before this figure, the initiates returned to their hamlet and, after resting, danced the panahlu through to first light.

As dawn broke, the initiators belabored their charges with stinging nettles, then led them down to the river, where they had prepared a small, dammed-up pool, its waters colored milky-white by the pith of a *hamberau* plant. With the enigmatic explanation that the rite would hasten their aging, they were each bidden to dunk their heads in the pool. Then began the *wangi* (eel) rite. With the initiates seated on boulders along the river bank, a woman decorated as a man appeared, holding at her pubes an *amba* shoot, a commonly recognized symbol of the penis. The initiates were warned that any laughter would subvert the whole purpose of their initiation, and the figure then solemnly stepped over each in turn. Afterwards, holding the shaft of a mature amba plant, they danced by the river and then returned home.

One or two mornings later, the initiates were taken into the bush and shown yet another wala, an ornamented display of shell rings similar to those constructed during narandauwa rites. As they turned to leave, though, they were told that now they would see the "real/true pana." Each initiate in turn was taken into the bush to confront a woman initiator painted black with white markings, and lavishly decorated "like a man." This encounter placed them under a set of taboos similar to those associated with the narandauwa wala, with intercourse proscribed in addition. After compensating their initiators for showing them this crucial wala, the initiates returned home. That night, they performed the *nangupana* (sago) rite: paired off in two lines, they clasped the hands of the initiate opposite, and an initiator wriggled along the line of forearms "like a snake."

For my main informant, the nangupana rite concluded her clan's main body of secret rituals. Other initiates, however, experienced the *kwazimpana*. Toward evening, they were gathered together in one of their hamlets, and a transvestite wala appeared, a woman decorated in male regalia with an amba tied at the base of her pelvis. Wagging this imitation penis up and down, she approached the initiates crying, "Here comes a man who wants intercourse!" Considerable horseplay ensued as this "man" grabbed at the initiates' buttocks and breasts. Afterwards, to the accompaniment of hand-drums and slit gongs, the night was spent singing frequently ribald, "women's *hworumbowanga*" songs.

The concluding phase of the second initiatory grade began at dawn some days later with the initiators roundly thrashing the initiates with stinging nettles. Perfumed and dressed in new banana-leaf skirts, they then went off to collect their husbands from the men's hworumbo. After a little ceremony outside the palisades in which each wife stepped on her husband's foot and splashed a little water on his leg, spouses were paired off with one another and led away to a hamlet where two enclosures had been built, one for the males, the other for the females. For the rest of the day, husbands and wives sat outside their respective enclosures with neither food nor water. This, they were told, was penance for past acts of obstreperousness and insubordination toward their parents. Eventually, at dusk, they were invited into their respective enclosures to consume the first of a series of soups prepared by their kin group's *gurli* and *gurlirauwa*—its exchange partners and their wives. Afterwards, the initiates returned to the piazza outside their enclosures for a night of singing and dancing. With the dawn, the husbands returned to their enclosure, and their wives were seated on a log in the piazza and given betelnut, pepper, and lime by their gurlirauwa. Then, as their menfolk were brought out to receive similar gifts, they were led back into their enclosure for a ritual feast that included the ningi shrub.

For the next month, the initiates' lives centered on the enclosures. Each day, they were sent out to forage in the bush for game to give to the gurlirauwa who provided their meals of taro and coconut soup. Failure to find game meant they went hungry. The rest of the time was spent either sleeping or dancing and singing hworumbowanga songs in the hamlet piazza with their husbands.

At dawn on the final day of their seclusion, the initiates participated in the *sarahuna* (polluted fire) ceremony. Surrounded by onlookers, a big man started a small fire to the side of the piazza, lit a brand from it, and called the name of a male initiate. The man's wife was then supposed to chase the big man around the piazza until she caught him and wrestled the flame from his grasp. After repeating the rite for each initiate, the big man then took a loop of cane sized to the girth of his waist and held it up to the assembled women. This, he challenged them, was how large their cooking should make their husbands in future. By way of response, the initiates fell on the man and, with derisive comments about how easy they would find it to fatten their husbands, grabbed the cane from his hand, broke it to pieces, and tossed it contemptuously aside. As a further challenge, each was then given the saucepans and plates from which her husband had been fed during his initiation to remind her of her duty to feed him well in future.

By symbolically conferring cooking fire unpolluted by the initiation enclosures, the sarahuna rite formally marked the end of seclusion. To remind them of the taboos incurred in witnessing their wala displays, however, initiates were obliged to wear their initiation apparel until they were released from their prohibitions. The *saka* rite, conducted about a month later, lifted their taboo on consuming cold water. As their husbands were led away for a similar rite, the young women were taken down to the river where an elderly initiator stood in the water, a hooked shell ring between her feet, with pieces of sugar cane, squash, and ginger root in its aperture. Each initiate in turn then dived beneath the woman's legs to take up and consume these morsels along with gulps of water.

About a month later, after their husbands' tuahrung had conferred pigs on its exchange partners, a second rite was performed to release the initiates from their remaining proscriptions on meat, eating at other fires, and sleeping with their husbands. As at the conclusion of their narandauwa rites, they formally transferred their taboos to Mount Hurun. In some cases, they were then given a soup containing certain bush ingredients; in others, they received a piece of ningi stem to chew. In either case, the rites released them from their remaining taboos and completed their panarauwa initiation.

THE SUWERO RITES

It is sometimes loudly lamented in modern Yangoru that no suwero men and women remain alive to organize the initiations of their descendants. Whether these latterday Rachels would actually avail themselves of this expertise were it still available is debatable. Certainly, though, with the passing of Yangoru's old folk, little information now remains about the suwero rites, the third and final stage of female initiation. What can be established is that they were far less elaborate than the panarauwa or narandauwa rituals and involved no physical ordeals. They also appear to have centered around a single wala display, which placed the initiates under taboo for about a year. According to one elderly suwero male, he and his wife were shown a tableau entitled *kambarauwa* (ancestral-spirit woman), though his request for confidentiality prevents me from publicizing his description of the event. According to another informant, he and his wife were separately shown the "secrets" of suwero. Given the variability in Yangoru's rites, both versions might be true, but beyond this we now can never know.

On graduating from the kwulirauwa and suwero rites, a woman could take a new name; usually, she chose one from the stock owned by her husband's or husband's mother's brother's subclan. As with kwulirauwa rites, the suwero rites further diminished a woman's age-related pollution. Consequently, on emerging from seclusion, she was obliged to give her blankets and kitchen and dining utensils to a younger woman and take new, unpolluted ones. Not until the initiation of her last daughter, however, did she and her husband became completely pana, or pollution-free.

THE NARANDAUWA REVISITED

When a young girl is secluded for her narandauwa rites, it will be recalled, her parents are secluded along with her. Since "their blood is in her," it is said, they too are polluted by her menstrual flow. Like their daughter, therefore, they are proscribed food, water, tobacco, and betelnut, albeit only for one day. Until her winjengi ceremony, moreover, they must avoid direct contact with their food on pain of contaminating it and rendering themselves blind or arthritic. This avoidance is lifted by the small wealth payments made to their mothers' kin groups at the winjengi (figure 3.1). Their seclusion ends the next day when, at dusk, they accompany their daughter to the riverside to rub softened wild pitpit shoots and the leaves of certain shrubs over their bodies (see earlier).

In contrast to the earlier stages of their initiation, nothing in these rites is said to "strengthen" the parents, to imbue them with the virtues associated with their gender. By now, for better or worse, their reputations have been long decided. Instead, the point of these final seclusions and rites is to cleanse them of their remaining age-related sara. With the rites for their last daughter, they become completely purified.

PRESTIGE AND THE POWER OF THE TAMBARAN

In describing how, in Yangoru eyes, female initiation rites imbue women with their gender-specific virtues, I have so far said little about the role of the secret wala tableaus. To judge by informant comments, however, these were the most potent forces instilling female "strength." It was these that initiators identified to initiates as the "true thing" in their initiations, the core of the rites. "I am sorry, my child," an informant muttered as nervousness caught at her throat in the middle of divulging the most secret of the pana displays. "I'm laying out [the secrets of] my heart now in teaching you this. This is the wala here."

Wala spectacles served several interests. By virtue of their expense and the support networks needed to stage them, the narandauwa displays contributed directly to a father's prestige and that of his tuahrung. For their part, women knew that once they had seen the kwuli and suwero wala, this knowledge would bring them sizable sums of wealth when, one day, they in turn acted as initiators. In local ideology, however, the central purpose of the displays was to motivate and empower the initiates. Separately and together, they were believed to turn the initiate's thoughts toward settling down with her husband as an obedient and hardworking wife, her impulses transformed from the gaiety of youth to the studied resolve of womanhood. They were felt to instill recognition of the jealousy and strife that her philandering would cause her husband's subclan. They were thought to motivate her for motherhood; and they were believed to move her to become the self-sacrificing provider who, regardless of the rain pouring from the heavens, journeys dutifully to the gardens, there to labor for long and hard hours over crops to nourish her family, and her husband's dogs, pigs, and sororal affines.

These notions about the power of wala displays are conceptually connected to the nature of wala spirits, the quintessential sources of power in the universe. Incarnated in certain mountains, trees, and stream pools, wala spirits are believed to be formed of a spiritual union of *kamba* or "spirits of the dead." These are agencies believed vital to their descendants' economic and political prosperity: they alert their heirs to impending good or evil; they cause their fields to yield abundantly, their pigs to grow large, and their bush to yield plentiful game; and they help them attract shell wealth to meet traditional obligations. As unions of the kamba, therefore, wala spirits are considered potent beings; but it is a dangerous potency, for they are also known to protest encroachments on their abodes by attacking the health of the offender or by "blazing up"—causing thunder, lightning, and violent winds to sweep across the night. Accordingly, the term *wala* is metaphorically extended to any bush agency believed hazardous to humans—toxic fruits and greens, poisonous snakes, and so on. To call artistic creations such as initiation displays wala, then, is to recognize that they incarnate power and menace (Roscoe 1995).

The wala displays confronting female initiates seemed designed to evoke emotions appropriate to the presence of power and menace. In a long-standing tradition of symbolic and semiotic anthropology, Forge (1966, 1979) has argued that ritual art carries cognitive meaning, "messages" about the basic assumptions of the cultural universe. While agreeing with Forge that art and ritual have "meaning," I suggest this meaning has as much to do with the evocation of affective states as with the communication of semantic "messages" (see also Maschio, this volume). In the case of the wala, the apparent aim was to evoke fear. By representing these displays as spiritual incarnations of the dead, of course, initiators thereby communicated to initiates that they were in the presence of suprahuman powers, an understanding that in itself would generate fear. After viewing these displays, moreover, initiates also knew that they would have to observe lengthy and arduous dietary and sexual taboos or suffer dire sickness or deformity, a realization that could only have added to their fears. The accompanying thrashings and scourings would have heightened their terror and, by inducing hyperventilation, the curious, sustained jumping that accompanied the panahlu wala may have exacerbated their anxiety. But the point I wish to make is that the formal artistic properties of these tableaus also seemed designed to strike fear and unease. Initiators who had helped stage the narandauwa malingatcha displays, for example, made it clear that in painting and decorating these statues they wanted "to make initiates afraid." This effect seems to have been achieved through the use of bright colors and grotesque form: against the backdrop of an everyday, rather drab, olive and brown forest environment, the sight of massed and gleaming shell rings on luminous beds of white menja leaves and of bright paint (and, in the postcontact era, shining can lids) on fearsomely wrought and decorated carvings could hardly fail to have a startling impact on a young observer. Likewise, the sudden appearance of disguised and strangely ornamented humans in a context of frequent hazing must have provoked significant unease among kwulirauwa initiates. Whatever the means, women uniformly reported that they experienced fear in confronting the wala displays. The "real/true pana" display of the kwuli stage, for example, so terrified my informant and her co-initiates that they wanted to run away. "I told my guardian, 'I'm very afraid sister.' We went and looked at it and we were absolutely terrified. What was it? A spirit of the dead or ... what kind of thing?"

The apparent aim of evoking this response was to commit the initiate to her own prosperity and that of her husband and his kin group. As one woman said of the malingatcha carving she saw during her narandauwa rites, it was meant "to frighten me, so that I would not drink water or meat and get a bad skin. It helped me become motivated to settle down [with a husband] and produce food." It is tempting to construe this sort of ritual intimidation as a means of mystifying male subordination of women (Godelier 1986). In this case, though, both sexes were exposed to the same kind of wala displays in their initiations; in both sexes, the aim was to instill fear so that initiates would become "strong" to the benefit of themselves and their kin groups; and, in both sexes, control of second and third initiatory grades was vested in senior members of the same sex. If the aim were subordination, then, we should have to conclude that it was subordination of junior males and females by their same-sex seniors, and a subordination that, by rendering these juniors "strong," ultimately served their own interests and those of the kin groups of which they were a part.

If subordination were the aim, moreover, this still leaves unexplained why wala displays were considered so efficacious in transforming female physiology and motivation to these particular ends. To begin with, as suggested already, they not only represented an ultimate power of the universe, an agency capable par excellence of transforming humanity, they also evoked the incontestable feeling of its transforming presence. Indeed, if we allow that fear and anxiety are potent tools of "behavioral surgery" (Herdt 1981:305), it is plausible to suppose that initiates actually were transformed by their experience.

Equally important, though, was the apparent "message" with which this experience was conflated, the merging into productive union of men and women. Wala displays were characterized by a striking androgyny: as one informant put it, they were supposed to "mix the marks of men and women." The shell rings, hook rings, *pali* fruits, hibiscus flowers, feathers, and bird of paradise plumes that figured prominently in many displays, for example, each cast a gender-specific shadow that, in combinatory display, merged male and female. Shell rings are explicitly recognized as "the mark of women" because their apertures symbolize the vagina. *Nararauwa,* or "pubescent girl," rings have small holes like vaginas yet to be stretched by birth; *panarauwa,* or "mature woman," rings have larger holes like the vaginas of parous woman; *forarauwa,* or "old woman," rings have large holes akin to vaginas that have produced whole families; and the smaller, hwala rings have hooklike projections that are likened to the clitoris. The pali fruits that garlanded the neck and base of the wala dance masks were also considered feminine because their orange plumpness conjured images of the red, "swollen" genitals of a young girl. According to some informants, the red, showy hibiscus flowers that figured prominently in many displays also represented the vagina, its petals resembling the labia and its pistil the clitoris. By contrast, bird of paradise plumes, which crowned the dancing masks, are considered quintessentially male, as are other types of feathers because their riblike barbs conjure images of the most ritually potent of men, those whom old-age has withered almost to a skeleton.

The androgyny these elements produce in combination is explicitly remarked upon: of malingatcha carvings, it is said that, "the male wala [i.e., male carving] steals the work of women [e.g., it includes rings and hibiscus], while the female wala [i.e., female carving] steals the work of men [e.g., it includes feathers]." Some of the kwuli/pana displays underscored the androgynous theme with figures demonstrably female in physique and dress, yet attired "as a man." In the most important of all the kwuli wala, the "real/true pana" rite, the woman who appeared wore a banana-leaf skirt, shell bracelets, and three net bags handsomely decorated with shell rings. Yet, along with these demonstrably female accoutrements, she also was decorated "like a man," a feather-garlanded comb in her hair, a cap of shells on her forehead, male decorative bands on her arms and legs, and male shell ornaments in her ears.

In addition to merging male and female through combinations of gender-specific elements, several other wala displays united them in depictions of intercourse. In the little panahlu tableau, a half-hidden woman was seen to hold aloft a hwala hook ring, symbol of the vagina, on a stick, said by some informants to be a penis. In one version of the wangi rite, a woman appeared naked save for a netbag decorated with hook rings slung across her back. Both netbag and rings symbolize the vagina and femininity, but her face was painted black, like a man's at a pig exchange festival. In her hand, she held an amba shoot, explicitly recognized as a symbolic penis; and, by stepping over the initiates, she was said to have "intercourse" with them as though she were a man. The kwazimpana rite featured a similarly androgynous figure, a woman with blackened face, skull-cap, chicken feathers in her head and pubic hair, and amba shoot tied at her groin—a female "man" who then proceeded to grab at initiates lasciviously and cry out for sex. Lastly, though I received no explicit exegesis to the effect, intercourse may have been at the symbolic heart of two other rites, the nangupana and a variant of the wangi rite. In the nangupana, an initiator referred to as a *hwarau*, a python, wriggled over the clasped forearms of the initiates "like a snake"; in the wangi or "eel" rite, initiates dived like an eel between the legs of their husbands' exchange partners. In Yangoru, the snake and the eel both serve as metaphors for the penis, and it seems plausible that in wriggling along a channel of outstretched arms or diving between the legs of exchange partners, these "penises" thereby simulated intercourse.

Given that spirits of the dead are both male and female, it seems appropriate that their representation in wala displays should thus "mix the marks of male and female." The deeper significance, though, may be the congruence between this gender merging and the acts of intercourse that wala displays also presented: it is, after all, in intercourse, more than in any other act, that male and female are brought together. By communicating an erotic mood, these sexual representations may have contributed to the experience of power emanating from these wala displays. The only exegesis I was offered about why wala spectacles embodied intercourse, however, was that they enjoined initiates against promiscuous behavior that might create jealousy and strife within their husbands' subclan, and ensured they would look after their families and their husbands' pigs, gardens, and relatives. References to sexuality are common in initiation, and La Fontaine (1985) suggests they symbolize fertility, a referent certainly congruent with the powers of the wala. In a sexually differentiated context, however, I suggest wala displays drew attention to the politico-ritual empowerment conferred by gender complementarity. As in intercourse, the merging of male and female—husband and wife—was the most powerful of productive endeavors. Thus were the specific acts of initiation brought to bear on its expressed goal: the production of "strong" men and women who, acting in concert, jointly elevated their own politico-ritual eminence and the reputation of the kin groups with which they were associated.

FEMALE "INITIATION"
AMONG THE NDU OF THE SEPIK BASIN

Equipped with these understandings of Yangoru Boiken female initiation, I now return to the explanatory challenge with which I began: Why should the scale of female initiation vary so dramatically among the Ndu-speaking peoples? Among the Yangoru Boiken, we have seen, female initiation was extremely elaborate: indeed, about as much ritual attention was lavished on females as on males. Less apparent, but important nonetheless, the initiation rites performed on females were paralleled by rites performed for similar ends on males. These parallels are readily apparent in the rites of first intercourse, first birth, and the initiation of daughters, which a married couple experienced together. But in undergoing their sumbwi, kwuli, and suwero seclusions, males—like females—also were shown wala displays and obliged to ingest ningi shrubs, other ritual foods, and the saliva of esteemed elders with the aim of acquiring the virtues of their gender. As with females, moreover, their seclusions, beatings, and the wealth paid to maternal relatives on their behalf were believed to ameliorate their sara pollution (Roscoe 1990a).

Abelam and Iatmul initiations differed significantly from these sequences. Until about 1880–90, according to Weiss (1994:243–244, 246–249), before European influence had significantly affected the area, Central Iatmul villages had a single-stage, female initiation that resembled male rites. Hauser-Schäublin (1977:178), however, feels the evidence on whether such rites actually occurred is unclear. Certainly, in oral societies, as Weiss (1994:237) herself notes, it is not always easy to establish whether events that supposedly occurred eighty to ninety years earlier are actually myth or history. Even if Weiss is correct, however, Iatmul female initiation was only performed on some women and, as Hauser-Schäublin notes (this volume), it had disappeared by colonial times. Both agree that, traditionally, a few women were made to undergo *male* initiation, but this was rare, undertaken for idiosyncratic reasons, and the girl became, in a sense, a male (Hauser-Schäublin, this volume, 1977:169–178; Weiss 1994:244–246; see also Bateson 1958[1936]:10). If the Iatmul did have female initiation, in sum, the emphasis they placed on it was limited and, by the time of colonial contact, it had all but vanished.

There is no ethnographic mention of rites at first intercourse among the Iatmul, but they do practice birth rites (Hauser-Schäublin 1977: 121–127). Women give birth in their dwelling house, remaining there for the next five to ten days. From Hauser-Schäublin's description of the associated taboos and washing rites, it seems that, as among the Yangoru

Boiken, the mother is viewed as polluted by the birth, but here the similarities end. There is no mention of any rites to "strengthen" the couple, to imbue gender-specific values. Nor, it seems, is the occasion part of the male initiation sequence as among the Yangoru Boiken, for the husband apparently is not secluded with his wife and child. In fact, he scrupulously avoids contact with her and the newborn lest the birthing blood contaminate, cripple, and age him prematurely.

The Abelam definitely do have female initiation rites, and these share some similarities with those of the Yangoru Boiken (Forge 1970a:274–275; Hauser-Schäublin, this volume, 1989b:148–151; Losche 1982:154–160, 324–334). Rites at menarche are believed to imbue female virtues, and they exhibit some parallels to male initiation: initiates are secluded in specially constructed structures; they observe similar taboos to men; they are decorated with similar finery; and they must present a similarly impassive demeanor to the public. Similar exchanges and consumptions of food also occur, and some of the same leaves and plants are used to whip and wash initiates (Losche 1982:324–334).[6] But there are also differences between the Abelam and Yangoru Boiken sequences. Among the Abelam, there is no ethnographic mention of special rites at first intercourse, no further initiatory stages follow the menarcheal rites, and there is no indication that menarche rites are simultaneously rites of passage for a girl's parents.

Like the Yangoru Boiken, the Abelam practice birth rites, and Losche (1982:271) suggests that, along with their menarche rites, these form a female parallel to male initiation. First menstruation, she points out (1982:324) is referred to as the *maira* (secrets) of the women, just as male initiation is called the maira of the men. Birthing, like male initiation, she suggests (1982:330, 334–335), has its secrets and age grades, and just as children are produced in birthing, so men and objects are produced in male initiation. Finally, birthing also seems to involve pollution and seclusion: it occurs in the menstruation hut, where wife and child remain secluded for five days or so; and washing rites performed on the parents at the end of the mother's seclusion suggest the pair are also seen as polluted (Losche 1982:331–335; MacLennan and MacLennan n.d.:9–15).

Granting that the Abelam may perceive a parallel between male initiation and childbirth rites, it is not clear whether the birthing ritual constitutes part of an *initiatory sequence* as it does in Yangoru. There is no mention of childbirth or its associated rites imbuing female virtues.[7] Nor does the event form part of male initiation as among the Boiken: although a husband should remain in his hamlet for about a week after the birth, he does not join his wife in the menstrual hut and, to judge from the fact that she sometimes goes to her *natal* home to give birth (Losche 1982:331–335; MacLennan and MacLennan n.d.:9–15), he may not even be in the same hamlet.

To summarize: The Yangoru Boiken devote about as much ritual attention to the initiation of females as they do the initiation of males. Their female initiation rites are coordinated with those of males; and they draw on many of the same ritual structures and forms. Among the Abelam, there is some structural and formal similarity, and possibly some coordination, between male and female rites, but to a much more limited degree than in Yangoru, and with much less ritual attention to females than to males. Finally, though the Iatmul may once have initiated females, the emphasis they placed on these rites was much less than they devoted to male initiation and, by the time of significant European contact, even this attention had evaporated.

An important clue to explaining these differences, I think, lies in what studies of male and female initiation often ignore: the reasons actors give for performing these rites. The Abelam and Iatmul perform male initiation for the same reason as the Yangoru Boiken, to imbue the qualities necessary for eminence in politico-ritual events. In Yangoru, it will be recalled, male eminence rests on success in pig exchange, generosity with wealth, oratorical ability, and, in the past, valor in war. Accordingly, male initiation aimed at producing individuals who were motivated and capable of performing with distinction in these arenas.

In Abelam ideology, male reputations depend on pig exchange and on providing lavish feasts. The sine qua non of male eminence, however, "the highest and best point of male aspirations" (Forge 1970b:264), is success in growing long yams for public exchange ceremonies (Forge 1970b:263–264; Hauser-Schäublin, this volume; Kaberry 1941:355, 1973:51–52; Losche 1982:81, 214, 233, 226–235; Scaglion 1978:316). Concomitantly, the Abelam see male initiation as producing men "who are magically powerful enough to direct and control natural events, most especially the growing of those species of long yams which are presented by men to their exchange partners" (Losche 1982:298; see also Kaberry 1941:357).

Among the Iatmul, male status depends primarily on possession of the esoteric knowledge of spells, secret names, and myths required to triumph in magic, sorcery, and ritual debates, and, in the past, on achievements in war and head-hunting (Bateson 1958[1936]:124–129, 139; Hauser-Schäublin, this volume; Metraux 1978; Silverman 1993:123). Unfortunately, Iatmul ethnographers provide few details of the specific virtues male initiation was supposed to instill. Bateson, though, gives the general aim: male initiation was oriented to "the adoption by the novices of the masculine ethos" (1958[1936]:132), to the production of a man who could "wield authority" and who was "what we should describe as an over-compensating, harsh man—whom the natives describe as a 'hot' man" (ibid.:131).

Among the Ndu, in sum, the ideology of male initiation stresses the production of men who can triumph in politico-ritual affairs. But what of female initiation? Among the Yangoru Boiken, as we have seen, a woman's activities are recognized as crucial to the politico-ritual eminence of her husband and his kin group, a circumstance underscored by the public participation of women in the performance of politico-ritual activities like pig and wealth exchange. If, then, male initiation is oriented to producing politico-ritually empowered males, we should expect the same of female initiation. This, as we have seen, is precisely the case.

The situation among the Iatmul is quite the reverse. Although a woman's status depends significantly on her husband's (Hauser-Schäublin 1977:136), men's reputations are virtually independent of women's activities. Women played no part in the central male political activities of war and head-hunting; nor, by definition, do they make any contribution to their husband's possession or use of esoteric, male ritual knowledge (Hauser-Schäublin, this volume). Bateson (1958[1936]:147) comments that a husband depends chiefly on his wife to raise pigs and catch fish "for the wealth which helps him to make a splash in the ceremonial house," but this appears to be a peripheral aspect of male eminence. As if to emphasize the politico-ritual exclusion of women and the independence of their husbands, almost all male ritual takes place within the confines of the men's house, "hidden from the eyes of women and children" (Hauser-Schäublin, this volume).

These differences, I suggest, account for the presence of elaborate female initiation rites among the Yangoru Boiken and their virtual absence among the Iatmul. Among the Yangoru Boiken, formal politico-ritual affairs incorporate males *and* females, rather than males alone, and so demand the ritual empowerment of both. Among the Iatmul, by contrast, women are divorced from formal politico-ritual affairs, and so efforts at ritual empowerment engage males primarily or exclusively.

Among the Abelam, male eminence in politico-ritual life is more dependent on women than it is among the Iatmul. As Losche (1982:213–215; 226–235) makes clear, women play an important role in producing the pigs men exchange and the cooked food they provide at feasts and exchanges. It is clear, too, that women view these contributions—especially those of food—as an index of their status (1982:214, 228, 232–233); and, in the case of feasts at least, men recognize their dependence on women (1982:242). Underscoring this interdependence, politico-ritual events like feasting and exchange involve the public participation of females as well as males. Yet Abelam men and women also subscribe to an ideology that males are entirely *independent* of women in the activity most crucial to male prestige, the growth of long yams (Kaberry 1941:355; Hauser-Schäublin, this volume; Losche 1982:197, 219; Scaglion 1986:156–159).

The recognition that men depend to *some* extent on women for politico-ritual success explains, I suggest, why the Abelam believe it necessary to perform female initiation rites and why these rites are believed to produce women who are successful food producers (Losche 1982:329).[8] But it is the notion that men are independent of women for success in long-yam growing, the very pursuit central to formal politico-ritual life, that explains why these rites fail to approach those of the Yangoru Boiken in their degree of elaboration and their coordination with, and similarity to, male rites.

NOTES

1. For funding the research on which this essay is based, I am grateful to the Emslie Horniman Scholarship Fund, the Faculty and Summer Research Funds of the University of Maine, the Ford Foundation, the Mudge Foundation, and the Rush Rhees and University Scholarship Funds of the University of Rochester. For sponsoring the research, I am indebted to the Department of Community Medicine at the University of Papua New Guinea and the Papua New Guinea Institute for Cultural Research. I thank Terry Hays for comments on a previous version. Finally, I express my deepest gratitude to the many Yangoru Boiken men and women who have shared their knowledge of initiatory practices with me, and I extend my thanks to the people of Sima Village for so good humoredly putting up with me.

2. For lack of relevant data, I am unable to include the Sawos in this comparative endeavor.

3. At marriage, women become associated with their husbands' kin groups.

4. See Camp (1979) for a description of the narandauwa rites conducted among the Yangoru Boiken of the Negrie region.

5. It was difficult to obtain information on these kwulirauwa rites because of my gender, the secrecy attending them, and their disappearance many decades ago. My main informant, a woman in her mid-fifties, was initiated into this stage around the age of fifteen—before she had menstruated and, thus, before she had undergone the narandauwa rites. She owed this extraordinary circumstance to an unusually early marriage to a man of about twenty-five: shortly afterwards, he entered the second grade of the male sequence, and she was

obliged to enter the equivalent female grade. In light of my limited competency in the Yangoru vernacular, this informant's great virtue was her fluency in Tok Pisin, which set her apart from other women who had undergone these rites. A second principal informant was a woman in her sixties who spoke no pidgin and with whom, therefore, communication was taxing. My third informant was actually a man. In his late fifties, he claimed to have spied on kwulirauwa rites in his youth and, because of a close relationship to a now-deceased male ritual expert, to have become privy to further secrets in later years. Although highly skeptical of his claims to begin with, I was eventually forced to credit them when it became apparent how remarkably well they conformed with what my two female informants were telling me. So strong was this concordance, in fact, that it provided some credibility for his assertion that, notwithstanding ideological claims to the contrary, a few elder males traditionally were privy to, and ultimate arbiters of, female initiatory ritual.

6. Among some Northern Abelam villages, menarche rites may have been coordinated with male initiation in so far as the girl was decorated with shell wealth at the next male initiation after her menarche (Forge pers. comm., cited in Losche 1982:224; but cf. 1982:224).

7. Following the birth, Kaberry (1941:245–246, 361) and MacLennan and MacLennan (n.d.:12) note, parents consume a soup prepared with magical herbs. This, though, is apparently concerned not with imbuing the virtues of their gender but with preventing the child from dying (Kaberry 1941:246) and/or the mother from further painful contractions (MacLennan and MacLennan n.d.:12).

8. Given that Abelam men also depend on women to raise pigs, one might expect their female initiation rites to imbue pig-raising abilities, but there is no mention of this in the literature.

Part III

ACHIEVING WOMANHOOD: THE LIFE CYCLE AS CULTURAL PERFORMANCE

4

ACHIEVING WOMANHOOD AND THE ACHIEVEMENTS OF WOMEN IN MURIK SOCIETY

Cult Initiation, Gender Complementarity, and the Prestige of Women

Kathleen Barlow

Among the principal outcomes of postmodern and feminist critiques in anthropology are heightened sensitivity to the question of voice in ethnographic discourse and persistent attention to the fit between analytic and "local" systems of meaning. The postmodern question addresses the terms of the dialogue between ethnographer and subject(s) and asks whose voice is represented in both "data" and analysis. Early on in feminist discussions, Ardener raised the problem of the muted voice of women in male dominant societies (Ardener 1975), a voice which may be silenced both within the culture studied and by Western theoretical paradigms. Rituals of initiation for women bring both of these issues to the fore. It is therefore important to ask whether descriptions and interpretations of women's ritual pay sufficient attention to women's voices within the culture, and whether the categories of analysis fit with cultural conceptualizations.

In the following analysis of women's initiation in Murik society, I try to show how indigenous metaphors of gender, person, and womanhood are deployed in female cult-initiation rites to express women's potential to achieve influence and prestige.[1] To do this, I situate these metaphors with reference to the analytical categories of economics, social organization, and politics, all well-recognized subsystems of culture that are nevertheless more clearly separate in anthropological discourse than in the activities and everyday discourse of social life. By juxtaposing local and analytical inter-pretations, I hope to show how these rites for women express a unitary concept of personhood in Murik culture that is enacted differently for each gender. First, I briefly derive the analytical perspective used here from previous research on female initiation and feminist discussions of gender and prestige systems. Prefaced by a summary of the historical and ethno-graphic factors that have influenced the information used here, I describe Murik expectations about gender and personhood and their role in econom-ics, social organization, and politics. Rites of initiation for men and women dramatize the core values of personhood—socialized sexuality, nurture, and aggression. I show briefly how this was and is enacted in the male cults, then, in more detail, how it was and is effected in the female cults. Finally, this material is drawn together to examine how Murik conceptualizations of gender complementarity and personhood, expressed as values in the cults, lead to actions that maintain and reproduce Murik society.

THEORETICAL BACKGROUND

In anthropology, the topic of female initiation rites first arose primarily in relation to social organization—kinship, marriage, and the transfer of status (Gough 1955; Richards 1956)—and in response to a perceived overemphasis on the study of male initiation rites (La Fontaine 1972, 1982, 1985; Roscoe 1990). The former analyses resulted in studies that related "the meaning of symbols to the structure of society," but they dealt with both more as gen-eralized social features than as internalized or intersubjective realities (La Fontaine 1982:xix–xxi). They were influenced by the same male-centered views of women that characterized social anthropology, namely women as male property, as apolitical in their actions, or as disruptive and dangerous to the social order. Women's initiation rites were explained in terms of institutionalized male authority, perpetuating a covert Western assumption that gender roles are defined by different and differently valued attributes of men and women which explain women's inferior position in society. Although male and female were recognized as complementary categories, more specifically and problematically women were defined with reference to men. Cross-cultural research eventually suggested that male and female are not always conceptualized in opposition or hierarchical relation to each other (e.g., James 1993; McDowell 1984; Strathern 1980). Analyses of female initiation rituals formulated on the male authority model did not seem to capture existing cultural variation in what it meant to be female, the relationship of female to male in conceptual symbolic orders, and the actions of individual men and women vis-à-vis cultural gender constructs (Lederman 1980; Strathern 1981b).

Feminist anthropologists, using these liabilities as a point of departure, have questioned the puzzling co-occurrence of *variation* in the cultural construction of gender but apparently *universal* subordination of women. For some, this meant a search for a convincing counterexample—a society in which women were clearly equal to or even dominant over men. To better understand cultural variations in gender constructs and egalitarianism versus subordination, they proposed a slightly different set of related cultural systems—kinship, prestige, production, reproduction, and the dichotomy of public and domestic contexts (e.g., Collier and Rosaldo 1981; Collier and Yanagisako 1987; Reiter 1975b; Rosaldo 1974; Sanday 1974; Ortner 1981). These analyses hinged upon the difference between power and authority, and whether influence in one arena could be transferred to others.

Symbolic anthropologists have questioned the cross-cultural validity of the categories themselves by asking whether members of non-Western cultures understand issues of gender, prestige, and subordination in the same or similar terms and how much difference the differences make. Ortner (1974), Strathern (1976), Whitehead (1981, 1986, 1987), and others have explored cultural variation in gender and worldview. They have looked at how symbolic expressions of gender, personhood, nature, culture, and so on affect relations of power and authority in different cultures (Ortner 1981; Strathern 1980). Although variation in the cultural construction of gender and other categories is by now well established, the search for evidence to contradict the universal subordination of women has resulted in much disagreement about what constitutes subordination and what criteria should be used to evaluate it (see Ortner 1990). As a result, many analytical categories are being rigorously examined with respect to their applicability in diverse cultural contexts, partially in the hope that attending to cultural variation in symbolic constructs might reveal greater variation in women's status.

Thus many researchers have asked to what extent the concepts and dichotomies (domestic/public, nature/culture, production/reproduction) used in our analyses are Western ones that obscure emic views organized according to other conceptual systems (Harris and Young 1981; Lamphere 1993; MacCormack and Strathern 1980; Reiter 1975b; Rosaldo 1980; Yanagisako and Collier 1987). To the relief of feminists, more egalitarian views of women in precolonial societies emerge when greater weight is afforded the priorities expressed in emic systems (Etienne and Leacock 1980; O'Brien and Tiffany 1984). Nevertheless, Tiffany (1984:1–11) reminds us, efforts to grasp emic categories or to insist on standard etic ones are motivated by our desire for particular kinds of explanations, such as alternatives to the male dominant status quo. Therefore, the relationships among emic categories and analytic ones must be a constant concern.

Recently, Ortner (1990) has evaluated the reigning analytical frameworks on male dominance, prestige systems, and gender categories. She differentiates the criteria for relative prestige of men and women into two categories; those expressed in terms of "hard" social realities, such as economic position and political dominance, and those defined largely in terms of cultural values, what is socially worthy and morally good. For Ortner, access to prestige differentiated by gender is, on the one hand, embedded in practices and institutions, and on the other expressed metaphorically in language and other symbolic representations. Whereas earlier analyses tried to average these prestige factors to render a verdict, male dominant or egalitarian, Ortner suggests it may be more accurate to view them in dynamic relation to each other—not as fixed categories but as parameters and resources by means of which hegemonies and counterhegemonies are claimed and maintained. Within a given society there may be significant shifts across contexts or historically over time.

Ortner's distinction between "hard social realities" and cultural values describes an analytical schism that does not necessarily exist in ongoing social life. While economics, politics, and social organization (the cultural subsystems emphasized here) have to some extent their own momentum, the "hard social realities" of a marriage system, economic transaction, or assertion of authority occur because individuals decide to pursue particular courses of action in relation to what is culturally recognized as "socially worthy and morally good" (Ortner 1990:42). For example, Murik women engage in subsistence fishing, ritual feasting, and food-sharing within their extended families in conformity with the accepted division of labor, political prerogatives, and kinship obligations of adult women. But they do these things because it is intrinsic to their identity as Murik women to feed others. By providing food resources and preparing food, they derive influence in allocation of resources and descent-group activities, and they acquire reputations and respect for fulfilling their obligations as sisters, mothers, and wives. Murik women do not, of course, analyze social actions in terms of related cultural subsystems, but they do perceive multiple benefits for fulfilling, and repercussions for failing to fulfill, the criteria of female personhood. Thus cultural values do more than provide commentary supportive or contestive of hard social realities; they motivate people to enact them.

My goal in shifting the emphasis to the linkage between cultural institutions and local metaphors is to demonstrate the relationship in Murik society of gender, a largely symbolic construct, to the institutional consequences of gender differentiation. Thus we return, in modified form, to the Weberian question addressed in early analyses of female initiation: What is the relationship of meaning to the perpetuation of society? In the Murik case, I address this issue by showing how specific cultural institutions are constituted through actions that maximize personhood. Understanding gender relations in Murik culture is facilitated by the insight that systems of meaning and cultural institutions are dynamically related to each other. There are many avenues of discourse and interpretation in Murik society, including frequent and strenuous negotiation of prestige using multiple strategies and lines of argument. Individuals and groups pursue and defend a variety of interests through cooperation and competition that are sometimes organized according to gender, even boisterously so. Prestige criteria provide men and women, individually and collectively, with arguments to offset hegemonistic claims by either gender, exploiting potential ambiguity and contradiction to influence situations in their favor. In affinal relationships, men plainly have greater authority and receive more respect, but the dominant form of prestigious activity, feeding others, is associated categorically with women. Thus, explicitly male prerogatives can be counterbalanced by opportunities for women to challenge and sometimes surpass men's influence and prestige. Women's initiation ritual dramatizes the meanings that compel women to participate in activities that maintain economic, social organizational, and political institutions.

HISTORICAL AND ETHNOGRAPHIC FACTORS

Living at the mouth of the Sepik River on the North Coast of Papua New Guinea, the Murik numbered in 1982 some twelve hundred to fifteen hundred fisherfolk and traders, exploiting approximately 350 square kilometers of mangrove for fish and shellfish resources. They speak a non-Austronesian vernacular and Melanesian Pidgin. By their own accounts, they migrated to this region from further up the Sepik River and actively intermarried with, and adopted members from, other peoples throughout the region.

The data for this analysis were gathered by several different researchers over the past eighty years, a postcontact period that has seen significant changes in the extent and nature of outside influence. From early on, explorers and missionaries in the Sepik River delta described the Murik as quick to investigate their intrusions and to attempt to initiate exchange. They have welcomed on their narrow shores a succession of visitors: German Catholic missionaries (1912–42), Japanese military (1942), Australian patrol officers (1948–75), Seventh Day Adventist missionaries (1952 to present), S.I.L linguists (1979–80), tourists (1975 to present), and anthropologists (1936, 1981–82). Their acceptance of outsiders stems from an opportunistic attitude toward the incursion of Western culture—desire for some of its wealth, material goods, knowledge, and technology. Most Murik desire these things as a means not of becoming Western but of gaining access to resources that can augment their status within the local prestige system. Thus, their orientation toward culture contact has been characterized by the extension of their regional role as traders. Efforts to missionize them have been met with the skepticism of a mercantile people who understand very well that interaction with culturally different people provides opportunities to learn and obtain resources, but who also know that superior resources do not necessarily represent a better way of life.

The earliest data on Murik society were collected by Father Joseph Schmidt (1923–24, 1926, 1933), a German missionary of the Society of the Divine Word who lived in the Murik Lakes from 1913 to 1943. Schmidt came to speak the Murik language fluently and gathered information on women's ritual from both men and women. He was told about the secret aspects of initiation that occurred within the cult house and witnessed preparations and public performances at the beginning and end of the rites. Unfortunately, this access was cut off in 1920 when he broke the sacred spears of the men's cult house in the village of Big Murik to punish the men for a head-hunting raid on a non-Murik village. (In the other Murik villages, district government officials burned down the men's cult houses.) As a result, Schmidt noted in a 1926 description of women's initiation, "This is as it was told to me before. Now I may not ask any more" (Schmidt 1926:54). His only account of scarification and symbolic defloration of initiates inside the women's cult house was written in Latin (ibid.:55).

In 1936, on the advice of Margaret Mead, who had been impressed during her Sepik studies by the Murik role in regional trade, Louis Pierre Ledoux visited the Murik Lakes for about six months. With a BA in anthropology from Harvard, Ledoux wanted to try his hand at fieldwork. Unlike Schmidt, however, he conducted his work in Melanesian Pidgin, and his stay coincided with a period of government and mission suppression of local culture. Nonetheless, he produced over six hundred pages of field notes, a manuscript, and several hundred photographs. These data include a description of the public phase of initiation into the women's cult. His account does not specify clearly the kin ties among ritual sponsors and other participants, and makes no mention of the secret aspects of the cult, either because they no longer were being practiced for fear of punishment or because they were being concealed from Western eyes. It was Ledoux's impression that traditional culture was giving way quite rapidly under colonial administration.

The final source of data is my own two years of fieldwork conducted with my husband, David Lipset, in 1981–82, 1986, and 1988—the latter trips involving regional surveys of Murik trade networks along the Lower Sepik River and North Coast. In 1981–82, four villages had conducted several women's initiations within the past years. There was a women's cult house in Big Murik, where women gathered for other ceremonies, but no initiations were held during our stay. Between our departure in 1982 and return in 1986, the Murik performed three more initiation ceremonies and built two new women's cult houses, though these had yet to be completed and consecrated. In two other villages, women were wearing palm-spathe caps in anticipation of their initiation. In 1988, I obtained considerable comparative information about initiation rites in other Lower Sepik villages. Among the Murik, I had further discussions with senior women about the privileges conferred by the cult and observed preparations for impending initiations. In Darapap village, four groups of sponsors were each planning to initiate small groups of women.

My data are neither as complete nor as sound as I should wish. In 1981–82, a combination of factors, including my own reticence and childless status, made it difficult to inquire about the secret aspects of women's ritual even though I had read Schmidt's account of them. Although senior men were eager to have their ritual recorded, they were reluctant to describe those aspects involving the exchange of women for sexual intercourse, intimating only that there was something "bad" about the women's ritual. For their part, senior women were happy to talk about the public aspects of their cult but, asked about its secret aspects, they resorted to allusions and metaphors that I was poorly equipped to translate or interpret.

Our return with a young child in 1986 helped to confirm our interest in the Murik and perhaps our sexual viability. Two senior women implied to me that there was more to learn about the women's cult. But the opportunity to pursue this lead evaporated when one of their grandsons died unexpectedly of appendicitis and our remaining days in Darapap were taken up with his mortuary ceremonies. In 1988, I obtained considerably more information about the regional sources of women's cult ritual, but the brevity of our visit and a lack of privacy prevented me from pursuing further its secret aspects.[2]

Compounding these difficulties were great variations in individual accounts of initiation. My informants were from different villages and descent groups, which have their own versions of the rites. One informant was initiated in her non-Murik mother's natal village and again, by her father's descent group, in Big Murik, the latter rites being abbreviated to save her from enduring similar ordeals twice. Some events had been disrupted by outbreaks of quarreling or violence. Despite a formal injunction against violence during ritual, preparations and performances frequently provoke disagreement and jealousy as goods are amassed, indebtednesses reversed, and magically enhanced sexuality paraded. Since those responsible must redress these breaches with a gift of pig(s) to the sponsors before the ceremony can continue, many initiations are interrupted for up to a year, thus altering the momentum of the event. In sum, for a number of reasons, only one of which is the historical decline of traditional Murik culture, the information presented here is but a partial picture of women's ritual.

PERSONHOOD AND GENDER IN MURIK SOCIETY

In Murik society, one runs afoul by asking such questions as, "Are women X?" and "Do men do Y?" Because personhood transcends gender categories, a question that fixes aspects of personhood in one gender category is answered with an offsetting claim, "Men too are X" and "Women too can do Y." Gender differences are expressed as contextualized behavior in relation to certain social alters. For example, a woman as well as a man may be overtly angry and aggressive, but the way in which she does this and the contexts in which she acts are not always the same as those in which he displays the same characteristics.

More importantly, men and women in Murik society are made, not born. In an unsocialized person, nurturance, sexuality, and aggression are merely appetites. Uncontrolled desires are potentially disruptive, but more often laughable. By contrast, high-status individuals (those who epitomize personhood) have mastered their own impulses to eat, copulate, fight, and acquire in the service of larger groups—siblings, descent groups, and the village community. Their appetite for food has been transformed into the ability to create debts by feeding others and mounting feasts. They establish alliances through magical seduction and know how to avert aggression by manipulating others' appetites. If need be, they can wait for vengeance by indirect magical and spiritual means. Thus a big man or woman offers hospitality, but does not eat; extends his or her kin network through constant generosity with food; dismisses a spouse's sexual infidelity or promiscuity, while maintaining power in the cults and trade network through seduction; and prohibits aggression by his or her physical presence, exacting a high "price" in pigs if this injunction is broken.

The socialized attributes of personhood and the raw material of humanity thus stand in sharp contrast to each other. By attaining the necessary control of one's appetites and converting them to constructive social purposes, an individual acquires prestige and access to leadership roles. The primary obligation of full personhood in Murik society is to actively promote, through ritual sponsorship, the perpetuation and increase in membership of the descent group. The model of full personhood emphasizes actions that in the Murik view are intrinsically associated with mothers—birth and nurturance. This is not, however, a reason to deny that men may also perform such activities, albeit in different ways than women. The possible advantage to women of reproductive physiology is offset by symbolic displacements of mothering, and emphasis on male influence over pregnancy and birth and on parenting as embodied in the social act of feeding.[3] By ritual acts, men symbolically give birth to canoes and initiates (Barlow and Lipset 1989).

Murik social life provides opportunities to display the qualities of personhood and evaluate others' efforts to do so. In the following sections, I describe these activities through the analyst's lens of cultural subsystems to show how Murik economy, social organization, and leadership are maintained by gendered expressions of socialized feeding, sexuality, and aggression.

GENDER AND THE MURIK ECONOMY

It has long been noted that women, even when they produce the bulk of subsistence goods, may be subordinate to men in economic arenas if they do not participate in the distribution of what they produce (Friedl 1978). In Murik society, all women are mothers who feed others (their hungry and dependent children). In order to realize this powerful image, they participate in every phase of subsistence production and food distribution, but beyond this their participation, direct and indirect, in all forms of exchange and extravillage trade is substantial. Murik gardens do not reliably produce any staple starch; therefore, men and women exploit the mangroves at a level that supports trade. Part of their surplus and manufactures are traded nearby for foodstuffs, but the remainder is deployed in a regional network of trade that far exceeds subsistence requirements.

The ability to produce and access resources is highly valued, and women very nearly outdo men in this regard. Murik women produce not only food for daily subsistence, namely fish and shellfish, but also the mangrove products and woven bags that establish the Murik role in regional trade. Men and women inherit trade partnerships in other villages and communities, and, as the primary producers of trade items, women receive and control the distribution of trade goods obtained with them. Only initiated women may travel to the offshore islands, where their reputations as basket makers precede them and they are received with some ceremony (Barlow 1985a). As in other parts of coastal Melanesia, successful trade is an act of magical seduction (Hogbin 1935; Malinowski 1922; Scoditti 1990).

An important asymmetry in gender prerogatives has to do with transportation for trade. Men manufacture canoes and sail the large outrigger canoes, but women are believed to have magical influence over the safe travel and return of overseas canoes (Barlow 1985a). Men possess the knowledge and magic for negotiating the waterways in various seasons, tides, and weather. For over twenty-five years, the Murik have used outboard motors for long-distance trips, and though women may own their own motors and canoes of all types, they still depend on male kin to pilot, maintain, and repair them.

In practice, there are frequent occasions for conflicting interests with respect to labor, resources, and goods, but the accepted ethic is cooperation for the mutual benefit and prestige of extended family and descent groups. A minor ritual dramatizes how competitive production between male and female groups can benefit the whole community. On a designated day, the women of a village fish intensively, combine their catch, and present it to one of the initiated women's male joking partners, her alter in the men's cult. He is obligated to make a trade expedition to procure some special garden produce for her. The whole affair gives rise to mutual challenges about what men and women can do, but even obtaining the displays of surplus requires cooperative efforts by men and women in order to maintain their households while their alters are absent on work parties. The perishable food surpluses are immediately distributed to those who assisted with the work and thence throughout the village.

GENDER AND SOCIAL ORGANIZATION

Social organization in Murik society is based on ambilineal descent groups (*pwang*), which are residentially dispersed throughout the villages and own corporate property such as outrigger canoes, cult houses, mangrove channels, and named insignia (*suman*). Sibling sets (*nag*) within pwang are ranked relative to each other based on primogeniture in the most senior living generation. Older siblings are responsible for the welfare of younger ones and inherit property that they manage on their behalf. They are revered as parental figures who ensure that younger ones do not go hungry. Gender differences are secondary to birth-order ranking. Firstborn women as well as men are entitled to claim leadership positions. Nevertheless, women are deferent to senior men, while men show respect but not deference to senior women.

Descent groups compete for members by sponsoring life-cycle rituals on behalf of individuals, especially firstborns. Among the most important for claiming or reinforcing descent-group affiliation is initiation into the men's or women's secret societies. Acquiring the membership of the senior sibling via ritual usually means acquiring the primary loyalty of most members of the sibling set.

Marriage entails realignment of descent-group priorities, based partly on the differential seniority of each spouse but also on practicalities. Parents of a new couple confer to determine that the pair are not related as second cousins or closer. There is no bridewealth, no official transfer of descent-group identity, and no ritual recognition of coresidence, but women and men practice certain forms of affinal avoidance. Adjustments in residence and work on behalf of particular descent groups occur over the course of a marriage. Thus, social organization establishes no clear priority between women's roles as sister and wife. Women and men are obligated to support natal and affinal descent-group affiliations. Women's productivity makes them important contributors to households and descent groups, and they manipulate their options to ensure their interests are considered and sometimes to express disapproval.

POLITICS AND LEADERSHIP

Initiation confers the right to assemble and present the suman insignia[4] that publicly represent the identity and authority of the descent group. A descent-group leader (*suman gwan* or *suman merogo*, literally "suman son" and "suman woman") is responsible for managing corporately owned property, sponsoring trade and ritual work, and building the membership and prestige of the group. Some of his or her important rights are control of access to mangrove areas for fishing and gathering; organization of trade expeditions; and ownership and management of outrigger canoes and cult houses. Once ritually validated, maintaining a position of leadership is a matter of personal ability to organize work and maintain loyalty among supporters. In all of this, women's rights are the same as those of men. However, there seems to be a tendency for brothers eventually to succeed their elder sisters as heads of descent groups. Nevertheless, an initiated firstborn woman may legitimately usurp her husband's work on behalf of her descent group and may sponsor her own sons' initiation into the secret society, with her brothers as their ritual sponsors.

In all contexts, women defer to senior male affines. It is important to note that even a suman merogo must show extreme deference and avoid direct contact with her husband's senior male kin. She may not cook for them, enter their houses except on her knees, or engage in joking behavior in their presence; and she must depart from a pathway to avoid them. These and other restrictions are only removed if a woman's husband becomes the leader of his descent group by ritually retiring all those senior to him. At this time, the change in her status as wife and affine is marked by a public ceremony. To achieve these prerogatives, a woman must work hard to help her husband achieve leadership status.

With respect to economics, social organization, and leadership status, men and women have many opportunities to fulfill the requirements of personhood, sometimes directly and sometimes by assisting a spouse or senior sibling of the opposite sex. Gender, however, is important in achieving personhood, and its effects are epitomized in cult rituals that dramatize masculine and feminine modes of achieving personhood and status.

MEN'S AND WOMEN'S CULTS
AND RITES OF INITIATION

Murik cults are an unusual example of single-sex secret societies that were organized along parallel lines and at one time had interdependent ritual cycles for initiating members into successive grades. The symbolism of the initiation rituals into the junior grades, the only ones of which we have accounts, dramatizes the socialized expression of the Murik triad—sexuality, aggression, and nurturance according to gender.

According to Schmidt (1926:48–53), men's initiations were organized by moieties and age grades. Formerly, the first men's cult initiation occurred in conjunction with the boys' first-dressing rite at puberty. Nowadays, competing claims on resources from Western institutions have resulted in less frequent initiations and greater age variability within the grade cohort. The first loincloth ceremony for boys has been incorporated into the first achievements rituals celebrated for some firstborns (Lipset n.d.).

The first initiation ritual involves hazing the initiates, including penis incision, and sleeping with carved figures of cult spirits who convey magical knowledge about seduction. At the end of their ordeals, the young men are dressed in descent-group finery and paraded through the villages, where they are honored and given gifts.

The men's cult creates a separate arena for male activity in which successive generations learn the powers of the mythical cult hero, Sendam. The potential paths to power of feasting, sexuality, and exchange are acted out through the rituals as boys are reborn as warriors and groomed for descent-group leadership. They learn to conduct warfare fearlessly, to compete for prestige through ritual feasting, and to conduct long-distance trade.

Homicidal aggression and the conduct of warfare are strongly associated with maleness, as nurturance is with femaleness. In fact aggression is conceived of as antithetical to nurturance.[5] Preparation within the men's cult for warfare is accompanied by an elaborate set of practices and symbolic references to detachment from women, including repudiation of dependence on mothers and possessiveness toward wives (ibid.).

In the context of the men's cult, the meaning of nurture is transformed by overtones of aggression. There, food-giving is competitive, and men challenge each other to greater displays by attempting to "kill" each other with plates of food. The quintessentially maternal act of feeding thus becomes a hostile and competitive act that indebts and challenges others. By framing feasting as competition, however, men do not usurp this form of prestige from women. They must come to terms with the fact that women who cook on their behalf are acting out the high value they place on their own productivity and nurture. Women's labor supports the feasting competition in the men's cult, and women require men to help by gathering raw foodstuffs, splitting firewood, scraping coconuts, and helping with child care. Men know they may not impose unduly on women's time and resources, for women have been known to collectively refuse to cook, thus forcing cancellation of men's plans. The similarity of men waiting in the cult house for plates of food and hungry children sitting around the hearth does not escape the women. They indulge men and children alike, but not without some humor at their expense.

The somewhat fragile drama of male nurturance that exists today was once a more tyrannous appropriation of the right to feed and indebt. In earlier times, the subordination of domestic feeding to the men's house was enforced by daily sanctions. In order not to offend the cult house, we were told, domestic cooking only took place before dawn or after dark, with plates from every meal dispatched to the cult house—these times are remembered as "very hard." These daily restrictions are no longer enforced, yet the consecration of the men's house dramatizes the appropriation of women's nurture by the male cult. As part of the ritual, women gather around its posts and attempt to shake it down. Having manifestly failed in the endeavor, they enter the house for a meal of clams and sago, female foods, prepared by the men. Each woman then gathers other food hanging inside the building and cooks for the community during the several days-long celebration. At the same time, every cooking fire in the community is extinguished and relit from one freshly kindled in the new men's house. In these ways, the nurturance of individual women is defeated symbolically by the greater power of the cult house, from which women's own nurturance then supposedly derives.

For men, learning to access the power of cult spirits for male enterprises (warfare, curing, seduction, and trade) is a long process of sponsorship through several initiatory grades. In this context, seduction is a metaphorical antidote to dependence upon women as maternal sources of affection and food, and the means to authority. For each advancement, initiates are required to send a woman (their wife, mother, or sister) to provide sexual services to members of the next highest grade in the opposite moiety. For one moiety to wrest authority from the other, key men in the reigning moiety are seduced by the wives of men in the other moiety (Lipset n.d.). On one level, men suggested, the seductions involved were intended to develop a detachment from the women on whom a man depended most—to make him fearless and invulnerable in warfare and head-hunting, capable of action uninhibited by ties of affection and dependence, including the opportunistic exploitation of trade partners.

Women avoided my questions about these sexual practices. Men reported to Lipset that although, in general, women are afraid of the male cult spirits, which have the power to kill them, the ritual sexual encounters with men believed to be possessed by these spirits cause greater concern to their husbands. Intimacy with senior men is the inverse of the extreme deference women owe to senior affinal kin, but one senior woman affirmed that she was not afraid, even when she went to the men's house for the first time.

THE WOMEN'S CULT AND FEMALE INITIATION

The organization of the women's cult parallels the men's, having four age grades and initiatory moieties. Schmidt (1933:349) reports that the women's first initiation into cult membership occurred in conjunction with the second initiation in the men's cult (see plate 4.1).[6] In 1986, Murik informants

4.1   Women dressed as they were for their initiation a few weeks earlier. The
skirt designs and other costume elements show descent-group affiliations.
Murik; Big Murik Village, 1984. Photo credit: Helen Dennett

acknowledged that the two initiation sequences used to be coordinated temporally but had not been for a long time because it was too difficult to amass the required resources and personnel to mount major rituals successively. They did not recognize what Schmidt had described.

Like the men's cult, the women's cult (*sambaan*) stands for emergence from the protection and dependence of the domestic scene, but it is neither hostile to, nor destructive of, domestic relations. The women's cult house (*sambaan iran*) is a large dwelling, inhabited in day-to-day life by a senior woman and her family. On ceremonial occasions, her male relatives and children vacate the premises, and a slit gong belonging to the women's cult is moved in front of the main post. The sambaan iran becomes the venue for curing, for propitiating female spirits as oracles, and for some life-cycle rituals, including female initiation.

In earlier times, a first-dressing rite was performed for every girl at menarche. Following seclusion in the birth house with her father's sisters, a girl was given her first skirt. This rite was not a part of cult initiation and has not been practiced for at least fifty years. The reasons are unclear, but may be due to the fact that the physiological change at menarche denotes no changes in social status that are not recognized more substantially by initiation into the cult. Under pressure of dwindling time and resources to maintain such rituals, this ceremony may not have been viewed as crucial. The bestowal of a skirt which displays a specific descent-group design is part of the cult initiation.

In complementary fashion to the men's cult, the sambaan teaches women how sexuality, feeding, and exchange can be used as paths to power. Initiations are precipitated when a father announces his decision to sponsor his daughter's initiation. Other fathers then deliberate about whether it is an appropriate time for their daughters also to be initiated, and those who decide to go ahead make a gift of food to solicit the cooperation and cosponsorship of their daughter's *mwara ngakeen* (literally, valuables father's sister(s)—i.e., classificatory father's sisters). These women are inherited ritual sponsors who share a joking relationship in mundane contexts (Barlow 1992).

For the preliminary initiation ceremony, the father(s) present(s) food, betel nut, and tobacco to the mwara ngakeen, who then shave the novice's head and put on her the plain palm-spathe cap (*karagap*) that she will wear until she is initiated. In earlier days, the young women were secluded in special rooms near the entrances to their fathers' houses (to keep them away from the cooking hearth) or in a separate room inside the women's cult house. During seclusion, their bodies were covered with a smelly black

4.2   The spirit Yangaron, a coconut-bast costume worn by men of a specific
       age grade to present female initiates with plates of food while taunting
       them with a burlesque of male sexuality. Murik; Darapap Village, 1988.
       Photo credit: David Lipset

paint that supposedly made men sick if they came near; their hair was allowed to grow very long, and they became fat from overfeeding and lack of exercise. Their female friends were obliged to visit them, but formally they were secluded from all men.

Nowadays, as in the past, during this preliminary period, the initiates' mwara ngakeen make the girls' decorations for them according to their parents' specifications: skirts and other elements are decorated with designs belonging to the sponsoring descent groups. Meanwhile, the girls' kin embark on trade expeditions to gather food for a feast and for gifts to reward the mwara ngakeen for their contributions to the ritual, and each of the girls starts to build a platform on which to display this provender.

The initiation rites proper begin one evening as the initiates wait apprehensively in their mothers' houses to hear the shell leg rattles that will announce the arrival of their mwara ngakeen coming to fetch them to the sambaan iran.[7] When the girls and their mwara ngakeen are gathered there, a senior woman announces the fact on the slit gong, and Yangaron, a masked figure clothed in a costume sewn from coconut bast, descends from the men's cult house. One in a series of age-graded figures, Yangaron is notable for the exaggerated male genitals his costume sports and for giving gifts when trade expeditions return (see plate 4.2). He goes to each initiate's mother, who asks him if her daughter is hungry. When he shakes his head, "Yes," she gives him a plate of food, which he delivers to the daughter in the women's cult house. The initiates, schooled in the modesty of mundane etiquette, act ashamed before his "nakedness" but accept the food.[8]

The mwara ngakeen urge the initiates to eat the food, "Quickly, before they come to beat you." Suddenly, the *mansarip* (literally, lances), an age-grade band of women, probably from the opposite moiety, burst into the house dressed as male warriors. They beat the novices, steal their food, and depart. During the ensuing night of singing and dancing, the mwara ngakeen call out the names and villages of their lovers as they place feathers in the novices' caps. The feathers are colored according to the lovers' residences— red for the islands, black for the coast, white for the inland bush villages, and yellow for other Murik villages. Later, the mwara ngakeen pin the initiates' arms to the floor of the house, and the symbol of the moon—concentric circles with radiating lines—is cut into the skin between their breasts. The mwara ngakeen whoop loudly so that men cannot hear the cries of pain. Schmidt (1926:55) provides a rather confusing Latin description of a symbolic defloration in which the initiates' vaginas are marked with white lime and small sticks inserted in them. Together, the symbol of the moon, associated with menstrual cycles, and the defloration certainly celebrate sexual maturity, but seemingly not the entailments of marriage, fertility, and childbearing.

Near dawn, the initiates are put into canoes, seated leaning forward and covered with palm leaves. They are taken into the mangroves and attacked again by the "warrior" mansarip to whom their mothers, standing along the banks, shout encouragement: "Beat them hard! Beat them! They never listen to us!" Eventually, the canoes capsize, and the initiates are brought ashore by their mwara ngakeen. In certain villages, according to some informants, the novices also crawl into a small house woven of thorny, sago-palm fronds into which initiated women shove sticks and spears before crushing it down on top of them. Others describe crawling through a gauntlet of arched sticks or through a large turtle figure woven in a black and white pattern of fronds.

According to still other accounts, the initiates are taken to a waterhole in the bush known as *dagosaar*, which represents the dwelling place of the female spirits. These spirits are portrayed as tricksters with a capricious sense of humor and the power to change the sex of a newborn baby from a boy to a girl or to afflict their custodian with violent itching if they feel neglected. They are held responsible for certain kinds of illness and dementia, the cure for which is revealed in a possession state by the woman who owns the spirit's statue.

Decorated with flowers and herbs, the statues of these spirits have been set up around the water hole and a small house built to cover the water itself. The novices are ushered into the house, but the floor is flimsy and gives way, dumping them into the water. Their initiators then clamber onto the house, collapsing it onto the novices. Then, as the initiates flail about, their "mothers" call their names and reach in to pull them out.[9] The initiates return to their village, pausing on the outskirts to wash and remove the pollution they have accumulated by contact with the female spirits. Schmidt (1926:55) gives a different account of this washing procedure in which the sponsors step over the initiates in a gesture that will protect them from wounds "when they are later beaten by their husbands."

Returning to the sambaan iran, the mwara ngakeen decorate the initiates, oiling their bodies with red paint. Their fathers then bring the suman insignia. The transfer of suman must be witnessed by the senior members of each descent group from all Murik villages. Accordingly, the initiates parade through the village and, as they pass, a member of each household breaks open a coconut in their honor and blows a fine spray of juice over their heads. This is the customary salute when suman are displayed and acknowledges the legitimacy of those who now carry them for the first time.

The initiates receive gifts of pots, basket reeds, and carved wooden plates, then sit on specially constructed platforms while the men present a festival of song and dance. The presentations of food and trade goods for the mwara ngakeen are displayed on other platforms. During the days that follow, the whole entourage makes a similar tour of every Murik village.

FOOD, NURTURANCE, AND THE SAMBAAN CULT

Communications about food in the women's cult initiation are complex and multivalent. Women are already heavily identified with food and feeding as a means of expressing and maintaining affective ties among family members. Even young girls learn to cook for and feed others, and become well versed in hospitality and exchange. By the time of her initiation, there seems to be little for a woman to learn about giving and receiving food.

The progression of food presentations in the ritual constitutes a statement of the initiates' new role as sponsors of feasts, a role clearly separated from the noncompetitive duty of mothers to feed their household. This distinction is communicated when Yangaron, the garish male figure, delivers plates of food to them, which their mwara ngakeen encourage them to eat. Then the mansarip attack and beat them for passively accepting the plate from Yangaron, whose maleness is associated with the men's cult and competitive feasting—a stern lesson that they may not eat just any food. Suman holders are susceptible to sorcery and defilement through food and, therefore, must always know who gives the food they eat, whom the debt falls on, and whether it is safe to eat. In the context of the cult, food-giving is not about women's mundane obligations to give food but about competition for power and indebtedness.

This theme is underscored for the new initiates by what they observe the morning after their ritual hazing and scarification. The sponsors of the initiation prepare two enormous plates bearing every kind of good food to feed the intervening grade who were novices at the last initiation rites. The recipients of this feast will in turn indebt the novices at the next initiation. The initiates, still unfed, witness the next higher grade as they experience at first hand the one-upmanship of ritual feasting. All initiated women are enjoined to create such indebtedness as ritual sponsors and exchange partners in the community and beyond.

When the decorated initiates walk through the village, they observe displays of cooked food and trade goods (various kinds of raw foods, betel nut, and tobacco) arrayed for their sponsors, the mwara ngakeen. Since the initiates now represent the groups sponsoring the event, they can only eat privately at home after the whole affair is done. Schmidt (1926:51) reports for male initiation that when finally the weary initiates go home to eat and sleep, their parents slap their arms as they reach for food, saying, "Now you come and take sago from your mother." A senior man described the end of the women's initiation to me with similar words.

Other lessons concern analogies between food-giving and sexuality, appetites through which others can be indebted and which, uncontrolled, reduce one to a drooling fool. For new initiates, this analogy is suggested by the figure of Yangaron who, with his oversized balsa wood penis, delivers their food. Because they are seated, his decoration and their food are simultaneously at eye level as he stands before them offering the plate. In the ribald dances staged by ritual sponsors throughout the night, the girls are repeatedly taunted with suggestions that they are hungry for food and sex. Shouting "Are you hungry?" the sponsors dance toward them, thrusting their hips as if to invite copulation or attempting to shove their breasts into the girls' mouths. The response to the sexual taunt is to grab whatever is handy as a mock penis and chase off the rapacious attacker; the response to the invitation to suck is verbal: "I have parents! Just wait!"—which means the initiate has kin who, by the end of the rituals, will render the ritual sponsors indebted and dependent with gifts of food. These taunts must be challenged assertively. So long as an initiate is passive, the mwara ngakeen escalate their insults. They are said to teach the initiates how to respond to challenges and to defeat rivals.

SEXUALITY AND THE SAMBAAN

In contrast to many societies, the Murik women's cult does not celebrate adult sexuality for its potential to transform a girl into a fertile wife and/or mother. Nor are women praised for remaining chaste. Although, in former times, initiation was preceded by seclusion from men, this was to protect men's health (against elephantiasis of the scrotum) rather than the initiates' virginity,[10] and nowadays it has been dispensed with completely. Instead, the women's cult deals with sexuality as a resource for controlling others by manipulating their desire.

In Murik, sexuality is assumed to be a powerful aspect of being human, but uncontrolled lust, which is viewed with a jaundiced eye, makes one vulnerable to slavishness. Openly seductive behavior and promiscuity are relentlessly mocked by senior to junior joking partners. Ambivalence about sexual pleasure and the responsibilities of parenthood that eventually result is expressed by women in their separate roles of mother and mwara ngakeen. Older initiated women, observing younger women going to and fro in the village, acting slyly flirtatious and engaging in trysts, comment wryly, "Just wait. Later you will know." They are referring to the double burdens that accompany adult sexuality. As mothers, women worry that their daughters will find themselves pregnant and saddled with the burdens of parenthood before they are mature enough to undertake them. As classificatory father's sisters, many women openly enjoy the requisite ribald joking but understand the work of exchange, feasting, and ritual that these relationships entail. Joking among initiated women is full of veiled references to sexuality deployed according to cult requirements (Barlow 1992).

What the young women learn when they are initiated is that their sexuality can and should be used in the service of prestige, access to resources, and spiritual power accessed through male-female intercourse in the men's cult. In the past, the female cult focused even more on enhancing the initiates' sexuality. During seclusion, they underwent a beautification process: their hair grew pleasingly long, their bodies became invitingly plump and their skin desirably pale. They became visually "big," as befit their new status, and they absorbed seduction and beautification magic from sleeping with female, cult, spirit figures. At the end of the rites, they were—and still are—scarified and decorated to make them so beautiful that onlookers honor them with gifts.

The initiates are instructed to use their sexuality to develop alliances that increase their network of resources. Thus, when their father's sisters—their ritual sponsors—place feathers in their caps and call the names of their lovers, they reveal secret sources of support throughout the lakes and trade villages. Initiated women pointed out their partners in other villages to me saying, "If I have to make a feast, he will help me."

Particularly intriguing is the moiety "warfare" described by Schmidt and to Lipset, in which women conduct sexual affairs on behalf of their husbands to assist them in becoming the senior moiety. There are substantial risks involved. The women may be prevented or beaten by their jealous husbands, made ill or even killed by male cult spirits. Moreover, the act contravenes, at least metaphorically, the prohibition against social and sexual relations between a woman and her husband's senior male kin. Yet, for both men and women, it also provides the greatest opportunity for access to spiritual power.[11] Not only is the husband promoted in the ritual hierarchy but the woman achieves prestige among both men and women. A child born of a cult encounter is revered as an incarnated spirit.

The senior women of the cult haze the initiates for their prior carefree and casual sexual affairs, and enjoin them as suman merogo to use their sexuality according to new objectives. Along with considerable sexual freedom, the senior women confer magical protection and use their authority (the suman) on their own and other women's behalf. As Kanjo, an initiated Darapap woman, told me in 1988:

> Once you have been initiated, no one may question you. If someone gets mad at you for having an affair you may say, "Where were you? You ate the pig(s) that my father paid, didn't you? You may not talk."
>
> If your husband gets angry and beats you [for an affair], you can come to me, a suman woman. I will keep you in my house and feed you. When you are ready to go home, I will send you there with the suman and he may not touch you, or he will have to pay in pigs. I can protect you. Later you will return the suman to me on top of a plate of good food.

Given such prerogatives, the more senior a woman is in the cult hierarchy, the less likely she is to be challenged. At the same time, initiated women are discrete so as to avoid confrontation. And if their own husband has an affair with another woman, they are expected to dismiss it, saying, "Let her have the children and the work, too. I have enough."[12]

AGGRESSION AND THE SAMBAAN

The Murik consider both genders likely to act aggressively under certain circumstances and judge both to be capable of enforcing peace. Men and women assault others over sexual infidelity or transgressions of ownership. Threats should be faced down with the response, "Go ahead. I'm ready." Sanctioned aggression within the women's cult communicates at least two important messages about the manipulation of power. The first is related to the issue of sexuality, already discussed. The initiates are encouraged to assert themselves sexually and are offered protection from a jealous husband or lover's wife.

A second message, about aggression, is conveyed by the male-garbed mansarip warriors, who attack and haze the initiates. Their transvestism might imply that aggression is a *male* attribute or that the senior women act out the father's authority (as sponsor of the ritual) over his daughter. The first interpretation is congruent with the view that gender is conceptualized in terms of contrasting attributes, a view I have rejected for the Murik case. The second supports the view that female initiation is motivated by men's need to control women, particularly their sexuality (e.g., Paige and Paige 1981:43–45). The problem with this rationale is that the mansarip appear to represent the opposite women's cult moiety rather than the father. The father's ritual representatives are his actual sisters, whose role is to coach and protect the novices, and his classificatory sisters, the mwara ngakeen, who escort each initiate through the ritual and dress her in finery at the end. Together, they represent the father's sponsorship and parental guidance, as well as his approval of his daughter's independent and socialized sexuality. Following her initiation, she is less under her father's control than before, although her new identity will ultimately contribute to his own prestige.

In this case, the maleness of the mansarip denotes aggressive sanctioning (see Douglas 1966; Strathern 1976). Aggressive action, associated in the male domain with warfare, refers to the dominance of the male cult over mundane attachments and to the antimaternal character of dominance through aggression. Dressing as male warriors, the mansarip claim dominance in the cult by threatening aggression and thus dissociate themselves from the maternal nurture that is otherwise expected of senior women. Their domination of the initiates is thus set apart from domestic nurturance and seduction.

THE ROLE OF EXCHANGE
IN PERSONHOOD AND GENDER

If personhood in Murik society is achieved by giving cultural form to the human impulses of sexuality, aggression, and nurture, exchange is the process through which these meanings and values are enacted. In the secret societies, men and women are empowered to engage in the most prestigious types of exchange. In so doing, they play an important role in creating and reproducing Murik society. The cult initiations create an elite group of men and women who compete for status, personally and on behalf of their descent groups, by sponsoring other life-cycle and community rituals. These activities require feasting and trade to compensate ritual sponsors and other workers, and confer spiritual powers that ensure the success and prosperity of the group.

Exchange is a process by which the sambaan initiation is produced and the status changes of the initiates are effected. The *mwara* relationships of ritual sponsorship are maintained by intergenerational exchanges among mwara ngakeen and sponsors. These exchanges entail the repayment of previous debts and the creation of new ones. Indeed, so critical is this dynamic that, when the mission and government combined forces to suppress the secret cult, the Murik continued to conduct the public feasting exchanges between groups of ritual sponsors as a means of reproducing the status of suman merogo (Ledoux 1936).

If a woman being initiated is firstborn, then, since early childhood, her ritual sponsors have presented a stream of valuables on her behalf, receiving in exchange gifts of food. Once initiated, she can incur and discharge debts in her own name and build up a reputation. Like all major rituals in Murik society, sambaan initiations depend on trade beyond the Murik villages to subsidize the feasts that reward the mwara ngakeen for their services. As is the case for men, initiation cedes permission to women to participate in these vital missions. Thus, an initiated woman can become known regionally, first by sponsoring extratribal trade excursions and later, once she has reached the senior grades of the cult, by going to the islands and trading in her own name.

The critical importance to women of participation in local exchange and active trading is underscored by the symbolic appearance of these themes in the plates, pots, and basket reeds that initiates receive on their promenade through the villages. The plates are obtained from the coastal trade network and are important serving dishes in all public food exchanges. A woman who wants to appear prosperous must present many beautiful plates of food on ritual occasions. Pots, also obtained through trade, are seldom seen outside the domestic household, where they are used to store sago, a trade commodity that a woman must have in abundant supply if she is to feed her family well and participate fully in public life. Basket reeds enable women to manufacture the main item of exchange in the coastal and island trade. In sum, the gifts presented to initiates during their processions around the villages are symbols of the industry and productivity by which a woman's reputation is made.

A second kind of exchange, that of sexual services in return for the ritual promotion of husbands, also occurred as part of the Murik women's cult, but the secrecy surrounding it makes it difficult to interpret. Clearly, though, the act confers prestige among other women and confers special privileges with respect to the island trade.

CONCLUSION

Despite the absence of important data necessary for a comprehensive and detailed interpretation of Murik women's initiation, some general points are clear, including certain contrasts and complementarity in male and female personhood. The women's cult elaborates the motifs of sexuality, feeding, and exchange as women practice them. It distinguishes domestic feeding, which denotes the dependence and security of the mother-daughter tie, from competitive feasting; and it establishes relationships of sponsorship and protection among women in the high-stakes gamble of sexual exchange. Sexuality is deployed as a means to achieve specific goals—including access to resources, prestige, and spiritual power—but it is sharply differentiated from promiscuity and procreative sexual relations. In the men's cult, as we have seen, similar themes are expressed with different emphases. Feeding is an aggressive competition to "kill" one's rivals with plates of food. Sexuality is portrayed as generative, producing warriors and trade vessels. A significant difference is the tutelage concerning aggression and warfare in the men's cult, which is not emphasized in the sambaan. For women, this is not a major path to prestige as it has been, and to some extent remains, for men (Lipset 1984). But the men's and women's cults do not merely define and focus separately the means to power for each gender. Ultimately, they portray a dynamic interdependence among men and women, premised on personhood as a unitary concept. The values maximized to achieve full personhood are actualized differently by men and women in relation to both production and reproduction, but full personhood requires both genders to enact the full repertoire of meanings.

Returning to Ortner's suggestion that gender and prestige are negotiated through metaphor and praxis as hegemonies and counterhegemonies, we see that in Murik society such processes are never concluded and seldom at rest. Although men do have privileges and occupy domains from which women are excluded, this exclusion is never absolute and male prerogatives and claims often are offset by the ways in which women exercise power. They do so to such an extent that men openly recognize and accommodate this ability.

Men's and women's cult rituals dramatize the issues occupying the main stage of Murik social life, such as food production, descent-group status, trade, and exchange, but they also instruct new participants in scenes played offstage, yet to great benefit. These alternatives preclude any routine enactment of gender roles but promote intense negotiation in which gendered ways to claim prestige are played off against each other in some contexts and, in others, used to associate oneself with the prestigious accomplishments of others.

Individuals learn to present themselves to best advantage as competent, hard-working, productive, and generous. To this end, they undergo intense and long-term tutelage by parents, siblings, and grandparents in the domestic household, and by the ruthless joking partners who publicly mock and exaggerate their *faux pas* (Barlow 1992). Mere control of appetites and impulses is not enough to become a person of prestige. One must be born into a relatively senior position, receive ritual sponsorship, and demonstrate the personal capacities required for leadership. Initiation into the men's or women's cult is essential to these accomplishments. Through initiation into the women's cult, Murik women learn the concealed arts by means of which they may, if they are able, transform their separate achievements as women into the achievement of womanhood. As they enact the prerogatives of suman merogo, Murik big women perpetuate the cultural dialogue of women's identity and prestige. By their actions and claims, they produce many of the resources and provide much of the leadership that maintains Murik regional trade, which in turn reproduces the internal social organization of Murik society. Through the women's initiation ritual, new generations of suman merogo are inducted into this ongoing process.

NOTES

1. The research reported here was financed in part by the Wenner-Gren Foundation for Anthropological Research, the Institute for Intercultural Studies, the Graduate School of the University of California, San Diego, the Sepik Documentation Project of the Australian Museum, Sydney, and the Graduate School of the University of Minnesota.

   I thank Paul Roscoe and Nancy Lutkehaus for their patience and assistance with this paper; Brigitta Hauser-Schäublin for her encouragement and comments; and Mac Marshall and Margery Wolf for inviting me to present this paper at the University of Iowa and for discussing it with me. As always, David Lipset has provided editorial help and a challenging alternative perspective on Murik culture. Most of all, I appreciate the opportunity to learn about womanhood in Murik society from the women of the five Murik villages, especially Darapap. I hope this discussion is a fair representation and that it is but one step toward understanding their way of life more fully.

2. The Murik have always trafficked in the exchange of ritual practices and objects. With this in mind, I collected comparative information about women's ritual in the Schouten Islands and along the Lower Sepik River during our 1986 and 1988 visits. These villagers agreed that Murik initiation had been adapted from puberty ceremonies practiced in several River locations. Murik rituals are also similar to those of offshore islands (Barlow, Bolton, and Lipset 1987; Böhm 1983; Hogbin 1970; Lutkehaus, this volume; Wedgwood 1933, 1934), and Murik women who trace descent to these islands wear decorations from these places.

3. With respect to actual reproduction, social factors are emphasized over biological ones, giving men and women mutual responsibility and opportunity to participate (see Barlow 1985b). The biological mother is not considered the spiritual mother of the child, which is called the *nabwag ngaen*, literally the "flying fox mother." The physiological birth process, clearly women's domain,

occurs in a birth hut on the periphery of the village or in the mangrove while men's magical influence is dramatized through couvade. Successful pregnancy and birth require vigilant observance of taboos by both the mother *and father.* In matters of parenting and adoption, those who feed a child have a greater claim than those to whom it is born.

4. Suman insignia are assembled usually from boars' tusks, bird of paradise feathers, fruit, leaves, and flowers, but may also be a basket, lime gourd, or other property. Most require that no physical violence occur in their presence. (A few are designated as war suman and confer fighting courage and strength.) The physical presence of an initiated person is itself a suman, with or without the assembled objects. A Murik man fluent in English translated the word to mean "authority."

5. If fighting breaks out inside a house guarded by a female spirit, the combatants are bodily thrown out and must present plates of food to redress the insult. Two cowives who fought were required by their husband and parents to exchange plates of food.

6. Schmidt implies that the women were then expected to have sexual intercourse with the senior partners of the men's second age-grade to pay their debt to them for their own initiation, but he also says that if a woman were too young or unwilling, another female relative could take her place (Schmidt 1926:52).

7. Schmidt (1926:47) reports that in 1918 the whole celebration lasted fourteen days.

8. When senior women encounter Yangaron in his public parades through the village, they engage him in an exuberant dance. Their demeanor is part of the different understandings about female sexuality and women's status that cult initiation confers and of the association of seduction with successful trade.

9. It was unclear from my informant whether these "mothers" are the senior members of the initiates' own moiety or their actual mothers. The difference is significant in terms of the mothers' role in the initiation and the resulting messages about mothers within the context of the cult and in mundane life.

10. Women I spoke to about the seclusion period said they were not supposed to see men but met their boyfriends anyway. In 1918, according to Schmidt (1926:47), two girls in "seclusion" got pregnant.

11. I do not know the precise relationship between a woman and her husband's senior partner in the cult. I know of only one retrospective statement, by a senior woman to Lipset, in her husband's presence, that she was not afraid to go to the men's cult house. Clearly, this is an important aspect of understanding the emotional and motivational potential of the women's cult for which my data are at this point inadequate.

12. On one occasion, a village moot decided against a young couple who tried to marry by taking up residence together. The man's first wife was an initiated woman who, despite affairs with other men, did not want to divorce him. The young woman who had taken up with her husband had already had his child. Her comment on the decision that she must go back to her parents' home was, "What can I do? She is a big woman. I am not."

5

TRANSFORMING WOMEN

Being and Becoming in an Island Melanesian Society

Deane Fergie

This essay is concerned with *rites de passage* in an Island Melanesian society I shall call Babae.[1] Despite a contact history of over three hundred years, the people of Babae maintain a major commitment to a complex and strenuous corpus of public ritual which they consider to be indigenous. This ritual corpus is composed of three major ritual sequences. One of these, a sequence of four festivals, is known as *vevene* and may be viewed as a context for female initiation. Its performance is dominated by women. It focuses on a woman's first childbearing experience and critical points in the development of her infant.

My aim in this essay is to show that an analysis of vevene would remain impoverished if it were to explore only those dimensions of the sequence that may be construed as female initiation. I juxtapose an analysis of the structure of the sequence situated within the corpus as a whole, with an analysis of important dimensions of the ritual experience through a focus on performance. I show that this exploration of performance enriches our understanding of the ritual sequence and adds importantly to our understanding of it as rites de passage.

In the first half of the essay, I explore the structure of the ritual and relate it to Babae conceptions of the human procreative process. My discussion highlights the fact that the vevene sequence is a rite de passage for the child as well as for the primipara. I then relate the structure of the vevene sequence to the corpus of public rituals—a corpus made up of the vevene sequence, the Death sequence, and the *lukara* sequence. I show how each sequence of the corpus may be viewed in its own right as a rite de passage. But I go beyond this to show that the corpus itself also may be considered fruitfully as a rite de passage for, as a totality, it takes an individual through all the culturally important dimensions and states of human existence, and in addition is deemed essential for the reproduction of the Babae cosmos.

By exploring vevene and the total corpus from this perspective, the analysis falls easily into a view of rites de passage that has its roots in Van Gennep's work. The second half of the essay, however, extends this view of Babae's rich ritual life by exploring also its performative aspects. Vevene is a context in which the frame of ritual (Bateson 1973; Handelman 1979) is coterminous with the frame of comedy. Here my analysis focuses on vevene comedy. In particular, I examine two kinds of identities that become particular targets of vevene comedy. On the one hand, I explore the dynamic, performative tension sustained between the two participating groups in the performance, and the fluidity of relatedness on Babae. On the other, I focus on young women who, on the cusp of puberty, become the targets of comedic actions. In performance, I argue, their sexuality is domesticated and appropriated by older performers, a conclusion I derive by attending to laughter, shame, and intoxication as they are played out in performance.

VEVENE

A vevene sequence is instigated when a Babae woman becomes pregnant for the first time.[2] Its four festivals celebrate the crossing of ontological thresholds by the developing child and the primipara. It is not just the engagement of the primipara's fecundity—attested by the development of her first child—that is celebrated, but also the precondition of that process—the engagement of her sexuality in pubescence.

As in much of Melanesia, it is assumed by many in this society that conception is the result of a number of sexual encounters. People also believe that the substantial form achieved derives from both male and female procreative substances: vaginal secretions and semen, which eventually gel in the womb. Yet the achievement of substantial form is clearly differentiated from growth because the former is considered prior to the latter. This is pointed up by women's explanations for the injunction on continued sexual relations after conception, which state that these procreative substances

TABLE 5.1   VEVENE FESTIVALS

Festival Gloss	Contingent Development	Process
		Sexual intercourse
"Conception"	Achievement of substantial form	Fetus begins to develop in utero
"Delivery"	Delivery	Start of birthing process
"Detachment"	Detachment of remnants of umbilical cord/cessation of postpartum bleeding	End of birthing process
"Weaning"	Cessation of breast feeding	End of growth by consumption of mother's bodily substance—child develops on food from wider environment

would dent the newly achieved form. Thus, a pronounced indentation in the fontenelle is interpreted as evidence that sexual intercourse continued after the establishment of a substantial form. Procreative substances cannot be broken down and incorporated into a new form because their a priori essence is form. This contrasts with nurturing substances, most prominently Mother's blood and, more generally, breast milk and food—whose essence is digestibility. These substances can be broken down and incorporated into another body to become a basis for growth and the maintenance of corporeality.

Thus, for the Babae, it is the child's mother's blood, and later her breast milk, that are the basis of a child's growth. This process begins after conception—that is, after the establishment of a substantial form—and the first vevene festival celebrates the transition between conception and the beginnings of fetal development in utero (see table 5.1).

Birth, in Babae terms, is a process spanning the period from delivery until the mother's postpartum bleeding has ceased and the remnants of the umbilicus, which is viewed as the last vestige of the child's in utero nurturance, has detached from the child's body. The beginning and end of this process is celebrated in ritual. Its beginning is marked by the Delivery Festival, which normally begins moments after the child has been safely delivered; its end is celebrated at the "detachment" feast, which takes place some weeks later.

Birth is believed to entail a change in the child's nurturance from blood (in utero) to breast milk (ex utero). Until it is weaned, usually 18 to 36 months after birth, a child continues to grow on its mother's milk: in effect, it consumes her bodily substance. This illuminates the implications of Babae birth-order terms. A first child—the subject of the vevene sequence —is referred to as just that, "first child." A second child is called "the child who follows." But, significantly, all subsequent children may be referred to as "child(ren) of an old woman." It is the process of feeding the corporeality of her children that ages a mother, and thus, in contrast to sterile women and men in general, mothers are believed to grow bodily old before their time.

Weaning thus marks a significant transition on Babae. Until that point, the child is "of" its mother's substance in a very direct way; after that point, the child ceases to depend directly on its mother's substance for its developing corporeality. It is the final festival in the vevene sequence that marks this important transition.

Table 5.1 summarizes the process of human reproduction and its implications for both the primipara and her child, and relates this process to the timing of the vevene festivals. The table also underscores how the vevene sequence can be profitably viewed as rites de passage for both the primipara and her child. For the primipara, it celebrates her transformation from preproductive to reproducing woman. For the child, it draws attention to important transitions in its mode of nurturance by its mother.

VEVENE AND THE CORPUS OF PUBLIC RITUAL

Vevene is a significant part of the corpus of public ritual celebrated in these islands. The other sequences of the corpus are the Death sequence and the lukara sequence. Like vevene, the Death festivals also mark important transitions. As birth is a process, so too is death. Whenever possible, the first of the Death festivals takes place in the period immediately preceding what we conceive of as death. It is said to "shake hands" with the dying person. The next festival occurs immediately after death and entails a vigil with the body of the deceased in which inmarrying women carry it across their legs as they sit on beds in the men's house. It is followed, usually the next morning, by a burial feast. Some weeks later, as many as three "taboo"-lifting festivals may be held. These end the community's period of concerted mourning.

Like the vevene festivals, the Death sequence ritually enacts critical ontological transformations. Death does not imply simply the death of the body. Rather, the end of corporeality is an extended process that may begin in the period before signs of life have gone and does not end until the body has decomposed. For many Babae, the critical nexus of here-and-now existence—a nexus between a breathing, corporeal form housing an animated spirit—is disrupted when breathing ceases, and a new set of processes begin: decomposition and, in consequence, a new metaphysical "freedom." The person's spirit can no longer find its home in the disintegrating body and instead becomes a potentially threatening named and proximate spirit that must be treated ritually and with caution.

It is in the final sequence of the corpus—the lukara sequence—that the spirit is ritually dealt with and this "unease" resolved. These festivals usually commence after decomposition is considered to have finished—in practice, as early as a year but often up to a decade after death. In this sequence, the named and proximate spirits of one or more dead members of a group are transformed into generalized ancestral spirits who then can be called upon to facilitate human projects—most prominently, engaging the fecundity of territory. Unlike the preceeding sequences, lukara ceremonies do not have a common sequence of festivals. Nor do they focus necessarily on the transitions of a single human subject. Rather, a number of dead can be dealt with in concert at the most public festivals of the sequence. Each of the deceased is represented by a particular ritual sculpture, and the early festivals of their sequences vary with the entailments for the reproduction of these particular sculptures. It is in the final festivals of each sequence, when the sculptures are publicly presented, that the ritual work of each converges in a common context.

Until the Second World War, lukara were also the context in which males were initiated. Thus, boys became men in the same context in which proximate named spirits of the dead became generalized ancestral spirits. The transformation of each body and each spirit was represented by a sculpture dedicated and produced for them.

Although each sculpture entailed a specific and unique sequence, all lukara sequences share a basic structure. In every sequence, there is what we may consider to be a festival of commissioning and a festival or series of festivals celebrating the particular shaping and adornment of the sculpture by, for example, painting, decorating, or emplacement of eyes. This is followed by the beginning of the most public festivals in which the sculpture is said to be "stood up": it is publicly and ritually presented as a finished work, and its particular identity is revealed. The final festival is one in which the "stood up," finished sculpture is decommissioned. This ends the ritual sequence, and the sculpture is disposed of in whatever manner is prescribed for it: burning or leaving it to rot by the sea or in the bush. This

TABLE 5.2   RITES OF PASSAGE AND THE PUBLIC
                                RITUAL CORPUS

Ritual Sequence	Festivals	Rite of Passage for . . .
Vevene	• Conception • Delivery • Detachment • Weaning	Infants and women (primipara and pubescent girls)
Death	• Shaking hands • Death • Burial • Taboo-lifting feast	Deceased persons
Lukara	• Commissioning • Festivals of adornment • Standing up • Decommissioning	Boys (formerly), deceased persons, and sculptures

common lukara structure leads me to argue that each sculpture in its particular ritual sequence undergoes an ontological transformation just as humans
do in this ritual corpus. Like humans, the beginning of their form and
growth as sculptures is celebrated, as is their achievement of fullness and
their demise. Thus, lukara sequences may be seen not only as rites de passage for the dead and for males, but also for each sculpture.

It is significant, then, that the juxtaposition of forms and materials used
in these sculptures represents dimensions and juxtapositions of the island
environment. As a corpus, therefore, all dimensions of this cosmos are ritually presented and, I would argue, facilitate the reproduction of that cosmos.

Table 5.2 summarizes the ontological transitions enacted by the total
ritual corpus of the vevene, Death, and lukara sequences. It outlines how
the vevene sequence provides the context of rites de passage for women—
both pubescent girls and primiparas—and also for the transformations
entailed in the development of infants while they grow on their mother's
bodily substance. The immediate ontological entailments of dying are dealt
with in the Death sequence, while the transformations entailed by death are
concluded in lukara ceremonies.

It is clear that while each of the three sequences that make up this public
ritual corpus may be considered productively as a rite de passage, the corpus as a whole also constitutes a rite de passage. This corpus of ritual takes
any Babae individual through the ontological transitions entailed by human

existence. I would argue, then, that the analysis of any of the component ritual sequences would remain impoverished if it were not also explored in the context of the corpus itself.

Similarly, the analysis of ritual in this Island Melanesian society would be impoverished if it failed to explore important experiential dimensions of ritual performance. It is to that aspect that I now turn, focusing on the vevene sequence.

VEVENE PERFORMANCE

Following Ortiz (1972), vevene is a ritual drama. But it is also a sequence for which the ritual "frame" is coterminous with a frame of comedy that is eagerly anticipated, engaged in, and gleefully recalled. The comedy is enacted through songs, costumes, dance, dramas, and jokes. As comedy, each of these "mediums" entails a play upon form (Douglas 1975:96).

It is useful in this analysis to distinguish between "standard" (i.e., precedented and well-recognized) and "innovative" comedy in ritual performances. Although standard comedy dominates any vevene festival, it is innovative comedy that sustains each event over the arduous hours of performance.[3] Innovative comedy is loudly applauded at the time and provides the highlights that people recall after the event is over. To give an example: a standard mode of costuming is to present oneself comically as a man, perhaps wearing shorts and always carrying a male basket. But the first time a woman came wearing the sunglasses favored by progressive Babae men, it created a real stir. I observed women sit around for days trying to think of some new play on form that would bring them renown. People were forever wanting to borrow this or that item from my "wardrobe" for a performance.

On another occasion, two young women stopped the show for several moments when they combined the standard comedic elements of short trousers, hats, and traditional decorative chestbands with a creative *pièce de résistance* dangling from their chestbands: several items of modern rubbish that included softdrink bottles, cigarette packets, crumpled envelopes, discarded meat and fish tins, and plastic rice bags. On another occasion, for which the standard costume is a large taro tuber hung around the neck, a woman suspended in its place a large piece of polystyrene she had found washed up on the beach.

Similarly, there is a standard corpus of vevene songs that are sung throughout a performance. But imaginative women may create a stir by composing and teaching their group an entirely new song for the festival, which then is likely to become part of the standard stock. It is also possible to assay impromptu plays on the words of song lyrics. And, whereas the standard vevene dance is performed upright on two feet, pelvis thrusting in imitation of sexual intercourse, one performance achieved new resonance when two women transformed the pose by lying on the ground. These are the sorts of highlights that "stop the show" and are the quintessence of these creative dramatic events.

Plays on form may not be encapsulated solely in the antics of performers. Frequently, they also involve other people and objects. One standard example involves lifting up the aprons of others, peering closely at their genitals, and asking, "Is your (domesticated) pig hungry?"—a formulation that posits the pig as a metaphor for the vagina and implies that it is hungry for intercourse. Another oft-repeated example is a performer dancing at, into, and upon the bodies of others. In a creative extreme, one woman who for some time had targeted another with her dancing eventually grabbed onto the rafters of the house and, hanging from them, held her target's head between her thighs as she continued the action of the dance.

The integral form of objects also may be played with. Thus, women freely take, destroy, or disfigure the possessions of others. For example, I attended a vevene festival at which women performers turned on the houses of their hosts and rampaged about inside, violently breaking up beds and seats and throwing saucepans about. Then they came back out, grabbed the long lines of roof thatch, and danced vigorously until the thatch ultimately was dislodged and broken.

There are also standard moments in a vevene performance when women invade the space of the men's house, rampage among its objects, destroying or damaging them; douse the men with water; rub them with ashes and other rubbish such as the greasy remains of the feast food; steal the remains of their food; and ultimately throw them out of the men's house enclosure, classically into a river, the sea, or the bush. As I will try to show, however, vevene is no simple rite of rebellion (Gluckman 1963) or rite of reversal.

Although it is tempting to focus on the apparent "transvestism" in vevene comedy, it should be kept in mind that the male decorations women may use to "make an entrance" into the host hamlet are usually dispensed with soon after, and women clothe themselves as much in decorations of ambiguous gender or neutrality as in any other. The point is that women play with the very categories of gendered, personal, and "becoming" appearance from every which way.

It also should be borne in mind that the victims of their comedy are both men and women. Indeed, given that men may choose to leave the host hamlet before a performance commences, it is intriguing that they stay—the more so since my cofieldworker, Rod Lucus, discovered that men anticipate their discomfort and humiliation and bemoan their fate to each other. But, by maintaining a presence in the hamlet, and by taking up particular rhetorical and performative positions themselves, men enact their complicity with the ritual. They also take on a dramatic stance themselves—active in its constructed anticipation, passive when the women focus their attentions on them.

Finally, the performative attention to men is never addressed to the abstract category, *men*, but always to a particular group of men—usually those of the Mother's group though sometimes those of the Father's.[4] In other words, the gender of these male "victims" cannot be separated from their group affiliation; when gender is played with, it is played with in this social context.

GROUPS AND THE DYNAMIC TENSION OF VEVENE PERFORMANCE

An important aspect of any vevene performance is the distinction between two participating groups of women, the Mother's group and the Father's group, frequently glossed as "us" and "them." Despite this "kinship" idiom, however, it is impossible to predict by simple reference to "clan" or "subclan" affiliation or genealogies who will align themselves with which group. Thus, it is not uncommon to record ten or more members of different natal "clans" presenting as a single group referring to itself (or referred to by others) as "the Fathers." Moreover, women who joined in the same group at one festival may be sighted on opposing sides at another. Like other aspects of Babae culture, these ritual festivals point up the fluidity of groups and "kin" relationships on Babae.

In this community, it is links of substance through nurturance that hold greater weight than links of procreative substances (semen and vaginal secretions) in the determination of peoples' relatedness. On Babae, the maxim, "You are what you eat," is no joke. Relatedness is a process in train from the moment substantial form is achieved in utero until a person is buried.[5] Although a child is nurtured directly on the corporeal substance of its mother until weaning and thus has its closest links to her and her group, the food it eats after weaning and the territory from which this food is derived become further important factors in its affiliation. Because the group burying a person can lay claims to his or her spirit and, in ritual, can transform it into a group resource for facilitating the fecundity of territory, burial is a time when disputes can arise over which group has closest affiliation to the deceased. Not infrequently, therefore, people are buried and their spirits claimed by nonmaternal groups. (I briefly discuss such a case later.)

This dynamic of fluidity and competitiveness among groups is reflected in vevene performances, not just in terms of who aligns with which group but also in the structure of performance itself. Since vevene performances celebrate human procreation, reproductive power, and group affiliation (and reproduction), it is hardly surprising that food and sexuality are dominant themes and that the two participating groups gloss their distinctiveness as the "group of Fathers" and the "group of Mothers."

For the first three festivals of the sequence, "conception," "delivery," and "detachment," the group identifying itself as Mothers are the hosts, providing and preparing the food. The Fathers take center stage as the performing comedians, frequently targeting the Mothers in their comic antics—invading their bodily space, disrupting their work, and damaging or destroying their houses. Mothers must sit and take it; Fathers in their comic antics give them plenty of stick.

The Mothers' demeanor throughout the festivals and especially when they are the target of comedic attack is critical to this discussion. In the face of considerable onslaught, they attempt to present a demeanor of detached indifference. And while Fathers fall about in their laughter, Mothers strive to show no reaction, as though they were deaf and blind. Sometimes, though, it is clear they are struggling to suppress a smile or giggle, most obviously when an unexpected occasion of innovative comedy is successfully staged. Thus, an important dynamic of vevene performance is that Fathers seek to provoke Mothers to share their mirth, while intransigent Mothers seek to reject it.

Mary Douglas has pointed out that laughter is an eminently social phenomenon. Indeed, she suggests, "laughter is a unique bodily eruption which is always to be taken as communication" (1975:86). She also notes that comedy is a rearrangement of form, while Hieb (1972:190) points out that humor is not simply a reversal but "involves an alternative pattern which makes sense to a sufficient degree for it to be entertained momentarily as a new and creative combination of the elements which comprised the original pattern."

So where does this leave us in exploring vevene comedy and laughter and its one-sided nature? In Kapferer's (1983:214) view, "laughter ... communicates that the members of the ritual gathering share a common and objective attitude towards the world whereby they can recognize the comic." We might draw from this that the Fathers share a view of the world by which they can recognize the ludic in their own antics but that Mothers do not.

Yet this is clearly untrue. After the performances are over, especially in private, the Mothers are quite capable of recalling and appreciating the comic moments that they appeared not to notice at the time. Clearly, the contrast in demeanor is a contrast that, for the duration of the festival at least, sustains a clear distinction between the two groups. This heightens the reality that is visibly expressed also by the fact that Fathers decorate themselves for these festivals whereas Mothers do not.

I would argue that what the Mothers are displaying is a "refusal," a refutation of relations that the Fathers seek to assert through their comedy. The issue around which this dynamic performative tension turns, I suggest, is the affiliation of the child at the center of the performance. Despite the antics of the Fathers, it is Mothers who have the last laugh, at least at the preweaning festivals, because until it is weaned the child is its Mother's substance and thus is more closely related to her and her group than to anyone else, including the child's Father.

Because nurturant substances—blood, breast milk, and food—are the primary building blocks of relatedness on Babae, weaning is a critical threshold in the relatedness stakes. Once crossed, it offers other individuals and groups their first opportunity to build links of substance with the child. This is a particularly potent concern if the family is resident in the husband/father's territory; if the child then is nurtured by food grown on this territory, the father and his group will be forging ties of shared substance with the child from the moment it begins to consume the food. As I have said, it is entirely conceivable that, over a lifetime, these links will transcend the early links of substance established through the mother to her group.

It is therefore significant that the dynamic tension I have described in the first three vevene festivals is radically transformed at the "weaning" festival, the final festival of the sequence. At this festival, the performative stances and inequalities are dissipated. Both groups bring and prepare the food that is pooled on a central platter of coconut fronds and, in contrast to the previous festivals, is eaten by Mothers and Fathers together. At the festival's climax, the two groups grab either end of the fronds on which the food was placed and play out a Babae version of a tug-of-war. They do so, I suggest, because this festival celebrates the child's weaning and so marks the point after which the child's closest affiliation is "up for grabs," when the mother and her group may well lose their preeminence.

It is worth pushing the cultural importance of this dynamic tension home with brief reference to an event that sometimes occurs at a burial feast. In this context, too, when the deceased's links of closest affiliation remain unclear, another battle between disputing groups may arise. One such case occurred while I was in the field, involving a woman who had left her natal territory early in life and, in the course of a long lifetime, had moved from one place to another. She had been living in the village where she died for going on ten years, and so it was at this place that preparations were made for her burial. In the hours after her death, however, her maternal relatives arrived to claim the corpse, and a dispute arose between the two groups. In response to my perplexity at this turn of events, a friend explained that the two groups were having a "tug-of-war"[6] over the body and that the deceased had "a foot over here with us, and another over there in her maternal territory. We are trying to decide on which foot she has placed most weight." In that case, the maternal group had the last laugh, but, as the performative tension of vevene festivals indicates, the laugh might as easily have been on them.

REFLECTIONS ON FORM

The previous section focused on the dynamic tension between the two groups that participate in vevene performances, and on the questions of why Mothers are the target of comedy at the preweaning festivals and of who has the last laugh. In this section, I return to the issue of laughter but juxtapose it with the shame of those girls, on the cusp of engaged sexuality, who have yet to join vevene as performers, and with the intoxication of young women in their early vevene performances.

I begin this discussion with the question of who comes to vevene performances. First, as I have already said, women who see themselves as "Mothers" and "Fathers" to the primipara and her child are the main participants. They are accompanied by all their young children, including boys under about five to seven years (older boys sometimes sit with their fathers in the men's house enclosure). Girls of all ages, however, remain as a kind of tacit audience to the performance until they reach the cusp of puberty and the possibility of joining the performance. It is this transition that concerns me here.

Reflecting on who does what at vevene performances, one is immediately drawn to the antics of the adult women, who always take center stage. Yet closer inspection reveals a couple of important points. First, young children may involve themselves in the performance but only in mimicry of the adult women, and rarely is any attention paid to their antics. One then notices that once girls reach the age of five or so, they rarely do anything but watch and, at the appropriate time, eat. Ordinarily, they do not even become targets of comedy. The situation changes, however, when they approach puberty, when they may become the periodic targets of performers' comedic forays.

Why should this happen, and what do these girls' fairly characteristic responses add to our understanding of vevene and the lives of women in this society? To answer these questions, I discuss the vevene "attacks" on a twelve-year-old girl named Yunami in my fieldtrip during the mid-1980s and her responses to them, and contrast them to the behavior of Taita, her eighteen-year-old cousin, whose first performances in a vevene sequence occurred at the same festivals. These two cases bring us back to the standard comedic action I have witnessed at all vevene festivals: the action of peering at another's genitals and asking, "Is the domesticated pig hungry?" The metaphor of pig for vagina is readily available in vevene performance. The focus of my question here is why vaginas are considered domesticated and how this is accomplished.

YUNAMI

Yunami was a quiet young girl whose mother was so enthusiastic a participant in vevene performances that for days after she bemoaned that her body ached from the physical exertion. Whenever her mother participated in a festival at which I was present, Yunami also was there. In the late 1970s, as a young girl, she would sit quietly on the sidelines while her mother danced and sang. In the mid-1980s, then aged about twelve, she found herself the occasional object of unwelcome attention in the performance. Older women would gibe her and go to rip at her apron, grab her genitals, and make other similarly provocative gestures. In response, Yunami's composure would dissolve, and she would hide her head in her hands or run out of the host house and hide.

At times, I noticed her trying to make herself inconspicuous by standing behind a tree or doorframe, peeking round to observe the goings on. But, paradoxically, when this defensive stance was noticed, it seemed only to provoke more unwanted attention. I found myself surprised to see in her self-conscious shyness a suggestion of a typical Babae stance of shame—surprised because, although I might have expected to see such a stance frequently at vevene, I never did see it among the adult performers, only among nonperforming, pubescent girls subjected to provocative actions.

TAITA

When I arrived in the field in the mid-1980s, Taita, who had been about eleven on my previous fieldtrip, was now eighteen and sexually active. At the first vevene festival during my second stay, Taita decorated herself in a standard vevene style and, when the dancing and singing began, danced tentatively on the sidelines, occasionally becoming the subject of forays from older performers. There is one, often sung song, in particular, that issues a challenge to a named woman to dance a solo, and Taita was always one of those challenged. Normally, the challenged woman gets up, dances, and, at the end of her solo, approaches the challenger, lifts her apron, and opens her genitals for inspection. This response is generally aggressive, and, at its conclusion, the other dancers whoop in delight. Taita at first danced solo, and only after a number of challenges did she finally respond in this manner. As the performance proceeded, however, she became less shy and more enthusiastic and, in the end, raised her skirts and thereby attested to the status of her "domesticated pig." Rather than humiliating her, the older women offered congratulations, and over a couple of hours her shyness dissipated.

A few weeks later another vevene festival was held, and we all traveled some hours to it. Taita's anticipation and her preparations for the event were obvious in the week leading up to it. As we walked to the host village, the women sang and played out several forms of vevene comedy—joking and play acting. Taita was one of the prominent performers. Older women warned that she was bound to become intoxicated at this performance and, indeed, when we arrived and joined the other performers, Taita frequently and without provocation took center stage with her outrageous antics. She danced and shook all day long, resting only occasionally. As night fell, her enthusiasm for performance appeared only to increase. When challenged to dance solo, she embraced the opportunity and her aggressive responses at the end of her dances drew great applause. When she sat for a while, she was even able to make a performance out of the mere act of sitting, and she would rise again sooner than any others to dance outrageously and with a gusto that defied the hours she had been already performing.

Frequently, it was Taita who initiated new songs and challenged others, especially those who were taking a break, to get up and dance again. She danced until just before dawn, when she and the handful of other young women who also had lasted the longest finally slept for an hour or so. As the warmth of the sun penetrated the ground on which these disheveled forms slept, however, she rose again to out-do and provoke the older women.

In the depths of the night, older women had solemnly informed me that Taita was intoxicated on vevene, and they renewed these opinions in the daylight hours. When most of the group went off to steal their hosts' betel nuts, it was Taita again who was among the most outrageous performers. In her intoxication, she had lost all shame and had become a wholehearted vevene performer, applauded for her antics by the congregation.

In succeeding vevene festivals, Taita retained this enthusiastic embrace of energetic, comedic performance. In the quieter moments of everyday life between vevene festivals, she spoke nostalgically of the excitements of past occasions and boasted of what she would do at the next. During performances, she rejoiced in her state of exhilarated intoxication and sought to repeat the experience again and again. Older women, too, reflected on these performances and would refer to Taita's energy and intoxication with great satisfaction. Taita had made a hit, and everyone was pleased.

BECOMING

Yunami and Taita, I suggest, were on either side of a threshold between performance and nonperformance in vevene. Clearly, when a girl approaches this threshold, she ceases to be relatively inconspicuous and begins to attract the attention of older performers. In effect, they goad and send up her shyness and shamed reactions. When she does finally take the step to performance, they challenge and congratulate her whenever she shows evidence of losing her self-consciousness and stance of shame. The actions of these older women may be seen as moves to incorporate young girls into the festivals as coperformers. In the one case, Yunami was shamed by her shyness, while her older and sexually active cousin Taita was embraced, drawn in, and heartily congratulated for her participation. Whereas Yunami has yet to be incorporated into the group of adult women who celebrate the reproductive accomplishment of one of their number, Taita is now incorporated. Yunami remains an untamed pig while, through its public revelation, Taita has been acclaimed as a domesticated one.

What happens at vevene, I want to suggest, is that a young woman's untamed sexuality is appropriated and domesticated by the congregation during her first vevene performance. Critical to this is the loss of shyness, especially at having her genitals touched or referred to by older women.

On my first visit to Babae, I became something of a *cause célèbre* at vevene performances because, when women dived at my genitals and asked whether my pig was hungry, I would blush from the roots of my chest, a phenomenon they found hilarious and sought to reproduce time and time again. By my next fieldtrip, having spent a great deal of time reflecting on vevene and Babae humor, I had—like Taita—ceased to be self-conscious in the face of such onslaughts. This transformation was greeted not by mirth but by quiet pleasure, for women assumed that, in the time between my two fieldtrips, my sexuality, like Taita's, had been domesticated.

COMPOSURE

There are three further points I wish to explore using the material from these cases. The first relates to Yunami's shyness and what was ludic about it. The issue here is as much about self-consciousness and shame as it is about laughter. Yet, I would argue, both of these human responses share some important features. On the one hand, what Mary Douglas has said of laughter—that it is a social phenomenon that is also communicative—can be said also of Yunami's responses of self-consciousness, shyness, and shame.

On the other hand, both responses undermine normal composure. In an important sense, in the Babae response I refer to as shame, the face disintegrates: one is apt to turn and "crumple" one's face and diminish one's body. Likewise, in laughter, the face bubbles out of shape. In recent years, much has been said of the relationship between humor and reflection. Because the ludic is a rearrangement of a taken-for-granted pattern or form, its recognition is predicated on an understanding of, and reflection upon, the taken-for-granted form. The ludic is a way of thinking about culture as well as playing with it. So what is funny about the loss of composure in a pubescent girl is her reaction—a reaction that means "not yet" and all that "not yet" implies in Babae culture. And that shamed response provides a poignant relief to the "already" that is bespoken by the laughter and antics of those women who have passed that threshold and become performers both in these rituals and, in a much broader sense, in this culture.

The second point I wish to consider is how, then, we understand intoxication. Following on from the foregoing, I would suggest that, like laughter and shame, intoxication is a loss of normal composure but a more radical loss than normally is achieved in either laughter or shame. It is a letting go, a radical transcendence of physical and psychological form. It is, I would suggest, the necessary medium by which a young woman in the context of these rituals can transcend shyness and achieve a comfortable mirth. It is the means by which the untamed sexuality of youth is culturally transformed into domesticated sexuality and appropriated by older women. It is how sexual activity in this culture can be represented as "sweet" and yet be appropriated in social reproduction.

A final point can be made about the composure, or rather decomposure, of men in vevene festivals. They are apt to be rudely awakened by having cold water poured over them as they lie deeply asleep in the night—their crumpled hair and disgruntled features the object of particular delight by their assailants. In the daylight hours of vevene performance, their space is invaded, their skins are rubbed with the most disgusting rubbish, any aspect of their being in the world is disparaged, and they may be thrown like rubbish into the bush in a heap or, with limbs and clothing disheveled, into water. In the same context that girls can become publicly composed as adult women, in other words, Babae men are decomposed and made most unbecoming by performing women.

CONCLUSION

In this essay I have sought to explore important aspects of the vevene ritual sequence in Babae. When I first saw these rituals, they left me totally at a loss. When I asked women why they performed them, or why they did particular actions that made no sense to me, the common and oft-repeated response was: "We do them because we are celebrating this new child"; or, "We do them because we are celebrating our reproduction." For me, the reproduction they celebrated could only be understood after I examined these rituals as they are set in the broader context of the Babae public, ritual corpus. It was my confrontation with this corpus that gave me a solid basis from which to explore the ontological transformations entailed by being a Babae person.

In the first part of the essay, I sought to relate the Babae understanding of human procreation to the structure of the ritual sequence. In this way, I tried to show in what sense these rituals can be seen as rites of passage both for the primipara and her child. But I also wished to make the point that our understanding of particular rituals or ritual sequences can be enriched by considering them in relation to the wider corpus of ritual in which they are embedded. By relating vevene to the other rituals of the Babae corpus, I sought to show that while each sequence can be seen in its own terms as a rite de passage, so too can the corpus as a whole. Seen from this perspective, it is possible to elucidate how the corpus takes an individual through the gamut of human existence as it is understood on Babae. The work of this ritual corpus is a cooperative effort between men and women. Through its performance, the environmental as well as social dimensions of Babae are reproduced.

In the first half of the essay, then, I took my lead in concentrating on "structure" from Van Gennep. In the last half, however, I sought to show how crucial is the experiential dimension of ritual. Here, I focused on particular aspects of performance in vevene and the prominent targets of vevene comedic performance. This enabled me to explore a passage that is not obvious in the structure alone, the threshold between puberty and socially responsible sexuality—which, in itself, is recognized as a precondition for human procreation. In a girl's early vevene performances, her sexuality is appropriated and domesticated by older women—her coperformers. For Babae women, this is a critical threshold to cross, and they cross it in a ritual sequence premised on a creative use of, and reflection upon, their culture.

NOTES

1. Babae is a pseudonym for an Island Melanesian society where I have under-taken nearly two years of fieldwork over the past decade and a half. I use pseu-donyms throughout this essay because discussion of some details of the women's ritual sequence and understandings included here is not appropriate between men and the women of this society and because of a concern that some outsiders might fail to treat this aspect of their culture with due sensitiv-ity and respect.

2. I also have seen cases when outsiders resident on Babae, such as Health Centre nurses, had vevene festivals performed for them when they became pregnant for the first time. In each case, the father was Babae.

3. In my experience, vevene festivals may take only a day of performance, though those that were considered most successful continued for more than thirty hours of exhausting, more or less continuous, performance.

4. I capitalize the terms Mother and Father to refer to groups that call them-selves 'mothers' and 'fathers' but whose membership is not exclusively deter-mined by 'real' or 'classificatory' relationships (see below).

5. Thus, if genealogy is to be a useful research tool on Babae, it must take into account that calculations of relatedness are not final until death and burial.

6. She used the English phrase here.

6

MYTHIC IMAGES
AND OBJECTS OF MYTH IN
RAUTO FEMALE PUBERTY RITUAL

Thomas Maschio

[D]iscourse and objects are not formulas or signs, and even less are they language, but rather tradition, that is, a way of translating the word in its perennity, a manifestation of being in its continuity.

—Maurice Leenhardt, *Do Kamo*

Sculpture of the habitat, prowboard of the canoe, earring, diadem, noise-maker or song, are a person's gesture manifesting some myth from which he draws his life.

—Leenhardt, *Arts de l'Oceanie*

During one of the last days of my first field stay with the Rauto, I saw a performance of the ritual that marks a woman's menarche. The ceremony took up one full day, from dawn to dusk, and its poetry and beauty both moved me and helped me understand the type of power a Rauto woman can draw on to express and construct her identity.[1] The rite also appeared to be a formal celebration of the part Rauto women play in helping to form the social identities of female adolescents, and it demonstrated that Rauto women are considered the producers and possessors of important aspects of their culture's religious imagination.

This last thought brings to mind contrasts between Rauto ceremonial for female adolescents and the initiation and puberty rites of many of the peoples of Highland New Guinea—where most of the recent work on adolescent ceremonies in Melanesia has been conducted (Godelier 1986; Herdt 1982b). A number of these authors argue that rites for both male and female adolescents invoke ideas associated with men's interest in the social control of women and youths (e.g., Godelier 1986:50; Hays and Hays 1981:234). There are no indications, however, that women are perceived as disseminators of aspects of the "moral tone" and aesthetic style and mood of their culture—what Clifford Geertz (1973:127) has called a culture's ethos. Nor do we have any examples in the Melanesian literature of women being involved in the creation and elaboration of a people's worldview—that is, "its picture of the way things in sheer actuality are," its "concept of nature, of self and society" (ibid.). The rites the Rauto perform to mark a woman's menarche, however, appear to provide just such examples.

This ritual has an extremely simple structure. During its performance two senior women—usually the initiates' paternal aunts or women classified with them—who are known for their skill in song magic and respected as women of economic influence, present the initiates with a number of objects associated mainly, though not exclusively, with subsistence production and the exchange activities of women. Other objects specifically convey ideas about the power, influence, and privileges of prominent, or big, women (*ilim alang*). As they are presented, special magical songs (*aurang*) are sung by the senior women conducting the ritual and by a rather large number of the adolescents' female matrikin. These songs are said to promote the adolescents' growth and enhance their beauty and health. Their poetry alludes to the uses to which women put the objects presented and represents a celebration of the aesthetic aspect of women's activities. The songs and mimetic acts of the rite also provide allusive encapsulations of some of the different phases or ages of a woman's life—from preadolescence to mature adulthood.

During the rite, the adolescents are instructed in the names—called *ikit*—and proper uses of the objects presented, instructions that outline the "picture" Rauto have of women's reality. By manipulating ideas and objects that define the nature of an adult woman—especially of a socially prominent big woman—aspects of Rauto ethos and worldview are drawn into relationship: the aesthetic feel Rauto women have for their way of life is synthesized with their "picture" of this life. For the Rauto, then, the ritual construction of gender is a way of expressing ideas about human nature, social and moral life, and power and status (see also Strathern 1988).

To say that Rauto women are "disseminators" of aspects of the moral tone and aesthetic style and mood of their culture is to say that they control an aspect of cultural, or, as Leenhardt might say, mythic memory. The significance of the acts and images of the puberty rite is that they place initiates in contact with cultural and personal memories that are contained by customary objects and events or scenarios that the rite mimes. The mimesis of the rite demonstrates in part, though only in part, that song, heirloom, necklace, diadem, and menstrual skirt are a woman's "gesture manifesting some myth from which" she "draws her life" (Leenhardt 1948:138, quoted in Clifford 1982:211). These myths are the stories of custom, the stories of collective and personal memory that explain the origins and original uses of the objects used during the rite.

In the puberty ritual some of these stories add meaning to the enacted song images, images that portray concretely experienced events in the lifeway of a woman. It is not wholly correct, then, to use the terms "symbol" and "symbolic" to describe the objects presented to the initiates and the acts and images accompanying these prestations, for really they stand for nothing. Rather, they appear to embody moments of experience and action through which the person realizes an aspect of identity. This last thought implies that each event mimed and sung during the rite, and each object given, reveals a moment of the initiate's attainment of identity, or personhood. And yet the initiates really do not receive formal acknowledgment during the rite that they have come into a completely new stage of social being; nor are new social and sexual responsibilities really taught to or imposed upon them by elders at this time. In fact they sometimes cannot even remember the simple ikit that are taught to them in the ritual. Rather, what is revealed to them is the feeling of what it means to possess the objects of cultural memory, to be introduced to the mythic patterns that give meaning to their use, to know that their use is a powerful gesture of the externalization of self.

While the images and acts of the rite portray moments of immediate experience and feeling that are "scrupulously externalized, clearly outlined, brightly and uniformly illuminated" (Auerbach 1991:3), their seeming naturalism and presentness represent only the most obvious aspects of a woman's social identity; they often simply seem to be women's acted or mimed valorizations of their characteristic roles and duties. As Roland Barthes (1990) has shown us, however, images and acts often have rounded, elusive, and evanescent meanings and countermeanings as well as obvious, seemingly naturalistic ones. The contexts that provide such meanings to the images of the puberty rite are the myths that explain the origins and original uses of the objects that elders present to initiates during the ritual. Exploring the full meaning of this ritual, then, and of the ideas of person and gender from which it draws significance, involves viewing the objects and activities of the rite in relationship to these myths.

In proceeding in this way, I hope to do more than simply provide an analysis of one of the rituals of a remote, Melanesian people. I mean to question a dominant style of interpretation and analysis. In other work (Maschio 1994), I have shown how Rauto religious and expressive culture often presents a wry face to classical Western forms of analysis, such as that represented by the explanatory models of modern symbolic anthropology. One of the central ideas of this approach is the notion of symbolic elaboration, or completion—the idea that symbols and expressive acts extract the essential meaning and emotion from an aspect of experience and then represent experience in such a way that its wholeness is revealed. The idea seems a straightforward translation of the classical realist understanding that art is, in part, a heightened expression or even purification of experience (Redfield 1975:219). That is, that art completes and clarifies the nature of an aspect of experience by deepening one's awareness of its life meaning. In this view art continually modifies, transforms, and models an understanding of the world by progressively adding depth and resonance to the character of this understanding.

One feels that such a theory of culture form would resonate with, and perhaps then, even draw explanatory power from, cultural systems where, as in the West, symbolic elaboration seems often to distinguish the character of expressive and religious life. One is reminded of Geertz's (1973:408) characterization of the Balinese as searching out and fashioning meanings in "significant symbols, clusters of significant symbols, and clusters of clusters of significant symbols." Yet, the involute character of Rauto expressive culture does not resonate with the elaborate and elaborating Western semiotic. Many of the central ritual events, metaphors, and mythic images of this people seem not so much "purifications" of everyday meanings, emotions, and experiences as restatements of them, "restatements that encourage a total, personal reinvolvement in their character" (Wagner, pers. comm.). The meaning of Rauto expressive culture seems to derive from the common events it represents and not from some exaggerated and abstract rhetoric.

This is precisely the sort of problem Leenhardt faced as he tried to understand and represent involute Melanesian culture forms and imminent forms of religious experience—forms of experience that did not seem to exist outside of "concretely experienced events" (Clifford 1982:214). His characterizations of mythic thought and experience were subtle responses to this problem. In Leenhardt's understanding, *la pensée obscure et confuse* of mythic experience communicated something of the nature of Melanesian being without recourse to abstract language and representation. Drawing on the work of Lévy-Bruhl, Leenhardt portrayed the Melanesians of New Caledonia as "image thinkers"—people who represented experience through the construction of images that retained an archaic primary form and, thus, a certain power to evoke the concrete richness of intuitive, sensuous experience (see ibid.:208–210). I use Leenhardt's suggestions in this essay to portray something of the nature of this experience.

ETHNOGRAPHIC BACKGROUND

The Austronesian-speaking Rauto number about 2,500 people and live along the coast and in the interior rain forest of the southwest portion of New Britain. Their lowland forest environment is crisscrossed by many streams and rivers, and the general topography is quite rugged. Unlike the neighboring Kaulong and Seng Seng, they are intensive horticulturalists, obtaining most of their subsistence from the slash-and-burn cultivation of taro, yam, and sweet potato, supplemented by banana and amaranth. Their diet is rounded out by coconut, breadfruit, and occasionally pork and wild game, such as cassowary or wallaby, with fish a frequent addition to the diet of coastal villagers.

Both coastal and interior groups usually live in hamlet settlements of twelve to thirty residents, occupying anywhere from five to ten family houses, with one or two large ceremonial houses. The number of residents fluctuates, however, since people frequently leave the hamlet to attend ceremonials or visit and take up temporary residence with trading partners or distant kin.

Social structure is organized around a principle of cognatic descent. Cognatic descent groups are called *rip* and are usually associated with a particular territory. Although people can reside and share the use of resources with either paternal or maternal kin, there is a bias toward patrifiliation. Coresident patrikin claiming close association with a particular territory also sometimes enjoy a marked political dominance over matrikin living with them.

Ceremonial life essentially consists of a series of song ceremonies performed for persons at major intervals of their life cycles. Most performances are religiously meaningful because they provide contexts for the expression of magical speech and of song genre such as the aurang.

SOME OBVIOUS SOCIAL MEANINGS AND FUNCTIONS OF THE RITE

One of the obvious social functions of the Rauto puberty rite is "to raise the name," or enhance the social reputation, of the adolescents for whom it is performed. The rite is most often performed for the eldest or most intelligent and socially promising daughters of prominent men and women, and marks the girls for assumption of a special social status, that of big woman. It also demonstrates the economic wherewithal of the sponsoring family and ramage, thereby becoming also a social marker for the girl's immediate family and extended kin group. Finally, it provides an opportunity for the senior women who perform it to demonstrate their knowledge of ritual and song scripts and, through their performance of various aurang songs, the power of their voices to promote the girls' growth and health. This expression of self is integrally related to the affirmation of the social and cultural identity of senior women. It is a demonstration that their voices have social, moral, and magical power. This is significant because of the particular importance voice and song have in this society (Maschio 1994): song is a social marker.

One of the most interesting aspects of Rauto female puberty ritual is that, by celebrating the role big women especially play in production and exchange, song serves as a leitmotif of ideals of female social identity. The songs also allude to the religious aspect of women's economic life, in particular to the important role song magic plays in their productive activity. Although big women never attain positions equal in power and status to those of big men, the Rauto recognize nonetheless that the power of a big woman approximates that of a big man. Female puberty ritual provides the most cogent formal expression of this notion. However, this is not really what is most significant about the ritual. What is, is what the ritual does not say, or rather what it does not *explicitly* say about women's power and religious or mythic identity. The ritual elides more often than it elaborates meaning. The meaning it elides provides as strong a statement of women's cultural centrality as does the rite itself.

THE PRESENTATION OF THE MENSTRUAL SKIRTS

Both male and female initiation among the Rauto are really part of a cycle of ceremonies, most of them achievement ceremonies, that parents arrange for their children a few years before or after puberty. What distinguishes Rauto initiation ritual from these achievement ceremonies is initiation's aim of celebrating and cultivating the physical attractiveness of adolescents. In fact, some informants said that puberty and initiation ceremonies could be considered forms of "love magic" since one of their primary aims was to make the initiate attractive to members of his or her opposite sex.

By all accounts, menarcheal ritual is and always was a more central part of Rauto religious life than male initiation. A number of Rauto even said it was the most important of all their ceremonies. When I asked one of them to explain this statement, he said simply that the ceremony was something his people "could never give up" however much introduced social change might alter the tenor of life. I took this to mean that the rite provided a particularly compelling statement about identity, one that, according to some, could not be dispensed with. The symbolism of the menstrual rite is somewhat more complex than that of male initiation. Though the latter is performed in three different stages—corresponding to Van Gennep's phases of separation, transition, and reincorporation, the major act of the rite consists mostly of a simple teeth-blackening ceremony. There are no grades involved in male initiation. Also, there are no hard and fast rules as to whether it should be performed for a group of initiates or a single one. Nor does its major aim appear to be the cultivation of a specifically "male" gender identity. A number of the elder women I knew had gone through the teeth-blackening ceremony along with their male kinsmen when they were young girls.

The menarcheal rites cannot begin until the girl's family has amassed sufficient wealth in the form of pigs, taro, and shell valuables to pay for the ritual services that will be provided. On the one hand, therefore, the rites may not take place until several years after a girl's first menses; on the other, they may be performed before the onset of menstruation if the family has accumulated the necessary wealth.

The major part of the ritual is directed by two "sisters" of the girl's father—either his true siblings or parallel cousins—assisted usually by the girl's maternal uncle and a large group of his classificatory female siblings. The night before the ritual proper, these officiants take the girl to a menstrual hut located on the outskirts of the hamlet settlement or, in coastal Rauto villages, on the edge of the sea. Throughout the night, these aunts and cousins bring the girl food and drink and they provide her with a special skirt to wear while she sleeps. This skirt, called the *agosgoso*, is made from the colorful leaves of a wild banana. More of these leaves are placed between her legs "to absorb her menstrual blood."

The next morning, at sunrise, the two aunts (*ado*) remove the skirt from around the girl's waist and throw it into the ocean or, if the ceremony is performed in a bush village, into the forest at the outskirts of the hamlet. In company with any other initiates, the girl then is led into the men's house of her father's ramage, where the two aunts scrape coconut meat and rub the extracted oil onto her breasts so that her skin will appear "shiny" and attractive.

The ritual I attended began when two aunts, officiating for two initiates, began to paint the girls' bodies. Red ocher was brushed onto their hair, and their faces were painted with red and white marks called *tinga tinga*. Next, the girls were taken to the center of the men's house, where their aunts presented each of them with a second, newly made agosgoso skirt and a skirt the Rauto call *yaoli*. The aunts painted the skirts with red ocher and then informed the girls that the yaoli were "their own grass skirts," which they should wear until the end of their lives. The plants from which they were made, the girls were told, represented their personal finery, which they should use to decorate their bodies whenever they worked in their gardens or attended song festivals. The two aunts then pointed out and individually named each of the plants making up the yaoli. The aromatic scent of the plants and the burning and effervescent quality of their sap are thought to stimulate the girls' skin and thereby promote their physical growth. The plants also have a variety of uses in other Rauto rituals; most, for instance, are used in the performance of taro magic. The implicit message of the aunts' instruction was that these important materials are controlled by women and their care and reproduction is a woman's privilege.

The girls were then shown and told the names of important cultivars that they should plant or harvest: these included a taro corm and stalk, two kinds of yam, amaranth, and sugar cane. The youngsters also were shown and told the names of the tobacco plant and the vine on which the betel pepper grows. They were instructed in the proper way to cut the taro corm from its stalk with a clam shell cutter, and told that if a nontraditional object such as a knife were used, the taro stalk would produce no food.

Finally, aurang for the new agosgoso skirts, also known as *lelme,* were performed. Like the agosgoso that were tossed into the sea, these ceremonial lelme are made predominantly from dark purple, bright red, and yellow wild banana leaves. The two aunts opened one up and then, holding a hemp tie each, brought it up to one of the girls' waists and began to swing it back and forth against her backside as they sang the song for the lelme:

Lelme, ngapapenwo lelme	Swing the skirt
lelme, lelme,	back and forth, back
lelme, ngapapenwo lelme	and forth.
Lelme lelme.	

After a few minutes of song, the lelme was fastened around the girl's waist and the act repeated for the second girl. The yaoli were raised up and fastened above the girls' waists, some of the leaves being slipped inside the

lelme, between their legs. As this operation was performed, the women all
sang the song for the yaoli:

Yaoli a yao a	The yaoli skirt,
yaoli a yao a	yaoli.
a komela aupua.	You put it on thus (it is yours now).

The significance of these first few activities in the puberty ritual lies in
their relation of a system of aesthetics to notions of physical development
and bodily health. Outlining this relationship, which is what I will do here,
means outlining the connotations or referents of the mimed actions and
activities of the rite. These correspond to a conscious ideology, an ideology
that makes up only a part of the meaning of the image of the presentation of
the menstrual skirts.

Informants told me that painting and anointing the girls' bodies makes
them healthy and their skin attractive. The scent of the yaoli plants and the
bright colors of the other skirts also are said to promote growth and health
because they are pleasing to the senses. The same was said of the senior
women's singing, but these women told me that the songs also "moved their
hearts" and sometimes made them cry by causing them to remember those
who had sung the aurang for them when they were young girls. The songs
allow elders to remember the poignancy of their own pasts at the very
moment that they invest their spiritual power in the next generation. These
statements made it clear to me that these first few rites are meant both to
impart physical sensation and to elicit sentiment from the girls and the
other ritual participants, and so sensitize and prepare the girls' minds and
bodies for the instruction to come.

A discussion of color "symbolism" will help support these points. Red
and white, the major colors displayed during the rite, express ideas of
health, growth, and personal power. The color red, which appears as ocher
paint on the yaoli and on the girls' bodies, is associated in several contexts
with growth. To begin with, red ocher is used to promote the growth of
young boys during male initiation and of the taro crop in a number of garden rites. Second, red is associated with beauty and sexual desirability, a
connection made most clearly during Rauto song festivals, when young men
and women enhance the beauty of their skin by painting their faces and
bodies with red ocher or *bixa orellana*. Third, red is also the color most frequently used to signal that a person has acquired an important bit of ritual
or traditional knowledge. After a child has seen or participated in a ritual

for the first time, for example, adults will paint it with a streak of red to signify its right to speak about the ceremony. Finally, red is also placed on
children or young men and women when they are in a ritual, or liminal,
state—a time when people are, in the Rauto view, in the process of aug-
menting the self either with knowledge or ritual power.

Red in the woman's puberty ritual appears to signify that the girls are
developing in both body and mind. Together with their anointment with
coconut oil, it also suggests a link to the development of their sexual attractiveness, a point I shall develop further in analyzing the next phase of the
ritual. White is also used in the puberty ritual. In Rauto culture, this is the
preeminent symbol of anger and warfare: thus, before going into battle
warriors would smear their faces with lime powder. But white also conveys
the idea of privilege: traditionally, for example, the young daughters of big
men or women had lime powder put on their faces during their ritual seclusion prior to marriage (see later). Since puberty ritual is about the privileges
and duties of women, white is therefore a very appropriate color with which
to express these ideas.

Notwithstanding the attention given to color, Rauto women told me that
the most important part of this first phase of the puberty ritual was the
girls' investiture with the "women's skirts." With these presentations, they
begin to acquire the outward signs of a new status. The skirts, especially the
yaoli, signify a woman's acquisition of new duties and privileges. But what
was fascinating to me was the way their presentation was related to a complex set of ideas about menstrual blood and the girls' developing power.

Almost all of the plants from which the skirts are made, and in the cultivation of which the girls are instructed, are also used in gardening rituals to
promote the healthy development of a taro crop. It seems, then, that the
grass skirts, most especially the yaoli, are not only meant to make the girls
grow well but are also a visual sign that they are acquiring a greater ability
to produce food. Yet the lelme and yaoli are, at least during the puberty
ritual, "menstrual" skirts. They denote the presence of menstrual blood,
which paradoxically is usually thought inimical to processes of human, animal, and plant growth and health.

A girl's first menses thus marks the fact that she now possesses a dangerous and sometimes destructive power. Yet the Rauto choose to mark this
event by celebrating her constructive economic, social, and moral influence.
One might argue that this paradox expresses the idea that women are influential partly because they are dangerous, especially to men. But this does not
satisfactorily explain why, in the context of puberty ritual, menstrual blood
signifies an increase in a woman's personal power while, in other contexts, it
is thought to lessen her productive powers and diminish rather than augment

her other abilities. I would point out, however, that it is men, not women, who most often voice fears about the polluting power of menstrual blood. Moreover, women certainly do not feel that menstruation places them at the periphery of social and cultural life. Rather, female puberty ritual suggests that the nature of women is partly defined by the fact of their menstruation, and women seize this opportunity to place themselves at the mythic center of Rauto life and draw strength from it. The ritual itself does not reveal the mythic character of the menstrual skirts and indeed of female identity. The myth that tells of the origins of these skirts, of menstruation, of women's objects and activities, indeed of the origins of the female sex, provides a more rounded understanding of the meaning of female identity and even, in fact, of female ethos than does the simple presentation described here. The story reveals how woman's possession of menstrual skirts and of female dress was her first gesture of assertion and female personhood. The myth reveals that woman had literally to wrest her gender from man:

> Men were not originally men. They followed women's ways. They carried around with them and used all the things that women now have: their oven stones, their oven tongs, their clam shell cutters for harvesting taro, their taro shell scrapers. They menstruated as women do and, as women, when they did, they left their garden work exclaiming, "Oh! I can't work now, I have my period. I'll have to rest." As women, they would comb the reefs for crustaceans and small fish and they would also collect freshwater snails. Then one day one of these supposed women came upon a real woman, and this real woman called out: "Hey you really large woman over there, where are you going?" And she answered, "I'm just going to comb the reefs for some small fish, although I wish I didn't have to do it all by myself. It's just that all my friends have their periods now and they are all much too exhausted to help me out. Do you see them over there resting on the verandas of their houses?"
>
> "Never mind them," said the real woman. "Come over here and let me get a good look at you," she said, eyeing this supposed woman suspiciously. "You know I don't think you're really a woman." As she said this, she lifted up the other woman's skirt, and after seeing what was hidden by the skirt exclaimed, "Hey you're not a woman. Is a woman so big as you? You don't even have breasts. And your genitals are hanging down there. You are a man. Give me my woman's skirt, give me my menstrual skirt, give me my woman's fishing net, my oven stones, my taro scraper, my taro cutter. And give me my menstruation." And then the real woman gathered up the things that were given to her, and she put on her female dress and her menstrual skirts. She then told the man about the objects that rightfully belonged to him, and she pointed them out to him. "There, there are your fishing and hunting nets, and your fishing spears; and there is the men's house. Go

> there now and give me my things. And menstruation, that belongs
> to me so leave it alone." And so the woman gathered up her things
> and the man gathered up his.

We have two images before us then. That evoked by the puberty rite presents a naturalistic scene and an obvious meaning; it pictures the initiates
being given their adult women's dress, their menstrual skirts, and a number
of objects this culture associates with women. The images and acts of this
opening phase suggest that women simply and naturally come to possess
these objects at the time of their puberty.

The mythic narrative belies this suggestion. It indicates that woman's
first act of authentic personhood consisted in taking her menstruation, her
women's objects, and her dress from men. The moment when she does this
portrays her immediate assumption of female identity. We see here a Rauto
"myth of identity" (Leenhardt 1979[1947]:23). Though this myth seems a
living part of the Rauto present, it contains a sense of the past. It was not
always so, it seems to say. Identity had to be won through a gesture of
assertion rather than simply put on, as a menstrual skirt is put on.

The myth expresses this insight as much by its psychological character
and humorous tone as by the sequence of events it outlines. The opening
sequences that describe men following woman's life-way, carrying out
woman's everyday tasks, and experiencing the state of menstruation, seem
to parody female personhood rather than provide an authentic mimesis of it.
The "she-males" portrayed seem grossly effeminate, frivolous, and clumsy
as they comb the reefs for food, run from their gardens at the slightest hint
of menstrual blood, and collapse exhausted on the verandas of their family
houses during their menstruation.

In contrast, the narrator's portrait of the one woman of the myth seems
an example of authentic personhood. This character quickly sends the man
on his way by pointing him to his own sphere of activity with absolute certainty. She assumes her own identity and asserts her claim to her woman's
objects with as much certainty. These are my things, she seems to say, I will
take them and be what I am.

A portrait of woman and of female ethos begins to emerge in the myth,
one counterposed to the narrator's weak parody of female personhood. This
ethos corresponds to the assertiveness seen in the puberty rite, yet it stands
in contrast to the rite's first sublime and simple act—the presentation of the
menstrual skirts. Or rather, the acts and images of the first presentations of
the puberty ritual are given meaning by two different, yet simultaneously
experienced feelings. The sort of pride evident in the women's clowning

and assertive, if ribald, celebration of the sexual parts of their bodies contrasts with the sublime plenitude of remembrance that is evoked by the aurang. The initiates seem the objects of these two emotions. In becoming these two emotions, they objectify two aspects of female ethos—assertive strength and a sort of sublime emotionality. It seems that the initiates come to objectify memory, emotion, and aspects of female ethos during this ritual.

THE PRESENTATION OF ARECA NUT

Following the presentation of the skirts, one of the two aunts took a large bunch of ripe areca (betel) nut in one hand, a lime holder in the other, and, handing the areca to her helper, began to rub lime powder on the girls' teeth. Both aunts then turned the girls' shoulders back and forth rhythmically, pulling the areca nut and its branches across the girls' front teeth. As they performed this ritual, they sang the aurang for the areca nut, songs in the language of the neighboring Gimi that refer to the harvesting and proper use of the areca:

Komsolei wirwiraei	Put the areca nut and the
komsolei wirwiraei;	lime together;
Komsolei warapmaei	the areca has fruit.
o komsolei warapmaei.	
Komsolei klokiaei	Harvest the areca (from
komsolei klokiaei.	its tree).
Komsolei abrumyaei	Remove the areca from its
komsolei abrumyaei.	stem.

As the following narratives make clear, areca has great mythic and emotional significance for the life of a woman:

> I was at a songfestival at Giring. When the festival was ending and the big men had begun to butcher the hogs, the young men and women were playing their games on the outskirts of the dancing ground. A woman from Aukur, my cousin-sister, sat down next to me, and we began to speak to one another. She held my arm tightly as we spoke. Another woman [whom this speaker later married] also came to sit down, and I told her that we really weren't doing anything; that I was just speaking with my little sister. This other woman than gave a pearl shell to my sister from Aukur and she told her to take the pay as compensation for her desire for me. Then she sat down between us. She took a red areca nut from her basket, chewed it for a moment, and then gave me part of it.

THE STORY OF THE ARECA NUT
AND THE YOUNG GIRL

A man and his wife left for the Woman's Sea, leaving their young daughter at home. A cannibal spirit then came upon the family's hamlet and spied the areca tree that stood in the plaza of the girl's house. He entered the plaza and climbed the tree to get at the betel; as he was climbing down, a single areca nut fell from his hand, hitting the thatch roof of the girl's house, falling through it, and then hitting the girl on her head. She decided to go outside to see if a bird had knocked it down from its tree. She looked up the tree and saw the cannibal spirit climbing down. She shouted at it: "Are you a man or a spirit? Are you going to catch and eat me?"

"No, I'm just a man; let's sit down and chew this areca nut together," said the spirit. The girl replied that she did not want any areca. The spirit then made a grab for her, and she jumped away from it and quickly climbed to the roof of her house. The spirit then pulled out one of its teeth and threw it at the house, thus destroying its roof, but the girl managed to jump away onto the trunk of the areca tree. He then extracted another tooth and hurled it at the areca-nut tree, knocking it down; but the girl managed to jump to the lower branches of the hamlet's ficus tree. The spirit extracted another tooth, which broke the lower branches of the ficus; she jumped to a higher branch. [Scenario is repeated a number of times.] The girl then began singing for her mother and father. They heard her song and began to rush back. They arrived back just in the nick of time. The father raised his spear, his wife her woman's fighting club, and together they dispatched the spirit.

Here we have three different images or representations of women's use of areca. In the first, evoked by the mimetic acts of the puberty rite, the initiates are simply presented with a bunch of areca and shown how to use them to make their teeth glisten. The image uses areca as a metonym. Here is your attractiveness, it seems to say, take it and use it as is your right. See how beautiful you can be. The image presents the naturalistic meaning of the use of areca and clearly celebrates the initiates' developing sexuality. One of the acts of this phase also involves naming the areca. As the naming of a person frequently signals a change of a person's status, so in this example the naming of the areca signals a change in the status of the object. It becomes, and is ritually marked as, a manifestation of woman's sexual being.

In the second image, contained in the recounted portion of a man's life history, a woman uses her areca to begin a sexual relationship with a man, and to compete with another woman for his sexual attention. This image draws meaning from the cultural connotations of areca's use and has the quality of a "coded message" (Barthes 1990:36). That is, the woman's use of betel alludes to a body of attitudes about the relationship between courtship, sexuality, and areca. These attitudes can be read from the image like a code. They include: (1) if a woman either continually gives or requests betel from a man, she thereby makes an indirect statement of interest in him; (2) if she forcefully pushes areca into a man's hand or, as in the above example, into his mouth, she thereby takes a more aggressive sexual stance.

These facts about areca's use underscore the point that women often take the lead in courtship. This is the case in the life history account: the narrator's future wife in effect makes a public announcement of marriage by offering him the charmed red areca she had previously put into her mouth. The narrator, whose name was Brumio, also alludes to this when he mentions the young men and women "playing" at the hamlet's edge at the conclusion of a song festival. Such "play" usually begins when a woman, moved by a man at a song festival, grasps his arm and refuses to let go of it. As "compensation" for the excitement he has caused her, the man must give the woman a pearl shell or meter of shell money. If the man does not wish the woman to loosen her grip, he will give her nothing.

The images of the mythic narrative of the cannibal spirit and the young girl seem to deny rather than augment the meanings that we have just discussed. This seems appropriate since the primary scenes of the myth describe a woman's refusal, rather than her acceptance, of a bunch of areca. This is consistent with a number of other ideas and themes developed by the myth.

The most obvious contrast that the myth provides to the puberty rite is its negative treatment and valuation of sexuality. For instance, the woman described in the myth is—like the female initiates—sexually mature. Yet the myth does not celebrate this quality; rather, it seems a cautionary tale of the danger that can be presented to women when they come to possess beauty and sexual capacity. On another, metaphorical level, one could view the girl's fear of the cannibal spirit as a refusal to acknowledge her sexuality. This in turn seems linked to the fact that the myth does not portray a moment of individuation, or development, in the life-way of a woman: it does not allude to any crossing of a social or cultural threshold. We can support this point by juxtaposing the girl's refusal of the areca nut offered her by the cannibal spirit with the mythic theme that the girl does not separate herself from the parental mantle. At the myth's end, she remains what she was at its beginning: simply her parent's child. Her temporary separation from the parents in the myth is simply a plot device, meant to portray her as being vulnerable to overly aggressive male sexuality and in need of being saved from it.

One detects a number of negative social attitudes about male sexual aggression in the portrait of the cannibal spirit. In the myth, his aggression takes the form of a desire for both rape and cannibalism. His dangerously exaggerated orality, expressed by the image of his jagged and sharp teeth, as well as by his wish to cannibalize the girl, seems a motif that equates sex with destruction—with the wish to harm, even obliterate the other by incorporating him or her into one's own body. Sexuality is indeed sometimes equated with violence in this culture. The association is often made for instance if a man, rather than a woman, initiates courtship. The proper male sexual approach is the indirect one.

This culture entertains other, equally negative images about sexuality that are opposed to the naturalistic and positive allusion represented in the puberty rite. One of these is the notion that excessive sexual activity can lead to lethargy, a general depletion of physical vigor, and even premature death for both men and women. The more rounded, fuller meaning of the prestation of areca in the puberty rite only emerges when we consider these negative valuations. The presentation seems to brush these attitudes aside with a simple gesture. It seems to say: here is this areca; it is a belonging of yours that is a blessing and not a curse. That is, the areca is a metonym for the girl's budding sexuality, and in the context of the puberty rite this sexuality is represented as a blessing.

THE PRESENTATION OF FIRE

In the next phase of the puberty ritual, the two girls were taught the proper care of fire, a process involving two rites, each accompanied by a magical song. First, the girls were seated on the floor of the men's house and instructed to sit with their legs crossed at the ankles. This, they were told, was the posture they should assume when tending a fire or simply sitting. The aunts then had them cross their legs at the knees and explained that this was the position assumed by women who knew the myths of Molyo and Alipo, the two culture heroes who originated the posture. Were those ignorant of the myth to adopt this posture, they were told, an elder might shame them by asking if they knew the meaning of their act. As the girls sat in this style, their aunts rocked their shoulders back and forth and sang one of the songs for fire:

Kamse kon Alipo,	Put your legs like Alipo
kamse kon Alipo.	taught us.
Kamse kon Molyo;	Sit by the fire as Molyo
kamse pe ayi langono	taught us;
tarango Molyo.	as elder brother Molyo.

The aunts then placed a small, smoldering log by the feet of each girl. Lifting the logs up again, they knocked some charcoal ash off the smoldering ends and blew on the embers until they were bright red and ready to burst into flame. They then replaced the logs on the ground and led the women in singing another aurang for fire:

Atrong lomo aii,	Make your fire,
atrong lomo aii.	make your fire.
Imbir, me aii	First the flame
yau me	comes then the smoke.

Fire is a sacred symbol throughout the cultures of Southwestern New Britain, sacred because of its association with women and domesticity. Thus, a Rauto metaphor states that a wife is the fire of a man. More accurately, a man's wife is the burning charcoal that transforms raw taro into food and provides nourishment for him and his children.

Fire and women are also symbols of peace. Thus, the sister exchanges that frequently concluded hostilities in prepacification days were described as "exchanges of fire," and the completion of the exchange as "the return of the fire." This symbolic equation, "fire = women and peace," is illustrated also in women's use of fire to stop men's fist or spear fights at song festivals, for instance. A woman can throw a burning log down between the fighters saying, "The fire flames"; or she can let fall her grass skirt, exposing her genitals and shaming the men. Commonly, though, she resorts to synecdoche, taking a piece of her grass skirt, or sometimes nowadays a piece of her cloth skirt, and waving it in front of the fighters who, duly shamed, should cease their fighting.

Another Rauto metaphor identifies fire with menstrual blood. The trope, *ilim apai ilo ayi,* "the marriageable woman's fire," refers to a red leaf said to have acquired its color when a nubile, menstruating woman stepped over and bled on it. In these examples, ideas about sexuality, menstrual blood, and power appear to be related and symbolized by fire.

The hearth, cookery, oath taking, menstrual blood, the control of violence by women, growth, and nurturance are only some of the more obvious associations of fire. The image of the rite explicitly refers to none of these things. We read them from the cultural context rather than the ritual image. All the image appears to say is: "Here is a woman tending her fire," a statement that can be considered a motif, rather than a picturing, of the many associations between fire and women. However, it is a motif that appears to assign women to the domestic realm. This seemingly naturalistic assignation seems a natural progression from the earlier ritual images and acts that celebrated the initiates' developing sexuality, and the phase of woman's life when she is permitted to adorn, beautify, and generally celebrate her developing body. Thus, two phases of a woman's life are celebrated by the simple ritual motifs of the presentation of areca and of fire: young adulthood and the full maturity which follows from the assumption of domestic responsibilities and duties. Some of the following prestations support the social assignment of women to the domestic realm, others represent forms of experience that make woman's domestic role seem a simple adjunct to the cultural or mythic importance that is attached to her person.

PRESENTATION OF THE COCONUT-FROND BASKET AND CORDYLINE

Following the presentation of fire, the officiating aunts took two coconut-frond baskets filled with areca nut, lime powder, tobacco, and other items and placed them on the girls' heads. As they did this, they turned the girls' shoulders back and forth, placing the girls' hands on top of the baskets to steady them. They then sang the first aurang for the coconut-frond basket:

Nga sun karei.	I carry the basket on my
Lolai karei	head. I carry the basket
muralmeia, muralmeia	in my hand.

As the other women joined the refrain, the two aunts removed the baskets from the initiates' heads and showed the girls how to carry them on their shoulders. Next, they demonstrated how to carry the baskets under the arm, cupped in the joint of the elbow. Finally, they showed the girls how to swing the baskets back and forth with their arms. Each act was accompanied by a verse of the woman's basket aurang.

After this, several species of cordyline were brought out. The first, called *anamoi*, had a dark red leaf. One of the aunts placed its base on the ground and began to rock it back and forth as though she were planting or harvesting it. As she did so, she sang its aurang:

Anamoi i wom mela,	The leaf of the red cordyline,
Anamoi i wom mela.	The leaf of the red cordyline.
Ngasok wom mela	I show the leaf of the cordyline to my
ngasokon aki,	cross cousin, I ask for a pig,
maieng oa	he, my cross cousin, is
ino vita. Nga karpan.	ashamed. I am angry.

To the accompaniment of another aurang, the act was repeated with a species called *ulu*, which had a small green leaf:

Luei ulu luai,	The cordyline's leaf,
keskesko aponmot	I cut the leaf, I cut
keskesko, keskesko.	the cordyline's leaf.

The first act of this ritual sequence, the presentation of the coconut-frond basket, appears to have a straightforward, if culturally coded, meaning: it alludes to a woman's role as dispenser of food and amenities such as areca and tobacco. Women's baskets are frequently filled with these commodities, which they should give to others. In fact, people often will scold those without their baskets because it means they wish to take from others and avoid sharing betel and food themselves. Thus, the basket is a symbol of reciprocity and sociality, and its presentation to girls during their puberty ritual is, in part, a metaphorical or coded statement that, as adult women, they must carry their baskets in order to "give things away."

These obvious meanings are ancillary to more powerful mythic insights about women's creative and social power. The first image of this series of prestations—the image that describes a woman simply carrying her basket as if it had no more significance than any other object of adornment—coexists with a powerful mythic image of the coconut-frond basket as a sort of womb. In one story a woman produces the objects of wealth, status, and political power that are such an important part of Rauto social life from her coconut-frond basket. I will recount this myth and discuss its meaning after describing the middle phase of the puberty ritual—the phase in which the initiates are presented with socially and politically prestigious objects.

The culturally coded significance of the rites involving the anamoi and ulu cordylines lies in their status as sacred representations of political and social power. In some contexts, the use of the anamoi is an expression of anger. When men wish to ask their kin for assistance in a feud, for instance, they send them the red leaf of the anamoi with a knot, or series of knots, in the leaf to indicate the number of days or weeks that must pass before assistance is to be rendered. The song of the anamoi refers to a woman who has asked her male cross-cousin (*vita*) for a gift of a pig. Unfortunately, he is unable to meet her request, a delinquency that can be a serious breach of custom and a denial of sociality. In the song the woman expresses her anger by showing the anamoi to him.

Rauto women have the right to point out this breach of custom because of their moral authority, which is formally recognized in the presentation of the second croton, the green ulu. This plant is cultivated around the bound-aries of the men's ceremonial house, the political and religious center of the hamlet or village, and it is a symbol of the political, ritual, and moral authority of the house's leaders.

In religious life, the ulu is also the preeminent symbol of the authority of *Varku,* a spirit thought to be incarnated in a carved wooden mask that appears during the performance of a special song festival. Varku is the most powerful spirit-being honored with song festivals. He is associated especially with adult men and buttresses their control over the ceremonial production, allocation, and consumption of pigs, one of the major symbols of big man-ship in southern West New Britain. Through the ulu, Varku expresses demands for pigs and other resources and honors those who accede to his request. For instance, a firstborn or promising daughter of a man who has honored such a demand will be "adopted" by the spirit as what the Rauto call an *aili.* To mark the adoption, the girl is painted with red ocher and taken into the men's ceremonial house where she stands before the mask. The man wearing the mask then puts his hand on her shoulder to place her under the protection of Varku, and she is given an ulu leaf to show that she shares in his authority and that of the spirit beings called *kamotmot.* She is now privileged to see the sacred masks of the kamotmot kept in the men's house, and she is allowed to aid men when banana-leaf costumes are made for these masks. No longer can she be struck by her parents or talked about critically, on pain of compensation to the society of men that controls the masks. The ulu does not just signify the protection of Varku, however; it also allows the girl to request resources and compensation from men, a privi-lege also accorded to prominent or big women. In sum, the formal presenta-tion of the ulu at the puberty ceremony marks a girl for a career of social influence and achievement. It is a ritual statement that she is to exercise the moral and political influence of a big woman.

But there is a mythic image that makes a much bolder statement of woman's religious and political influence. This is contained in the myth of the capture of the kamotmot spirit beings. It is a myth revealed to boys and just a few women—those women marked for a career of social influence by events such as the puberty rite. The myth reveals how, before their capture, the spirit beings had originally helped women with their garden work. It then tells how they were captured and possessed by women and recounts how men envied the women's new possession and stole it. Thus, the myth reveals that the political power and authority that accrued to men because of their posses-sion of the spirit masks was originally stolen, and thus derived, from women.

While the naturalistic image of the cordyline presentation simply indicates that some women have the right to share with men the political authority that derives from possession of the masks and cordyline, the image of the myth indicates that this is rather inadequate compensation for the power and influence lost by women when men stole the masks and used them to buttress their own power. The contained and simple images of the puberty rite elide this meaning rather than state it. This elision itself has meaning, however, especially if we consider that some of the big women who direct the puberty ritual know the myth of the spirit masks. The simple presentation of the cordylines—emblems of these masks and their power—seems to say: "You men understand the full meaning of our right to possess and use these emblems—a right that you gave back to us. The sacred or mythic center of our custom is our, rather than your, invention."

THE PRESENTATION OF COCONUTS

After the presentation of the cordylines, a number of coconuts were brought out, and the initiates were instructed in the names of their various parts, in how to plant them, and in how to bunch them together to carry them. Unlike the earlier rites, however, these instructions were not accompanied by an aurang.

In traditional discourse, ritual, and everyday use, coconuts are another "symbol" of domesticity and of the nurturing abilities of women. Because of its importance in cookery, for instance, coconut cream is referred to as women's breast milk, and a family's coconut palms usually are planted close to where its womenfolk tend their fires and prepare food. Indeed, in the myth explaining the origin of the coconut, a culture hero specifically instructs people to plant their palms near the cooking area so that women will have an easy time harvesting the nuts for food preparation.

The myth tells of the adventures of a lastborn child who has, like many other characters in Rauto myth, lost his father. Being physically unable to provide as much for his mother as his older brother, he decides to compete with the brother by inventing a long bamboo blowgun. One day, a big man persuades the boy to take him to the small island where he keeps his creation and show him the blowgun. The big man then steals it and leaves the boy stranded on the island. The boy fashions a small raft made of banana leaves and launches himself toward the shore; as he drifts in, a shark attacks his raft, chewing bits off it and then, finally, bits of the boy's body. Finally, only the boy's head is left bobbing on the waves and singing for his elder brother. The brother spears the head as it comes close to shore. The head tells his brother to plant him near the plaza of their mother's house so that the nuts of the coconut palm will fall close to her; thus could the younger brother continue to provide for his family.

The myth, then, represents the coconut as a woman's child. Together with the puberty rite, it also represents the coconut as a gift and blessing offered to women, and themes of the myth appear to justify aspects of the division of labor in this society. Thus, the boy's invention of the blowgun, and the theft of the gun by adult men, squarely assign the labor of hunting to men. The boy's second invention, the coconut, appears to assign women squarely to the domestic realm. This is consistent with the myth's apparent valorization of the closeness of the mother-child bond, a closeness that is elaborated further by the following series of coded associations. As is suggested by the myth, the growth and development of the coconut palm serves as a metaphor for the maturation of children. This is seen most clearly during a brief magical rite that a woman performs at the end of the first year of her child's life. The rite involves the bark cloth used to wrap the head of the newborn child in order to elongate it and make it aesthetically pleasing to the Rauto eye. The child's mother buries the bark cloth underneath a newly sprouted coconut, expressing as she does the wish that the growth of the coconut palm should aid the growth and development of the child—that the child grow tall and strong like a coconut palm. Thus, the child's life is juxtaposed to the life of the mythic coconut boy, and the child draws something of its life from this mythic participation.

By entrusting initiates with the "care" of coconuts in the puberty ceremony, senior women appear to be making an allusion to the girls' future domestic duties, the most important of which will be their care of children. Speaking both mythically and practically, one could say that one of the reasons children grow is because women plant the coconut palm and prepare food with its fruit.

SUMMARY: THE FIRST PHASE
OF THE PUBERTY RITUAL

Many of the objects presented in the first phase of the puberty ritual are objects of subsistence production, commodities upon which Rauto physical survival depends. More than this, however, as the material embodiment of mythic experience and cultural values, they literally must be propagated and maintained if moral and cultural life is to have a meaning that the Rauto would recognize. Their use in economic, political, and ritual life represents a way of expressing value and of motivating or influencing people, as well as of representing the concrete immediacy of mythic experience. In the puberty rite, girls are formally entrusted with these sacred objects and so, in a sense, become agents for the expression of the core of Rauto cultural and social life. Women thus become formally identified with this cultural core; one could say that ideas about the nature and activities of women are celebrated by the Rauto mythological and cultural system rather than denigrated, as seems the case in some other parts of Melanesia.

The next phase of the rite alludes primarily to elder women's political, economic, and religious centrality and involves the presentation of prestige objects to the initiates. The objects convey ideas about the political and social influence of people and their families.

THE PRESENTATION OF WIDOW'S SHELL MONEY AND OTHER PRESTIGE ITEMS

The ceremony continued when two different types of shell-bead valuables were brought out and presented to the initiates. First, about forty meters of blackish or dark brown shell money called *tili asap* (the widow's shell money) was brought out and waved before the girls. With the girls facing them, the two aunts placed the tili around their necks. As they made the presentation, they and other women sang what is perhaps the most beautiful song of the ceremony—the song for the tili:

O tili a o tili a	The *tili*
tili asap, wom ina	oh mother your
lom tili asapo o	woman's *tili*
tili o asap	woman's *tili*

A red shell-bead valuable, the *tili lua*, was brought out. This was waved before the young girls while the women sang.

The girls then were shown two necklaces, called *musmusu*, made from cassowary feather quills. As the women sang, the two aunts swung the necklaces rhythmically against the girls' skirts, then placed one around each girl's neck.

Dog's-teeth headbands were brought out and placed around each girl's forehead, and they were given woven hemp baskets covered on one side with rows of dog's teeth. Then, the aunts outfitted the pair with black, tortoise-shell arm bands.

At this point, the presentation of precious objects halted for a few minutes as one of the aunts painted the girls' faces with white pigment and their shoulders and backs with white marks called *gegeo*. In this instance, the gegeo serve as a symbol of privilege or rank. The aurang accompanying this activity was as follows:

Anei ilo itar	She stays in her house
ama kainei	alone (she won't work,
anei.	she won't carry).
O, ilim sikonong	Oh, *ilim sikonong* [see text below]
yo apu o	woman
tarang ama	the garden will wait;
kainei anei	she stays by herself

The objects presented to the girls are called *alul*, a word I translate as "heirloom." Alul are the prize possessions of family groups. The oldest and most valuable are individually named, and these names and the general history of the valuables are known by most elders in Southwestern New Britain. Alul are said to represent the ancestral history of specific kin groups and are referred to as the "memory of the visage of the ancestors"; in a sense, therefore, they symbolize the social history and identity of their owners' groups. Perhaps because of this, they are said to be also the "backbone" or "strength" of a family group or ramage, a metaphor alluding to the economic and political power they symbolize as well as their political and economic uses.

Valuables like those presented in the puberty ceremony are usually the most important items offered in a brideprice. A mere two meters from a famous black shell-bead necklace is said to be enough to "sever" a bride from her natal group; two meters of a famous white shell-bead valuable is enough to buy the services of a sorcerer. In the past, they were usually the possessions of prominent men and a few prominent women. Their use in the puberty ceremony formally marks the right of the initiates, who are being prepared for the status of big women, to possess them. Thereby, the initiates are advantaged because they are now entitled to use valuables not only for decoration but also for their own political and economic purposes. Later in their lives, for example, they may contribute some of these items to the brideprice of their sons. I have also heard accounts of big women using high-ranking valuables to buy the services of sorcerers. Because of these advantages, most of the puberty songs about the alul convey the idea that initiates strongly desire them. The songs for the red and black shell-bead valuables, for example, are meant to conjure an image of a young woman looking with anticipation and delight at her aunt's valuables. Equally important, when the initiates are presented with valuables such as the tili asap, they formally exhibit the wealth of their ramage and family and thus reassert the identity and power of their group. Thus, through possessing and wearing alul, big women become guardians and "exemplars" of the social, indeed the mythic, identity of groups.

In addition to its other referents, one of the songs accompanying the presentation of shell valuables also alludes to the traditional expectation that, at a later date, the initiate would become an *ilim sikonong*, a secluded woman. In traditional times, when a father considered his daughter marriageable, he had her secluded in a special house that she was not allowed to leave during daylight. She did neither garden nor domestic work, and her food was prepared and brought by a number of female attendants, who also provided her with firewood. When she went to her toilet, these attendants shielded her from the view of men with a pandanus mat "coat."

An ilim sikonong was almost invariably the first daughter of a big man. Her seclusion signaled that her father now would entertain offers of a suitable brideprice. He and his family would sponsor a round of song festivals, to which suitors from other hamlet groups would come and sing the warrior's chant on a dancing ground or plaza cleared next to the girl's house. The young men would sing from sundown to sunrise, trying to entice the young woman out of her house with their singing. If she emerged, it was thought that she wished to elope with one of them. Usually, however, her seclusion did not end until a match had been arranged, when another series of song festivals and a large pig slaughter followed, culminating with her being taken to her new husband's hamlet. The expense of honoring one's daughter as an ilim sikonong was considerable and more easily met by prominent families. Hence, like the puberty ritual, the practice was a marker of social rank.

Because of the importance of women and women's ritual in Rauto society, acquisition of the valuables displayed by women during ceremonial events still is an essential part of the successful attainment of high status. I suggest that it is because women are associated with ideals of cultural and moral life that, during important ritual events, they serve to exemplify the developing renown of family groups.

The religious significance of this phase of the rite is somewhat more profound however. The songs and the presentation of alul highlight the sacred character of the relationship that links the identity of the Rauto female person to important cultural objects. Also, in presenting the girls with the objects of initiation, adult women express and construct an ideal of personhood. As elders sing the names of these objects and present them to initiates, they reveal that the character of the person's nature is contained within a series of "participations" or spiritual relationships. In fact, because some initiation objects can be said to memorialize the identities of past owners, when the initiates have them placed on their persons their own identities participate in, and are augmented by, ancestral identities. This is why the sight of bedecked initiates often allows elders to remember those who performed their own rites of initiation and to weep because of the poignancy of these memories. The image of the young initiate becomes for an instant an image of the ancestress: it becomes the face of the dead. During the rite, initiates enter the spatiotemporal domain of the ancestors; simultaneously, they remain in their own time and space and live the moment of their initiation when the elder women who sing the aurang transfer to them the spiritual power of their song, and the material, political power of their objects.

The senior women are the subject of this rite, the initiates its object. The initiates seem transformed by the prestations into objectifications of the senior women's memories and into the central objects of the seniors' nostalgic emotions. It is only through the memories and feelings of the senior women that the initiates can enter the sociomythic domain of the ancestors and thereby take on an augmented social, or sociomythic, identity.

PRESENTATION OF THE PAIDELA

In the final presentation of the puberty ceremony, each aunt placed the curved pig-tusk ornament called *paidela* around a girl's neck, raised it to the girl's mouth, and then shifted it to the girl's back. Next, they rhythmically twisted the girl's torsos as they sang the aurang for this object:

> *Paidela pane*   Bring the tusks to your
> *ya gronso mo augopme.*   mouth, hold them at their base.
> *Ya gronso mo lepesme.*   Hold the tusks, they curve sharply.

Afterwards, the aunts instructed the girls in the names of each of the different parts of the ornament.

The obvious significance of these acts lies in the dual meanings paidela carry in Rauto culture. On the one hand, to wear paidela is to express anger. Thus, during a song festival or prior to a spear fight, men challenge each other by putting paidela to their mouths while brandishing spears. Likewise, big women don paidela during several ceremonies in which women express anger toward men by chasing them with sticks or spitting chewed areca at them: the ceremony of "routing the men" after the birth of a child; the ritual honoring of children; and the ceremonial passage of a new bride to a distant hamlet.

In the Rauto view, then, paidela symbolize both the aggressive anti-
social aspect of the self as well as its socially constructive, "network-build-
ing" capacities. The ritual presentation of paidela is a sign that initiates are
acquiring both a personal right and a social duty to cultivate these two
aspects of self. Thus, women—or at least those who are initiated—are
ritually accorded the right to act "aggressively," but at the same time an allusion is made to their role as caretakers and producers of pigs, and thus to
their role as important transactors of wealth and forgers of social networks.

The myth of paidela origins imparts a religious significance to this "role."
It tells of a mother's magical power and of the way she uses it to secure a
bride for each of her two sons. The opening scene recounts how a prominent big man has announced that his daughters are to be offered in marriage
to the most worthy suitor around. He devises a contest: the suitors must
scale the giant tahitian chestnut tree growing in his hamlet and then harvest
it. All fail the challenge save the two sons. Their mother enables them to
scale the tree by using her magic to make a nearby areca-nut palm grow to
form a bridge across to the canopy of the great chestnut. After this task is
accomplished, however, the other suitors complain that the boys are "rubbish men" unable to offer sufficient brideprice to the great man's family.
The boys' mother then takes a squealing piglet from her coconut-frond basket and throws it to the ground, where it promptly transforms itself into a
giant tusked pig, a pig with paidela. She does this nine more times, amass-
ing a great brideprice for her sons.

As the mother produced the boys physically by giving birth to them, so
now in the conclusion of this myth she gives birth to their social identity by
producing the needed objects of wealth. This mythic image provides a
stronger statement of woman's relationship to the political and economic
centers of Rauto culture than do the songs and activities of the puberty rite.
It suggests that women are, in a sense, the actual producers of the objects
that are such valued symbols of male political and economic identity, a
point to which I shall return.

THE CONCLUSION OF THE
WOMEN'S PUBERTY RITUAL

After the presentation of the paidela, the two girls were taken down to the
shore and a few steps out onto the reef (see plate 6.1). Here, their aunts
handed them some pronged fishing spears and bade them make a few casts.
The implicit message was that young women should spend some of their

6.1   A young initiate is taken down to the shore and a few steps out onto the reef. Rauto; New Britain, 1986. Photo credit: Thomas Maschio

time fishing and combing the reefs for food for themselves and their families. The two girls also were shown how to bathe away their menstrual blood and how to adjust their fiber skirts if they wished to urinate or defecate. The aunts then made the only *direct* reference to either a woman's sexuality or reproductive capacity that I observed, telling the girls the Rauto words for "vagina" and "breast" and informing them that after giving birth, they should feed their child with milk from their breasts.

The women then formed a procession back to the village, where the aunts conducted the girls around the ceremonial house, naming its external sections. At the entrance to the house, the other women threw down several pandanus mats, while others placed mats over the heads of the girls, shielding them from onlookers as they entered the house. Once inside, the aunts instructed their charges in the names of the inner sections of the structure. This instruction is another example of the privileged status of female initiates, representing one of several claims that prominent women make on the ritual and religious knowledge possessed by big men.

CONCLUSION

Geertz (1973:113–118) has written that religious traditions find their most forceful and dramatic expression during the performance of ritual. In his view, ritual manages to dramatize and thus empower religious belief by "setting before the eyes" the sense and meaning a way of life has for a people, and by powerfully evoking their moral and aesthetic "feel" for this life. In the setting of ritual, ethos is experienced more intensely and a people's worldview pictured more vividly and completely than in the activities of everyday life. On the one hand, ritual points "beyond the realities of everyday life to wider ones which correct and complete them" (ibid.:42). On the other hand, it directs participants' attention back to the world, enabling them to view it with more profound understanding by revealing the ontology on which their views of the world are based. Among other things, then, ritual in Geertz's view is a form of heightened discourse about the world that sanctifies its perceived character by relating this perception to a culturally specific ontology or metaphysic.

We can perceive here how the classic understanding of art as a heightened imitation of experience has influenced Geertz's theory of cultural representation. There especially appears to be a relationship between the visual character of Geertz's theory and the ideas of purification and heightening that inform classical theories of representation (see Abrams 1971:35–46). That is, in Geertz's view, ritual appears to complete experience not only by rendering it emotionally comprehensible but by allowing one to view all of its most significant or thematic contours, as these are acted out as it were. But what of "*la pensée obscure et confuse*" of mythic experience, the allusive and evanescent thoughts, meanings, and countermeanings that may enable us to see further and deeper into the nature of experience by representing it as something more than meets the eye?

The puberty rite does create and valorize a "picture" of the everyday world by celebrating some of the Rauto world's most common objects and activities in song. But this picture is only the obvious meaning of the rite and the simple song images that accompany the presentation of objects. It is really the more evanescent and obscure meanings and countermeanings of the rite that express something of the ontology and the aesthetic on which Rauto concepts of person and gender are based. This ontology suggests that the worldview and the ethos that are given expression by the simple acts and images of the puberty rite are understatements of the extent to which women are associated with creative power of various sorts. It is in the rite's counternarrative, in its elusive and allusive meaning, that we come to understand something of the nature of female personhood.

The picture of the world and of a big woman evoked during the rite is composed of elements and objects that the Rauto associate with both men and women. Thus, during the course of the ritual, we see big women invested with symbols that demonstrate their access to big men's "power" over special valuables and exchange activities, as well as their access to "woman's power" over garden production and the reproduction of people. The point to stress is that a big woman's access to both "male" and "female" forms of power does not make her an anomalous figure in Rauto society. Rather, it is precisely because she possesses both forms of power that she is perceived to embody an ideal of female social identity.

However, the more rounded mythic images and meanings associated with the objects of the rite suggest that women represent an ideal of human, rather than simply female, identity. We see this assertion first in the mythic insight that men stole their political power from women. Thus, men's political and cultural primacy is derivative and rightfully woman's possession. Perhaps the most subversive or carnivalesque mythic suggestion is that there is neither a specifically male nor female "gender identity." The myths tell of how women took their sex, their menstruation, and the objects signifying female identity from men. They tell of how men took their objects of power and their influence from women. Neither possessed a "natural" gender identity; both simply possessed a mythic identity. As Leenhardt well knew, there are no absolute boundaries or categories, such as male and female, in the domain of mythic experience. There are simply juxtaposed emotions and forms of being.

These mythic insights are of note since, in other realms of Rauto ritual life, men have to acquire and demonstrate some of the mythic attributes and powers associated with women (see Maschio 1994:152–166). That the concept of the person and views of the world evoked in the female puberty rite in particular, and in Rauto ritual life more generally, are composed of both male and female symbolic elements demonstrates that the ritual activities of men and women, in this particular society at least, evoke "models" of the person and the world that are not antithetical, as the work of others might lead us to conclude (Ardener 1975; Ortner 1974). Neither can these models, as they are evoked during the female puberty ritual, be considered pale reflections of the models presented in male ritual activity. Rather, Rauto ritual and mythic life demonstrates that a particular view of the world and person acquires a compelling meaning when male and female symbolic elements, categories, and powers are brought into a complementary relationship. It is not so much, then, that Rauto women's "powers are considered innate and natural, while men's power is associated with the practice of 'culture'"—i.e., ceremony and ritual (Strathern 1980:212). Rather, in defining ideals of personhood through ritual activity, Rauto express the notion that "neither sex can possibly stand for humanity as against 'nature'" (ibid.). Thus, rather than "defining" Woman by demonstrating the way her nature differs from Man's, the female puberty ritual conflates male and female realms and thus indicates that the Rauto ideal of humanity is represented by an amalgam of male and female powers.

Equally important, the rite reveals the sacred character that the concept of the person has for the Rauto. An aspect of this character is contained in the relationship—underscored by the ritual—between the person and important objects of both the natural and cultural world. In presenting initiates with these objects, and by singing them their names, female song leaders forge a series of "participations" or sacred relationships. For instance, since some of the objects stand as tokens for people of both past and present generations, when they are placed on the initiates' persons they participate in the identities of these others. Moreover, as the presented objects and their names constitute an aspect of tradition and memory, their possession by the initiates signals the incorporation of a concept of cultural memory into the very structure of a person's social identity. And, of course, the presentation of foods, plants, and finery to the initiates underscores the series of participations or relationships between person and world. For the Rauto, the locus of the sacred is contained within these manifold participations as well as within the instrument of their creation: the human voice.

NOTE

1. The fieldwork on which this essay is based was carried out in Southwestern New Britain during two field trips, the first from September 1985 to December 1986, the second from February to May 1990. I thank the Fulbright-Hays program and the Institute of Intercultural Studies for support, and Nancy Lutkehaus, Jim Roscoe, Roy Wagner, and Coralie Cooper for criticism and advice. Finally, I am deeply grateful to the women of Southwestern New Britain for teaching me about their custom.

Part IV

THE FEMALE BODY
AND LIFE-CYCLE RITES
AS METAPHOR

7

THE WASHED
AND THE UNWASHED

*Women's Life-Cycle Rituals among the Saniyo-Hiyowe
of East Sepik Province, Papua New Guinea*

Patricia K. Townsend

A girl's first menstruation and the secular ceremony that concludes it are public and clearly marked in Saniyo-Hiyowe society.[1] While menstruating, the girl remains in a small shelter built by her father or brother in an area slightly away from the main hamlet site. During her week-long seclusion, she is fed generously. At the end of the period, her mother and all the other women of the hamlet bring water, wash her, and deck her in shell ornaments and beads. She then works some sago, pounding, scraping, and leaching starch from a palm cut in the nearby swamp forest. This batch of sago can only be eaten by women and small children (see plate 7.1). Though she is not likely to marry for several months or even years, the girl who thus has "washed" (*sa'i huwei*) is marriageable, in contrast to a prepubertal girl (*ruwasei*), and indeed the common way to refer to young single women is to refer to their having "washed."

The Saniyo girl's puberty ritual is thus a ritual in the best Rappaportian sense, a display that transmits information about a girl's physiological and sociological state (Rappaport 1971). It converts information about her grad-

7 . 1   A young woman who has recently undergone the washing ritual preparing
         sago pudding. Her necklaces are predominantly of shells with some
         trade-store beads. Saniyo-Hiyowe; Wourei Village, 1967. Photo credit:
         William H. Townsend

ual maturation into unambiguous, binary, yes–no form: yesterday a girl, now
a young woman. It transmits information not only about her readiness for
marriage, but also about the support she enjoys from the local group of kin
who feast and adorn her as she enters a phase during which she and her
family will review prospective mates.

  After the death of her husband, a widow is subjected to a series of ritual
observances that dramatically unmakes all that was made in the menarcheal
ritual. Secluded in a back room of her house, under severe food taboos, she
is starved rather than fed. Forbidden to wash, to wear bodily ornaments, to
work, to appear in public events, her role is a dramatic reversal of the newly
nubile girl's. Only gradually, over several years, does she return to full participation in social life and become eligible for remarriage.

  In general terms, as enunciated by Marilyn Strathern (1987b; 1993), the
Saniyo menarcheal ritual transforms a passive, androgynous person into an
active, single-gendered, and nubile female. The bundle brings out of the girl
the bundle of social relationships of which she is composed. In contrast to
Strathern's New Guinea Highlands model, these social relationships are not

exclusively agnatic. Yet the point remains the same: from the whole set of social relations that comprise the girl, the puberty ritual decomposes the set that will carry forward into establishing her eventual marriage and the new social relationships that derive from it. Even more conspicuously, the severe restrictions that comprise the widow's mourning ritual not only undo what was done by the puberty rite but also decompose the whole set of social relationships that were built up throughout the marriage into a narrow set centered on the husband's heirs, who control the future remarriage of the widow.

This essay discusses the details of these two female life-crisis rites, both of which have a distinctive political dimension. Their participants publicly reaffirm their allegiances just when they face the two most dangerous points for potential outbreaks of violence in Saniyo society: the negotiation and payment of bridewealth; and the execution of a suspected cannibal witch, accused of responsibility for the death of a person who dies suddenly of illness in the prime of life.

THE SANIYO-HIYOWE

The practices here described are those of some two hundred speakers of the western, or Hiyowe, dialect area of the Saniyo-Hiyowe language of the Sepik Hill language family, a grouping of some fourteen languages spread across the foothills and tributaries south of the Middle and Upper Sepik (Dye, et al. 1968). The population was first studied between 1966 and 1967 (Townsend 1969); by the 1980s, it had regrouped from several smaller hamlets into the settlements of Yapatawi, Mapisi, and Wourei (Taunapi) in the Walio Sio Census Division of the Ambunti District of East Sepik Province. Subsistence is based on sago, hunting, and fishing, with only minimal planting of crops or care of domesticated pigs (Townsend 1974). Saniyo descent groups are named, nonexogamous, totemic patriclans segmented into landholding patrilineages. These patrilineages are designated by a binomial that includes the clan name and a second term usually derived from the birth order of the lineage founder: for example, Oparu Wariari lineage is descended from a fourth-born man (*waro*) of the Oparu clan. Residence is nominally patrivirilocal, but frequent visits and changes of residence to wife's and mother's places of origin occur (Townsend 1978).

SA'I HUWE: THE MENARCHEAL RITUAL

The Saniyo-Hiyowe sa'i huwei "washing" ritual is a community-wide celebration of a girl's productivity, nubility, and value as an individual. Its stages are those of the classic rite of passage: separation, liminality, and reincorporation. While she is in the menstrual hut, the girl is isolated—though she is not literally alone because she is visited by women and young girlfriends, but not normally by males. After the washing, she is part of the community again, accessible to the admiration of men and women, visitors and residents. In seclusion, she wears a dirty old "grass" skirt (usually, in fact, made of shredded leaves) and is unadorned. After washing, she is attractive, dressed in a fresh skirt, and decked with ornaments. In seclusion, she is passive, fed not only with sago and other day-to-day foods, but also with especially desirable animal foods such as sago grubs, pork, and fish, which her father and other male relatives make an extra effort to obtain for her. After washing, she is active; *she* feeds others by working sago that is eaten by women and children of the community.

By stringent definitions of initiation rituals, such as those of La Fontaine (1985) and Allen (1967), the Saniyo ceremony is merely a puberty rite and not an initiation (see also Roscoe's conclusion, this volume). It is held for an individual rather than a group of girls, and it is closely tied to the biological event of menarche. Unlike her male counterpart, who may be initiated individually but is more often one of a pair or small group of young men, she is not initiated into anything comparable to the ritual secrets of the men's house cult of ancestral spirits and flutes.[2] Nor is she initiated in secrecy into a "discrete group of individuals who cooperate in certain activities, share common property and are conscious of their existence as an organized body" (Allen 1967:7). Although the social category of those who have "washed" is conceptually discrete, the kinds of activities in which women cooperate most intensely, particularly sago work, also include younger girls who have not yet "washed." By the less stringent definitions used by Brown (1963) and Young (1965), however, Saniyo rites do qualify as initiation rites. The amount of community involvement is substantial, including not only the immediate family but the whole hamlet of fifteen to forty or more persons (see Townsend 1978 for a discussion of hamlet structure).

MENSTRUATION AND PURITY

Insofar as the usual term for unmarried young women refers to their having washed, bathing seems to be the central feature of the girl's puberty ritual. Because I have never been in a settlement when this event was taking place, however, I do not know how prominent it is in practice among the other events. Bathing has the double significance of making the girl attractive and purifying her of menstrual contamination. By New Guinea standards, however, the Saniyo-Hiyowe are not extreme in their concern with menstrual contamination and, after this initial ritual attention, concern with menstrual pollution is little marked. At subsequent menstruations, the teenager may spend a day in cheerful seclusion, sitting in the bush with young female friends for company. Because of pollution fears, women have their own entrances to houses, but men are sometimes careless and use them, and a recent rainfall is considered sufficient to cleanse them. In addition, women have their own sitting areas: I was once chided for my carelessness in exposing my husband to possible harm when I set a stringbag I had borrowed from him on a woman's *limbum* mat, even though, to outward appearances, the mat was not soiled.

After marriage, menstrual pollution ceases to be an issue since married women and widows are said not to menstruate (privately some will admit this is a fiction). Of course, pregnancy and prolonged lactational amenorrhea do account for long stretches of time during which women do not menstruate (at least two years for each surviving infant and at least one year for infants who die). But the denial goes beyond this, since fertility is moderate—five or six births per woman of completed fertility—and women are not, therefore, constantly pregnant or lactating (Townsend 1971; 1985).

THE GIRL'S ORNAMENTS:
THE PUBERTY RITE AS
THE FIRST STAGE OF BETROTHAL

Although washing is the central symbol of a girl's puberty ritual, the most conspicuous public feature is her arrayment with ornaments (see plate 7.2).[3] Like the washing, the ornaments beautify the initiated girl. They also display the wealth and generosity of her parents and advertise her marriageability to those who visit the community in subsequent weeks and months. Prior to the 1960s, ornaments consisted of necklaces of dog's teeth, buttons, or shells, often conus shells or cowries. More recently, trade beads have become most important. Although few were seen in 1966–67, by the 1980s they were abundant. People made long trips to trade stores at Frieda River and Hauna on the Sepik to obtain beads, among other things, and we were encouraged to bring them as trade goods on our return visits. Red and white beads are the most valued, strung on strands of nylon fishline and twisted into multistrand chokers.

The types of ornaments girls wear after their ritual washing are the same as the secondary categories of bridewealth items, those most often given and received in bridewealth distributions by women and younger or more dis-

7.2   A young woman who has recently undergone the washing ritual standing
       in a garden with her married elder sister. Her necklaces are predominantly
       of beads. Both wear cassowary quill earrings. Saniyo-Hiyowe; Nikiai
       Village, 1967. Photo credit: William H. Townsend

tantly related persons. In contrast, the major categories of bridewealth—
long strings of cowrie shells—are not worn but simply hung from a rafter
for display during the exchange and then rolled up and hidden away again
in their owners' net bags.[4] This is not to say that the girl's puberty ornaments are used in the transaction surrounding her marriage; although they
may subsequently enter into other women's bridewealth,[5] at her marriage
they usually go with her as personal ornaments.

After the menarcheal ritual, the girl is marriageable. In recent years, several
girls have moved from menarche to marriage within months, with bridewealth
payments and first pregnancies following soon after. This was unusual in earlier years. In the 1960s there were several young, single women who had
"washed" some years previously but were in no hurry to marry, enjoying
their freedom as much as their families appreciated their companionship and
contribution to family labor requirements. Even in the 1980s, one of my oldest Saniyo friends, a new bride when I met her in 1966, was reluctant to have
her eldest, seventeen-year-old daughter marry soon because she appreciated
her help with the younger children. Suitors described the mother as "fierce,"
and her attractive daughter was in no hurry to marry either.

In the last few years, however, several factors seem to have accelerated
marriage arrangements for local girls. One is the stepped-up pace of social
interaction generally. As small, isolated hamlets have consolidated into
fewer and larger settlements, including the large airstrip-community at
Mapisi, there are more opportunities for both young people and their elders
to get together. Consequently, the flirtations and discussions that lead to
betrothal proceed more rapidly than when people were more isolated.
Another factor is the windfall of earning opportunities that the Ambunti
Akademi with its airstrip and school at Mapisi began to offer in the late
1970s. Young men with cash incomes have been able to marry girls from
poorer communities. These young men and their brides are younger than
was usual when the wealth in bridal exchange came exclusively from elder
relatives of the groom. Beginning in the 1980s, moreover, bridewealth has
come to include banknotes, and cash is now also used to purchase cowries.
By 1984, the largest brideprice included about K100 (about 100 U.S. dol-
lars) in banknotes, though most still included much less.

A final factor pressing Saniyo-Hiyowe girls to marry young in the 1980s
is a quirk of small-population demographics. In 1967, the population pyra-
mid showed an imbalance of twenty boys to ten girls in the under five-year-
old age group (Townsend 1969). The small cohort of survivors among these
girls came to maturity in the 1980s, and their scarcity encouraged many
young men to look outside the local population for brides. This demo-

graphic pressure also depressed girls' marriage ages, though not so low that betrothals were occurring prior to menarche, which is very rarely done. The single exception I know of was a girl who married prior to menarche in the early 1960s. She is cited by informants to illustrate that it is not completely unthinkable for a man to raise his child-bride to maturity, particularly if—as was true in this case—her parents are dead.

The washed and ornamented girl is very much on display, conspicuous to visitors to her community. Not only is she only on display to potential suitors, however, but also to potential contributors to, and recipients of, her bridewealth. Mate selection ideally involves mutual agreement by both partners, though there is a convention that a man may grab an unwilling woman by the wrist and drag her off. On the other hand, in at least one recent case, it was the groom who was reluctant and his mother and the bride who initiated the arrangements. However the selection actually occurs, a new bride is taken to her husband's home where the pair remain for the first several months of marriage. One to several months later, the bridewealth having been assembled, the bride's relatives arrive for a feast, from which they carry away the wealth objects.[6]

The Saniyo-Hiyowe view bridewealth as a long-term investment. Relatives of the groom, as individuals, contribute strings of cowries or smaller items, and these contributions are remembered: when the daughters of the marriage are themselves married, they or their descendants will expect a share of the bridewealth. As they are growing up, a man who has contributed a major item tells his children: "See that little girl over there? When she grows up and gets married, you will get part of the bridewealth." In a population with such high mortality, these investments are risky enough (Townsend 1971, 1985), but the risk is compounded by variability in the assets of prospective husbands, who do not all have the same kinship networks enabling them to amass bridewealth. The adornment of the initiated girl in shells, beads, and dog's teeth thus forecasts the eventual payment of bridewealth for her. It also opens up the possibility of moving toward betrothal, though this may be delayed for some time.

HISTORY AND PERSISTENCE OF GIRLS' PUBERTY RITES: A COMPARATIVE NOTE

The menarcheal ritual described above has persisted into the 1980s without apparent need for reevaluation after Sepik evangelists introduced Christianity in the mid-1970s. This contrasts with the abandonment of male initiation, which was rejected as inconsistent with Christianity because of the spirit cult associated with the flutes (Tok Pisin: *tambaran*; Saniyo-Hiyowe: *nahe awe*). The last male initiation in the area under study was held in 1976.[7]

That female puberty rites persist unquestioned while male initiation has been rejected is the strongest indicator of the substantially secular nature of the female ritual, though there may yet turn out to be some hidden sacred dimension that has escaped me. Speakers of the Bahinemo language to the east, linguistically and culturally related to the Saniyo, adopted a similar version of evangelical Christianity a decade earlier at Wagu village. They too decided that male initiation was in conflict with Christianity but that female initiation was not.[8] After discussion, it was decided that only small modifications in the girls' rite needed to be made but that the boys' rite was unsuitable because devotion to spirits rather than God was at its core (Dye 1974). Even so, male initiation was too important to be abandoned easily, and there has been constant tension and discussion for many years over whether Christians should participate or not, resulting in an attempt to create a Christianized version that would fill similar social functions (Wayne and Sally Dye, pers. comm.).

The Bahinemo girls' initiation rite is slightly more elaborate than the Saniyo-Hiyowe version, though similar in general outline (ibid.). The ritual requires a sponsor, and not every girl who reaches puberty is sponsored. The sponsored girl and her patron derive prestige from the ceremony, a variation from Saniyo practice that is consistent with the slightly greater emphasis on leadership and prestige at Wagu (Dye 1990). Three or four other girls approaching puberty are initiated along with the sponsored girl, and the ceremony is another occasion for one of a series of affinal exchanges that make up childprice, the prior one being a grass-skirt ceremony for prepubertal girls of ages ten to twelve. In the ceremony the Dyes observed in the 1960s, the initiates were hidden from view for a month. During this seclusion, the girls were said to be with spirits who were giving them growth.

In the 1970s, Wagu village reduced seclusion to about ten days, dropped a disciplinary switching (on the grounds that it was said to be disapproved by the government), head shaving, and body painting. They retained the postseclusion washing and bodily ornamentation that are also core features of Saniyo initiation.

The Yimar (Alamblak) of the Upper Korowori River speak Alamblak, the easternmost of the Sepik Hill languages. Like the Saniyo, the Yimar marked a girl's first menstruation with an individual rite but initiated males in groups (Haberland and Seyfarth 1974:332–334). The Yimar were first contacted by Australian patrols in the mid-1930s, twenty-five years prior to the

TABLE 7.1   SANIYO-HIYOWE WIDOW'S RITUAL AS THE
ANTITHESIS OF PUBERTY RITUAL

Ritual Element	Girl at Puberty	Widow
Bathes	+	−
Shell/bead ornaments	+	−
Skirt	short, bright	long, dark
Seclusion	brief; in menstrual hut away from house	prolonged; in apartment within house
Feeds others (sago)	+	−
Food taboos	−	+
Fed by kinsmen	sago, vegetables, game, sago grubs	wild yams, rats
Role in public events	+	−
Use of personal name	+	−
Danger to men	menstrual contamination	cannibal witch

Saniyo, and underwent substantial social change after World War II. When studied ethnographically in 1963, they had last initiated a group of males in 1958 and did not anticipate that the ceremony would be revived (ibid.:279).

In their menarcheal ceremony, the Yimar collect the first menstrual blood in a leaf and bury it to assure magically that the girl will not continue to menstruate—a concept, if not a practice, consistent with Saniyo ideas.[9] Like the Saniyo-Hiyowe and Bahinemo, they do not cicatrize women. In this, the Sepik Hill peoples contrast with better-known Sepik peoples such as the Kwoma, Abelam, and Iatmul (Williamson 1979; Hauser-Schäublin, this volume).

Among the Sepik Hill peoples, in sum, somewhat similar female puberty rites were practiced from east to west by the Yimar, Bahinemo, and Saniyo, and these rituals were more persistent than male initiation in the face of contact with Australian administration and missions.

RITUAL OBSERVANCE OF WIDOWHOOD

When her husband dies, a Saniyo widow goes into seclusion and assumes a set of behavioral restrictions that point-for-point are a reversal of the Saniyo puberty ritual (see table 7.1). It is as though the nubility and femininity attained and celebrated earlier in her life are abruptly terminated. Only slowly is her feminine identity rebuilt by the lifting of taboos and the gradual resumption of women's work over the several years that pass before she may remarry.[10] It is a tense time. In addition to her grief, the widow experiences fear, for she may be murdered by her husband's grieving relatives. In the early 1960s, it was said, a widow at Oteni was killed by her husband's sister's sons "for not giving sago to him," and in the late 1950s a widow from Yareno was killed by her husband's relatives for eating fish in violation of a food taboo.

Unlike a menstrual or birth house, the widow's place of seclusion is not separate from the main dwelling. She stays in the same multifamily house that she lived in when her husband was alive, but to avoid being seen—particularly by her husband's male relatives—she remains out of view of the main room, in a back room with its own hearth (*tevi wesi*, literally "part-house," i.e., apartment). As recently as 1967, her most complete seclusion lasted while her husband's corpse decayed nearby on a platform, awaiting secondary burial in the earth or a forest pool. Now that public health rules require burial shortly after death, burial no longer marks the end of this phase of mourning. After the first months, seclusion is not as extreme and consists mostly of exhibiting a quiet demeanor and avoiding public gatherings, even such routine and modern ones as church services. Many years after her husband's death, the unremarried mother of a bride or groom is excluded from receiving or giving bridewealth, although by then she may be taking an active social role in other respects.[11]

A girl ending puberty seclusion washes and is dressed in a new skirt and ornaments. In contrast, a new widow is not allowed to wash and becomes noticeably grimy. Even after she surreptitiously begins to wash her skin, she still will not cut her hair. (Bending the rule, one widow of several months appeared with a patchy haircut, having cut out the lice.) In puberty ritual, the girl wears knee-length, bright green or yellow reeds. Widows wear ankle-length skirts of dark, gray-green shredded leaves. Whereas the newly pubescent girl is decorated with ornaments, widows are barred from wearing them.[12] The girl in menstrual seclusion is fed especially desirable foods: game, fish, and grubs obtained by her father and brothers. The new widow obeys harsh food taboos; initially, she is not even allowed sago, the staple that normally provides 85 percent of the caloric value of the diet. Even after this proscription is lifted, a widow continues, out of sentiment, to avoid the particular variety of sago that she and her husband were eating at the time of his death.

Like the relatives of a menarcheal girl, a widow's family brings her special foods, but of contrasting types: Raru's son found bitter wild yams for her when she could not eat sago. She may eat no animal foods except a few types of rats that no one else would eat—my husband was expected to give the rats he trapped in our house to widows. At puberty, the girl works and shares out a special batch of sago; the widow is forbidden to work sago for several years.

The mourning taboos on food and work are lifted only gradually, and the removal of the most important is signaled by an exchange. A relative of the deceased makes a gift of a formerly prohibited item—for example, a serving of a particular kind of fish—and the widow reciprocates with a payment—for example, a small handful of cowrie shells. Once a sago pounder or sieve is given, she can start working sago again. When she receives a palm spathe bucket, the container in which water is boiled by adding hot stones, she can make sago pudding again. The removal of less salient taboos, however, goes unmarked: once the main taboos have been lifted ritually, she progressively and quietly takes up other foods and activities.

Taboos are removed by one or more kinsmen of the deceased. The food taboos are removed one at a time by the deceased's matrilateral cross cousin (*ofay rame*) or other close matrilateral kin who receive the funeral payment. The taboo on sago work is lifted when an agnatic kinsman gives the widow a sago pounder; he is said to be acting on behalf of the ancestral spirits of the husband's lineage (*nahe awe*), whose voices are the flutes.

Circumspection is called for in lifting the taboos, particularly if the husband's death was unexpected. A young widow with two small children, whose husband died suddenly in his early thirties (probably of pneumonia following influenza), was still severely restricted four years after his death. In the same community, by contrast, an older woman whose frail and elderly husband's death was not unexpected was back at work within two years of his death, helping provide for her grandchildren.

The logic of natural symbols might lead us to expect that a ritual celebrating menarche would be paired with a ritual marking menopause. Can Saniyo widowhood be seen as a kind of social menopause, even though women frequently are widowed in their childbearing years?[13] At first blush, it would seem awkward to insist on this, since it is held that married women do not menstruate, but a closer examination lends credence to the idea.

One of the women most adamant in insisting to me that local women do not menstruate after marriage was a young widow. Although she had given birth to an infant shortly after her husband's death, the infant had died. Consequently, she had been neither pregnant nor lactating for most of the four years since her husband had died, and therefore surely would have been menstruating if anyone was. Yet she adamantly denied that she and other women menstruated. She persisted in her denial even in a confidential conversation with me and another young married woman who was all along hinting broadly to her that it would be all right for them to be candid with me about menstruation. Now this young widow was still obeying severe widow's taboos on food, dress, and appearance at public gatherings. She was not yet allowed to work sago, cook, or do other work, even though this meant that her two small children had to be fed by other women. The point is that her denial of menstruation seemed consistent with the symbolic nature of her taboos, which symbolically denied her sexuality and marriageability. In other words, though she was probably physically menstruating, she was scrupulously careful to present herself as *socially* postmenopausal. Although she was physically young and healthy, her presentation of self and dependence on others made her socially appear an elderly woman, even a crone.

In her essay "Space Crones," Ursula Le Guin laments the loss in modern society of rituals of menarche and menopause:

> The entire life of a woman from ten or twelve through seventy or eighty has become secular, uniform, changeless. As there is no longer any virtue in virginity, so there is no longer any meaning in menopause. It requires fanatical determination now to become a Crone. (Le Guin 1989:4)

Le Guin celebrates the Crone, the old woman who has "experienced, accepted, and acted the entire human condition" (1989:6).

> Men are afraid of virgins, but they have a cure for their own fear and the virgin's virginity: fucking. Men are afraid of crones, so afraid of them that their cure for virginity fails them; they know it won't work. (Ibid.)

Saniyo men have their own response to their fear of crones: accusing them as cannibal witches and killing them. The most recent killing of a widow accused as a witch resulted in a prison term in Wewak for a man who had thus avenged the death of his stepbrother. He and his dead brother were both young, married men, but the accused witch was not the young widow of the deceased but an older widow in another community. Indeed, when the killer returned from prison, in 1981, he polygynously married his brother's widow, then in her late twenties.

The Saniyo conception of the witch is bound up with values related to food and eating. The witch is a cannibal who kills to eat the brain and internal organs of a living person, the damage being recognizable in the corpse on the burial platform, whose insides appear to contain "nothing but sago." The witch then returns to eat the remaining flesh on the burial platform. A person becomes a witch by eating human flesh, perhaps inadvertently, having been tricked into doing so by another witch. Witches eat other repulsive things as well—worms, eels, and snakes, which are eaten through the nose and ears rather than the mouth. A witch's gluttony and greed may be hidden, but the seemingly minor infractions of a widow's food taboos may be taken as a clue that she is really a witch.

It is not just widows, however, who are accused as cannibal witches; men, too, may be considered witches, especially if they have big bellies that testify to a lust for flesh. The difference is that men are not often executed outright as witches. At least, the only tales of male witch killings that I heard were stories of hunters who had shot a pig or bird that failed to die; if the hunter later heard that a suspected male witch in another village had died, he could infer that he had shot a were-animal, which had then changed back into human form and returned home to die.

For a period of months or at most a few years, the virgin and the crone are each sources of possible danger to Saniyo-Hiyowe men—the young girl because of her menstrual blood, and the widow because of the possibility that she is a witch. With female danger contained to these two relatively brief periods in the life cycle, gender relations are not antagonistic and women's participation in community life is enhanced through most of their lives. In this, the Saniyo-Hiyowe contrast with Highlands societies, where gender ideology declares women to be a danger to men throughout their reproductive life. As we shall see in the following section, the two female life-cycle rituals occur at phases when societal tensions are high and outbreaks of violence are very likely. It is therefore necessary to look at the political context within which the rituals occur and which they help to shape.

THE POLITICS OF WOMEN'S LIFE-CRISIS RITUALS

Paige and Paige (1981:43) assess reproductive rituals as a "continuation of politics by another means," and the Saniyo-Hiyowe menarcheal ritual is a reasonably supportive case. Although the Saniyo-Hiyowe have patrilineal descent groups, they form generally weak fraternal interest groups whose effectiveness is continually undercut by dispersed, flexible residence and the weak resource base of an essentially foraging economy. Under these social conditions, according to the Paiges, menarcheal ceremonies are "mobilization rituals," occasions for bargaining and creating community support in preparation for making the best possible marriage arrangements for the nubile girl (1981:78).

Although the Paiges' formulation generally rings true for the Saniyo case, in some details it does not fit. The Paiges emphasize the girl's father as the one motivated to protect his interests by these rituals, but for the Saniyo-Hiyowe the girl's mother and the whole bilateral kindred with claims to her brideprice are included in the bargaining unit, and the father does not necessarily dominate the proceedings.

Puberty ritual opens up marriage negotiations on the bride's side by beginning to identify the men, women, and children who will be the claimants to a share of her bridewealth. These will include both male and female heirs of the contributors to her mother's brideprice as well as others of her kin who came into the picture later (e.g., her stepfather). Because the bride-giver is neither the girl's father alone nor a corporate group such as the patrilineage, but rather a bilateral coalition, these claimants now must begin to identify themselves. Consequently, people scattered by the Saniyo pattern of multiple and flexible residence begin to visit and become involved as potential participants. It is also frequently the case that, in addition to bridewealth, marriage negotiations will complete a sister exchange, albeit one that may have been long delayed. While, on the one side, the parties to the exchange may be actual or close classificatory brother and sister, on the other side they may be fairly distant kin. Bargaining time is needed, not just to find suitable mates, but to work out who will make up the wife-giving unit or units. Care in this process is required to minimize subsequent conflict.

Conflict arises when people who have been left out of marriage negotiations or have received only token items later assert claims. Thus, the politicking that begins with the menarcheal ritual is important. The men who supply food to the girl in seclusion and the women who wash her thereby are beginning the discussions that will form the bride-giving unit, a stage of negotiation that is not only prior to the choice of a husband but much more likely to lead to trouble.

The potential for conflict is substantial; in fact, marriage negotiations are a major—if not *the* major—cause of conflict in Saniyo-Hiyowe society and, in the past, killings have occurred at weddings. Indeed, the first wedding we attended in 1967 threatened to end in an early-morning brawl after a night of dancing. Our companions, who were matrilateral relatives of the groom, rushed us to the canoes to leave quickly, and the visitors from the bride's party also all left to avoid escalating the fight. More recently, bridewealth negotiators, worried that conflict was unavoidable, have been ready to call in police from the station at Ambunti months before the wedding.

Elsewhere, I have described a bridewealth distribution that left two women angry at being excluded when their brothers received the payment due to the heirs of men who had contributed to the bride's mother's bridewealth a generation earlier. After making a fuss, both of these women eventually received payments (Townsend 1990). But the most extreme expressions of anger at being cheated of bridewealth are cases in which the malevolence of brothers who feel they have been inadequately compensated for their sister's marriage is said supernaturally to cause the death of her children or even her barrenness or death in childbirth.

Like a teenager, a widow also is newly available for marriage, and the political implications are therefore similar. In the case of a widow, however, marriage is delayed not by her parents' reluctance to give her up but by fear of her husband's jealous ghost, which is a danger to all but is especially likely to bring illness to any man presumptuous enough to marry her. In contrast to the amorphous bride-giving unit for a young woman, the right to give a widow away in marriage is held by her husband's group. Although the males of this group have leviratic rights to her, they rarely exercise their prerogative. More often, she is married to a recent widower, who pays a small brideprice of one or two strings of cowries to the closest agnate of the deceased—his brother or perhaps his grown son—the woman's own relatives ceasing to have claims on her brideprice after her first marriage.

This assertion of control over the widow's productivity and fertility by her deceased husband's patrilineage is reflected in the enforcement of her taboos by its ancestral spirits, as discussed earlier. If she asserted her own interests, her husband's kin would withdraw their protection and increase her vulnerability to being accused as a witch and killed by her husband's relatives or by outsiders.

CONCLUSION

The Saniyo-Hiyowe girl's puberty ceremony and widow's observances are simple rituals that nonetheless draw the participation of the whole hamlet. They form occasions to communicate beyond the hamlet to potential spouses in other communities. The structural elements of the puberty ritual are each mirrored in the ritual observances of the widow. The girl is washed; the widow is required to remain dirty. The girl is ornamented; the widow is stripped of ornaments. The girl is fed and feeds others; the widow is starved and forbidden to produce food or work. Despite the surface contrasts, however, both widow and girl are now available for eventual marriage exchange. Both sets of ritual observances mark out the interested parties to negotiations that must proceed very slowly, for no situation is more fraught with conflict for the Saniyo than the establishment and reestablishment of affinal exchange.

NOTES

1. For assistance in fieldwork my debts are many. I would like to thank my husband, William H. Townsend, for assisting me in the field in 1966–67 and our daughter Alison for helping both of us during the five shorter field trips we made in 1980–84. Fieldwork in 1966–67 was supported by an NIMH fellowship and an NSF dissertation grant. The 1980–84 field sessions were taken as holidays from my work at the PNG Institute of Applied Social and Economic Research. This nonapplied part of my work was sponsored but not funded by IASER, and I thank the members of the Institute and the government bodies who made this time in Papua New Guinea possible. Members of the Summer Institute of Linguistics were also helpful, including Wayne and Sally Dye, who led us in the initial choice of a field site, and Ronald and Sandra Lewis, who generously shared their hospitality. This paper was improved by the comments or encouragements of Terry Hays, Jim Roscoe, and other participants in the ASAO sessions at which it was presented.

2. In contrast, male initiates, who, I am told, are also bathed before they emerge from seclusion, are referred to as having seen the ancestral spirits. Also, in contrast to their sisters, their food consumption in seclusion is restricted and they are subsequently subject to many food taboos on game animals. Because initiations occur infrequently and irregularly, initiates may range from small boys to married men.

3. On many occasions, I have visited hamlets and noticed or had pointed out to me girls who had recently gone through the puberty rite and were all decked out in ornaments. But except for one brief encounter during the seclusion period, I have not personally observed other phases of the ritual. This is one of the penalties of working in a small and scattered population. There may well be aspects of the ceremony that no one thought to tell me about. Sadly, my experience of widows' rites is more complete, because of the deaths of the husband and son of my sister, Heniye-Weinamei.

4. Townsend (1990) supplies more information about the involvement of women as transactors in bridewealth.

5. An instance occurred during a bridewealth distribution at Mapisi in 1984. At the last minute, stung by criticism that the wealth was insufficient, the groom's mother's brother rushed off to where his own daughter was in seclusion (for a later period, not her first period). He took one of the shell ornaments from her neck and dramatically added it to the brideprice.

6. Virilocal residence at the time of marriage is the norm, but subsequent residence is bilocal and shifts frequently. Consequently, the Saniyo-Hiyowe do not conform to Judith Brown's hypothesis that female initiation establishes adult status for girls who remain in their natal communities after marriage (Brown 1963). The temporary, patrivirilocal residence during the time when the bridewealth and feast are being accumulated would mark the adult status of the bride, even if the couple later returned to stay with her family.

7. The Papua New Guinean Christians with whom the Saniyo-Hiyowe have had most contact have come from Hauna, Yessan-Mayo, and Washkuk, all along the upper Sepik around and above Ambunti. They have links to the Assemblies of God (headquartered in Maprik), the Summer Institute of Linguistics, and the independent Ambunti Akademi (Pacific Islands Ministries). As late as January 1984, a group of young males was undergoing initiation within the eastern dialect of the Saniyo language group. This was at the village of Sio, at its new site called Karanoko on the lower Wogamus River just above Biaga, where the Seventh Day Adventist mission established a presence sufficient to discourage other missions from working but was unable itself to maintain a continuous presence.

8. Wagu is under the supervision of the same Assemblies of God missionaries as the Saniyo-Hiyowe.

9. The Sepik Hill cultures are not the only Melanesian cultures to contain female pollution by the denial of menstruation. The Bush Mekeo achieve the same end by "preventing" menstruation. Believing that women menstruate only when having sexual relations, they consider that as long as women are kept chaste or pregnant they need never menstruate (Mosko 1985:68–69).

10. Although regional comparison of widow's rites is beyond the scope of this paper, it is striking that Yimar widows wear men's clothing for a month after their husband's death and go about with downcast eyes because their gaze is dangerous (Haberland and Seyfarth 1974:388).

11. Widowers are not excluded from bridewealth exchanges following their wives' deaths but, in most other respects, they are subject to the same observances as widows. Their taboos are neither as severe nor as fear-driven, however, since female ghosts are regarded as less dangerous than male and there is less reason to fear action by their wife's relatives or accusations of witchcraft.

12. In 1966–67, women did not have cloth, though men did have at least a loincloth or a ragged pair of shorts. In the 1980s, when all women possessed some clothing to wear on special occasions, such clothing was still categorized as an ornament and thus not to be worn by widows.

13. Nine of the twenty-five women past the age of childbearing in 1967 had been widowed, remarried, and had born children by a second husband (Townsend 1971). Women are more likely than men to be widowed because they are several years younger at first marriage. Both infant mortality (Townsend 1985) and adult mortality remained extremely high throughout the 1970s.

8

GENDER METAPHORS

Female Rituals as Cultural Models in Manam

Nancy C. Lutkehaus

The "Coming of Age" of Wazike

April 18, 1933

In the afternoon met Wazike just having finished washing by the Tsokali waterholes and put on her petticoat of coarse banana leaves which was just new, or at least the top layer looked it. With her were Sagido, Idoge (Tsedam's daughter), and several other little girls all wearing green petticoats. They were all newly oiled (*bureng*) and felt very pleased with themselves. They wanted to oil my face but said unfortunately they had thrown the remains of the preparation into the sea.

Camilla Wedgwood (n.d., notebook 5:31)[1]

Thus begin the British anthropologist Camilla Wedgwood's observations of the *imoaziri*, or first menstruation rites, performed in 1933 for Wazike, a young woman from Zogari (Tsokali) village on Manam Island.[2] The key elements of this phase of the rites include the women's ritual washing of the initiate in the sea, the girl's donning of fresh banana-leaf skirts (*saresare*), and the oiling of her face with coconut oil (*bureng*) mixed with special herbs and leaves (*aduma*). These activities all relate to the girl's physical condition

of menarche and her new state of sexual maturity. The bathing purifies her
from the danger of contamination from her menstrual blood. Banana-leaf
skirts—easily fabricated and readily dispensable—are worn by all Manam
women when they menstruate in place of their regular *baligo* (grass skirts),
or, at present, cloth sarongs or skirts. The aduma mixture the women rub
on the initiate's face is primarily to enhance her beauty. These rites, which
are performed twice a day for a week, involve women only. They are the
private and secret dimension of Manam female initiation and contrast with
the public rites held at the conclusion of the imoaziri ceremony where men
as well as women are present.

In his book, *Male Cults and Secret Initiations in Melanesia*, Michael Allen
(1967) argues that Melanesian initiation rites are fundamentally concerned
with the creation and maintenance of separation between the sexes. He also
suggests that the presence or absence of these rites and the form they take is
directly related to a society's social structure. Allen based his analysis of the
Manam rites on Wedgwood's published descriptions of Manam culture
(1933, 1934, 1937, 1938), including a description of activities similar to
those described for Wazike (1933).

Allen concluded, however, that unlike most Melanesian societies, Manam
maturation rites (his terminology) are only secondarily concerned with male-
female relations (1967:65). As evidence, he cited the fact that Manam male
initiation did not include incision or any other form of blood-letting common
in many Melanesian male initiation ceremonies (ibid.). This relative lack of
emphasis on physiology and sexual symbolism in Manam was even more
apparent in girls' puberty rites, where little attention is paid to their physiological condition (1967:66). According to Allen, girls' puberty rites are "primarily social affairs that mark a change in individual status [from
adolescence to adulthood] with little or no sexual connotation" (1967:65):

> A menstruating girl is not considered to be unclean or to present a
> danger to men, she defiles nothing and nothing defiles her, the rites
> have no real connection with menstruation as a physiological event,
> with ideas about menstrual blood, or with the dangers most Mela-
> nesian societies believed to be inherent in such overt manifestations
> of a girl's sexuality. (1967:66)

The key to understanding this lack of emphasis on physiological change
and sexuality, Allen explains, "is almost certainly to be found in the presence of what is, for a New Guinea society, an unusually well-developed
hereditary class system" (1967:66). Thus, "instead of ritually reinforcing the

social and physiological differences between the sexes, [Manam] ceremonies emphasize the privileges of the aristocrats" (ibid.).

In contrast to other, more egalitarian New Guinea societies, Manam is unusual in possessing a system of hereditary social groups that categorize individuals on the basis of birth, adoption, or marriage according to one of two named social groups: *gadagada* (commoners) or *tanepoa* (elite). Although there are differences in how initiation rites were conducted for tanepoa and gadagada children, I argue that, in the past, the expression and perpetuation of prestige relations was *not* their dominant feature. Contrary to Allen, I also argue that cultural notions concerning the body and physiological processes—in particular, menstruation and sexuality—are important symbolic and ritual foci of the Manam female rites.

I suggest that Allen's description and analysis of Manam male and female "rites of maturation" lead to a misinterpretation of the significance of these rites in Manam culture and society. I take exception to Allen's interpretation of Manam initiation rites not simply as a point of departure for a more culturally grounded interpretation and analysis of their meaning, but more significantly because an understanding of the limitations of his interpretation—in particular, its unidimensional focus on social structure—allows us to better appreciate the multiple levels of meaning and relationship between cultural notions of gender, sexuality, power, and prestige that were salient features of Manam male and female initiation rites.

As Roscoe points out in the conclusion to this volume, differences in the definition of initiation rites are rife in the anthropological literature. According to Allen's definition (1967:7), initiation rituals include only those rites in which several initiates are incorporated into a discrete group of individuals who cooperate or participate in specific activities. In addition, the rites, activities, and group itself must be characterized by a degree of secrecy (ibid.). Although organically related to initiation, Allen states, puberty rites are rites of passage that involve a change of status for only one individual, are public in nature, and do not result in admittance to a discrete social group (1967:5). Thus, like many others, Allen's definition differentiates between initiation and puberty rites on the basis of whether the rituals are collective or individual. According to this definition, the Manam traditionally practiced male initiation rites since groups of youths—who became agemates (*dzugu teke*)—were initiated into a secret male cult based on the performance of sacred bamboo flutes (*embeki*) and participation in activities centered on the men's house (*keda*), from which women and children were forbidden. On the other hand, according to Allen, since rites celebrating a girl's first menstruation were performed individually, the imoaziri rites are simply a female puberty ritual. Indeed, Camilla Wedgwood (1933) followed the same categorization in her article, "Girls' Puberty Rites in Manam." Following the argument presented in this volume, I prefer to use the term "initiation" to describe both sets of rites, whether they involve groups of initiates or single individuals.[3]

Initiation rites have changed substantially since Wedgwood was on Manam. Male initiation per se is no longer practiced, and although female initiation rites (and some male rites marking the onset of the transition to adulthood) are still performed, their form and function have altered. At present they are usually performed only for firstborn sons and daughters of the elite. In the discussion that follows, I describe and analyze aspects of the traditional first menstruation rites for women using information that Camilla Wedgwood collected on Manam in 1933 in the course of observing four such ceremonies (Wedgwood n.d.). These data are supplemented by the records of Karl Böhm and Georg Höltker (Böhm 1983), Society of the Divine Word (SVD) missionaries on Manam in the 1930s, and by information I collected in 1978–79 and 1983.[4] I conclude with a brief discussion of changes in the rites as they are performed at present, and comment on the significance of these changes and the transformation of male initiation rites to contemporary Manam society.

AINE IMOAZIRI: FIRST MENSTRUATION RITES

The Manam phrase, *aine imoaziri*, is used to describe both a girl who has just reached menarche and a girl who is celebrating her puberty rites. Although social recognition of a girl's achievement of sexual maturity is prompted by the onset of menarche, parents sometimes delay the public celebration of the imoaziri rites until they have sufficient food to hold the feast that marks its conclusion. Wedgwood reports (1933:135) that a girl who had started to menstruate before her imoaziri rites had been performed was not socially recognized as sexually mature (i.e., she was not considered to be, or referred to as, a *barasi*, a woman capable of childbearing), although she was required to observe taboos specifically associated with menstruation (e.g., on planting taro, traveling in overseas canoes, and cooking food). Whether or not they were held in conjunction with her first menses, however, the rites remained the same.

According to Wedgwood, early in the morning of the first day of her imoaziri rites, a group of women gather at the girl's homestead to take her down to the beach to be ritually bathed. The group is comprised of close adult female paternal kin—the girl's real or classificatory father's sister

8 . 1   An *aine imoaziri* with her "followers" (*tagataga*) dressed in banana-
leaf skirts (*saresare*). Manam; Kuluguma Village, 1978. Photo
credit: Nancy Lutkehaus

(*poapoa*), her father's mother, and the wives of her father's brothers. On her maternal side, the girl's mother's brother's wife sometimes joins them, but her mother is always excluded. The group that gathers at the beach also includes three to five young girls close to pubescence, usually the girl's father's brother's daughters, who call the initiate *toka* (i.e., classificatory elder sister). Throughout the next seven to ten days, these young girls— referred to collectively as her "followers" (*tagataga*)—accompany the aine imoaziri wherever she goes (see plate 8.1).

The women and young girls lead the aine imoaziri down to the women's section of the beach, secluded from the view of men, where they have erected an arch of coconut fronds (*goara*) decorated with garlands of orange *poapega* fruits and sweet-scented leaves along a pathway or clearing near the beach. With her kinswomen holding her hands, the initiate is supposed to run toward the arch, duck underneath it, and continue straight into the sea.[5] The one arch that I saw was approximately five feet wide at its base and about six feet tall. It, too, was decorated with poapega garlands and fringe made from young coconut fronds. Böhm (1983:92) also describes construction of the arch and adds that the initiate is then supposed to "turn around and look at Manam [the volcano]. If she fails to do so, she risks becoming sick" (1983:89).

Once in the sea, women who have celebrated their first menstruation perform the rite of washing the girl, carefully bathing her face with the broad leaves of the *paru* tree, which are then cast into the sea. At this point, the tagataga are forbidden to touch her. Far from solemn, the women celebrate this part of the ritual with laughter, singing, and horseplay. After emerging from the sea, the women discard the baligo skirt the girl has worn as an adolescent and give her five or six freshly made banana-leaf skirts, the type of skirt worn by all Manam women when they menstruate. (The term in Manam for menstruation is, *saresare o'o'o*, "to put on a banana-leaf skirt.")

Women still wear these skirts, which they make very quickly by simply shredding (*sare*) large banana leaves into layers of fringe, hence their name saresare. When new, they look very attractive with their shiny green color and layered fullness. On each subsequent day, the initiate is given a new set of saresare after bathing, the old ones usually being thrown over the branches of a tree near the edge of the beach where they are left to shrivel, turning from bright green to parched brown. Although they have yet to menstruate themselves, the tagataga also wear fresh banana-leaf skirts to indicate their special role as assistants to the aine imoaziri.

On the first day, the aine imoaziri is also given a saltwater drink made with special leaves valued for their medicinal properties. This infusion is believed to protect her from the potentially dangerous effects of her new condition. From then on she is prohibited from touching her body on pain of sores appearing at the spot, or from directly handling any food, tobacco, or betel nut she might consume, lest she fall sick. Since these prohibitions prevent the girl from scratching herself, an aine imoaziri is given two wands—sticks about sixteen inches long from which the bark has been peeled—with which to scratch herself. In order to eat her food, she must use a special, long-handled spoon or metal spoon, and cigarettes and betel nut are prepared and handed to her on a special holder. It is her tagataga's duty to ensure she is supplied with tobacco and betel nut throughout the day.

Washing the initiate is a central part of the imoaziri rites (see Townsend, this volume, for a similar emphasis on first menstruation rites and washing). Morning and evening baths are administered daily during the entire ritual period. Böhm reports that if the girl was a *moaede* (i.e., the daughter of a tanepoa), she was also "washed" by the *embeki* flute spirit:

> For the first menstruation of a *moaide* [*sic*] a fence (*babari*) is made near the sea inside which the bamboo flutes are blown.... The *moaide* may walk around inside the fence, but other women may not approach her. She is washed by the men and since she has been near the spirits (flutes), she may not eat pork that day. The following day she is washed by the women and may eat everything again, but she cannot yet touch food with her hands. (Böhm 1983:89)[6]

In her notes, Wedgwood states that theoretically each day a different group of women, representing each of the separate clans in the village, should take the girl down to the beach in the morning to bathe her and wash her face with paru leaves. The evening bath is less ritualized since no paru leaves are used and often only the tagataga accompany the initiate. They give her fresh skirts and oil her body with a mixture of coconut oil and sweet-scented aduma plants to make her attractive. As Wedgwood's remarks at the beginning of this essay indicate, the tagataga also oil themselves and toss any remaining oil into the sea. If an initiate is betrothed, according to Böhm (1983:89), the groom-to-be has to remain in the forest during these first days of her rites:

> There, along with other men, he prepares a love potion. When the girl returns from the sea, on the third or fourth day, she is attacked by the men and the love potion given to her. Should she not want to take the potion, she will be forced to by the men. While in the bush, her future husband can only eat things which have been roasted—nothing that has been boiled. He may also not drink anything. Once

he has given the potion to the girl, he may then return to the village and eat everything again. After having received this love potion, the girl will not want any other man except for the specific one who gave her the potion. (Böhm 1983:90)

During the course of the imoaziri rites, the initiate is not confined to a special place, nor need she avoid being seen by other villagers. This contrasts with her future menstruations, when she should be seen as little as possible. She and her followers do little other than relax, eat, and talk. Like any menstruating woman, she is prohibited from the work she normally would be engaged in, such as gardening, child care, cooking, and collecting firewood and water. A girl's mother cooks and serves the first meal—usually stew made from taro, sweet potatoes, and fish—that her daughter and her companions eat after the initial ritual bathing. On subsequent days, other women in the village, beginning with her poapoa, should invite the initiate and her tagataga to their homesteads for similar meals.

On the evening of the first day of the imoaziri rites, women from the different clans in the village, but especially from the girl's own paternal clan, gather outside her house to sing *tang rang*, literally "crying songs"—i.e., mourning songs. Except for her father and perhaps his brothers, no men are present at this event. The initiate's father is expected to provide the visiting women with gifts of tobacco and betel nut as a gesture of his appreciation for their singing.

Depending upon the girl's status, the daily bathing, oiling, and eating continue for seven to ten days.[7] In the past, during this time, an aine imoaziri received cicatrices on her chest and back. The scarification was performed by a woman, preferably the girl's father's sister, and it was done out in the open, in the girl's homestead.

> On Wazike's back was the beginning of her scarification decoration—two short lines of parallel, vertical slits, just on the left shoulder-blade and sloping down towards the spine. They were rubbed with white ashes and she said they hurt rather, but she made no fuss about them.
>
> She seems to be pleasantly conscious of her being the center of interest just now. In Abonai's hamlet Mandau was busily making a waist belt for Wazike of red or brown (black) *karia*. (Wedgwood n.d., notebook 5:32)

Incisions traditionally were made with a bamboo knife, or, after contact, with a sliver of glass. Wazike's were made with a razor blade, the tool used for most of the operations I know about. Ash was then rubbed into the cuts to raise the scars as they healed. The designs were not usually completed in one sitting, and the process extended over several days or longer. Only women over the age of thirty still have the keloidal designs on their bodies. These women are proud of having bravely endured the ordeal of scarification. At present most Manam girls reject the practice, protesting that it is too painful.

On Manam only women were ritually scarified. Although youths were beaten until bloody welts appeared on their backs and chests during initiation, the scars were meant to be only temporary wounds that would disappear after they had healed. Women were also tattooed, though not in a ritual context. At present, girls are still often tattooed, having stars, initials, or other designs tattooed on their faces, arms, and hands. But tattooing and scarification are not analogous practices. The former is based on personal preference and an individual's ideas about feminine beauty, while scarification, like other forms of bodily mutilation associated with initiation rites, was a culturally prescribed practice. The marks it produced, although also considered attractive, were primarily significant as a permanent, public sign that a girl had celebrated her imoaziri rites and now was socially recognized as a sexually mature young woman, a barasi.

The last two days of the rites—usually days six and seven—are characterized by the oiling, painting, and adornment of the girl with special ornaments and her public presentation at a feast sponsored by her father. On the day before the feast, village men skilled at plaiting rattan ornaments (karia) are asked to the girl's father's homestead to begin plaiting a special belt and neckband for the aine imoaziri and arm and leg bands for both her and her tagataga. In the late afternoon, after the girl has bathed and the plaiters have left for the day, the girl's poapoa and other paternal female relatives gather at her homestead to prepare umuna, the congealed sediment extracted from cooked coconut oil. When the umuna is ready, the initiate's poapoa takes a wad of leaves soaked in the umuna and anoints the girl's shoulders, back, her lower back, and her palms and knuckles, pressing the leaves against her skin. Next, coconut oil siphoned from the container in which the umuna has been prepared is used to "oil" (dibureng) the girl's body and she is "painted" (didara) with taro, a red pigment made from the crushed seeds of the bix orellana bush, which the Manam frequently use for personal adornment (see plate 8.2).

Wedgwood notes that an aine imoaziri's oiling and painting was no solemn occasion, but, like the ritual bathing in the sea, an opportunity for joking and horseplay, especially among women related as in-laws (ia). This was certainly true of the event when I witnessed it. Participants gleefully "attacked" their sisters-in-law and, slathering them with swathes of red pigment, grabbed at

8.2   A father's sister (*poapoa*) decorating an *aine imoaziri* with
       dog's-teeth and shell ornaments. Manam; Oaia Village, 1979.
       Photo credit: Nancy Lutkehaus

their genitals and breasts, and inquired teasingly about the condition of their private parts, insinuating that perhaps they had been engaging in sexual intercourse. After the raucousness subsides, women and children take the tender leaves of taro plants and scrape the remains of the bureng from the bottom of the containers, the sweet oil being a favorite snack.

Umuna is a different substance from the scented coconut oil, aduma, applied daily after the girl has bathed, and is used as a prophylactic to protect her from harmful effects of her new condition (Wedgwood 1933:145). A woman performs a similar ritual anointing when she emerges from the birth hut (*boaruku*) at the end of her confinement, and both men and women anoint themselves with another substance after contact with a dead body. The Manam believe that these anointings release a person who has been in contact with some form of pollution—in the case of the menarcheal girl, her menstrual blood—from the dangers of contamination. Hence, the umuna rite is performed near the close of the imoaziri ceremony to purify the girl for a resumption of normal life. Aduma, in contrast, appears to be used simply cosmetically. The practice of oiling and painting the initiate, though also believed to have supernatural effects, is concerned with the girl's sexuality and beauty. Glistening skin, whether female or male, is believed to imbue an individual with power (*marou*) and make them especially attractive to the opposite sex.

The lightheartedness and gaiety of the girl's painting and oiling contrasts sharply with the more solemn rituals of the following day. This final day begins very early. After bathing, the aine imoaziri and her tagataga return to her homestead, where the men who are plaiting have arrived to finish their work. For several hours, the girls must remain almost motionless while the men plait the rattan into bands decorated with intricate designs directly on their limbs. Once completed, the bands are smeared with red pigment and sometimes decorated with shell disks and dog's teeth. The men who perform the plaiting are paid for their services with food, tobacco, betel nut (and, in the past, with dog's-teeth valuables). During their work, they are obliged to observe taboos against touching themselves. (According to Wedgwood, this prohibition is not related to their contact with the aine imoaziri but to the powerful magic associated with the plaiting of the bands.) With their task finished, they go off to wash in the sea, rubbing themselves with special leaves in order to release themselves from their prohibitions.

Meanwhile, the aine imoaziri's head may be shaved and she is taken down to the beach to be ritually washed one last time. In the water, she eases her way into a new rattan belt, soaking it to expand the freshly woven fibers. Upon emerging she removes her old banana-leaf skirts and is given a new adult women's baligo skirt to wear. Back at her homestead, fresh umuna and bureng have been prepared. Once again the initiate is anointed with umuna and, together with her tagataga, oiled and painted with the bureng and taro. At this time, she usually receives several more new skirts—gifts from her mother, poapoa (father's sister), and other female relatives—which she also puts on, one on top of another. After she has been oiled and painted, she is seated on a plaited coconut-frond mat (*regina*) placed in the center of the homestead, and the women decorate her with her family's heirloom shell valuables (*kuta*)—bands of cowrie shells, dog's-teeth necklaces and earrings, and a headdress of feathers and cowrie shells. If the initiate is a moaede, she will also wear at least one pair of curved boar's tusks (*zongo*), the insignia of the Manam tanepoa.

While the girl is being bathed and decorated, preparations are afoot in her homestead for the final feast in her honor. Ideally, her father will have provided a pig, which has been slaughtered and distributed to the households of the initiate's various kinswomen to be cooked. The guests at the feasts I observed included both men and women—consanguineal and affinal relatives of the girl's father, as well as neighbors. At this point in the proceedings, women were relegated to the background; after having decorated the aine imoaziri, they returned to their own homes to finish cooking. Later, bringing plates of food with them, they returned to the girl's homestead and gathered together in a group separate from the men.

Wedgwood's notes describe the final day of Wazike's imoaziri rites:

> I got up to Tsedam's place at c. 5 pm and found a considerable gathering there. Several *reginas* had been spread out just in the middle of the ground and on these were sitting Wazike heavily ornamented with dog's teeth, shell rings and *tsa* [bands of cowrie shells] and with her a number of small girls—I think those who previously had been going about with her in saresare [banana-leaf petticoats]. These, too were ornamented but not so heavily; most had on necklaces of dog's teeth and very short little *baligo*. Some had arm-bands with shell discs too. . . .
>
> For the most part only women were present—with of course the usual crowd of babies. . . . The wailing had been going on for a little while before we arrived and Wazike was eating with a spoon from a dish. . . . Tsedam, Kurum and another man which I did not recognize sat apart under a tree chewing betel nut and looking on. . . . For the rest the men kept strictly in the background. . . .
>
> I went to look more closely at Wazike and was invited to sit down. The child was not looking her best for her good looks were somewhat marred by her heavy ornaments. She had on an exquisite baligo, on her arms were many armlets with shell discs. Her ears

were completely hidden with dog's teeth as was also her chest and back. On her wrists and ankles were the regulation karia and on her right wrist was also a cuff of red plaited rattan decorated with cowrie shells. She held a slender stick c. 16 inches long, stained orange-red and with this she occasionally wiped away the tears which trickled down her cheeks. She might not touch her skin with her hands, but she pushed up the heavy armlets from time to time with her hands. She looked tired and a little doleful but occasionally produced a smile. (n.d., notebook 5: 49–55)

The imoaziri rites end just as they began—with the singing of mourning songs. This is a sad time for a girl, for if she is betrothed, as was often the case in the past,[8] she will have to leave her parents' home at the conclusion of the feasting and singing for the homestead of her future husband. There, on the following day, in a ceremony similar in form to the previous day's imoaziri rites, she will be married. If she is not betrothed, after the singing has ended and people have dispersed, the imoaziri rites are over, leaving her free once again to touch herself and consume food directly, and to take off her several skirts, remove her ornaments, and resume her daily chores. From now on, she will be referred to as a barasi or young woman.

To Wedgwood, the girl's tears appeared to be ritualized behavior expected of her at this time as part of the performance. However, from my own conversations with young women, it appears that this is also a genuinely sad time for them, as they must renounce their childhood and take on the added responsibilities of adulthood and, very often, motherhood soon after.

THE CULTURAL CONSTRUCTION OF GENDER: THE IMOAZIRI RITUAL AS TRANSITION

Following Van Gennep's (1960[1908]) classic tripartite division of rites of passage, we can identify the aine imoaziri's first ritual washing and her investment with the saresare as a rite of separation that marks the disjuncture between her former adolescent status of *aine mogangang* (prepubescent girl) and her new status as an aine imoaziri. The days she spends with her tagataga engaged in bathing, visiting, eating, sleeping, and relaxing, rather than in the normal female tasks of adolescence, form the rite of transition from childhood to adulthood. Her liminal status during this period is indicated not only by her withdrawal from normal female productive activities but also by the prohibitions she must observe against touching herself or any substance she may consume or bring into contact with her body.

The final set of imoaziri activities, public and social in nature, constitute the rites of incorporation that reintegrate the girl into the community as a mature young woman. At this point, she is no longer called an aine imoaziri but a barasi, a woman of childbearing age. She is expected to work at the same tasks as before but with a new sense of responsibility and seriousness of intent. If she is already betrothed, she soon will have to work alongside her mother-in-law; if not, her work habits will be scrutinized by others interested in whether she will make a good wife and mother. Rather than instructing the girl in the correct performance of her secular productive role, as occurs in some female initiation rites (Comaroff 1985; Maschio, this volume; Richards 1956), imoaziri rites emphasize the powerful, almost supernatural, aspects of her new physiological condition.

Other elements also characterize the imoaziri rituals as a rite of passage. For example, the entire ritual is framed at beginning and end by women singing tang rang, or mourning songs, a form of social recognition that accompanies various Manam rites of passage. In the past, women also sang tang rang during the final public stage of male initiation ceremonies, and they still sing them at funerals and when a girl is married. In the case of a girl's first menstruation, it is the loss of her childhood self and her rebirth as a sexual woman that is being acknowledged.[9] As residence after marriage is virilocal, the attainment of adulthood also foreshadows her imminent separation from, and loss to, her paternal clan relatives when she marries. The women who sing the tang rang come from various clans in the village, representing the village as a whole and signifying the community's recognition of the girl's new status. The singing also separates the public from the private aspects of the rites that take place on the beach, and demarcates those aspects of the ritual concerned with the initiate's social identity from those focused on her physiological maturity.

From another perspective, however, the imoaziri ritual can be seen as part of an ongoing process of transition rather than one of complete transformation. It is but one in a series of female rites of passage practiced between childhood and old age that are concerned with aspects of female gender and sexuality and with the transition from the asexuality of childhood to the sexuality of womanhood. In Manam, I would argue, male and female sexuality are not simply natural phenomena but states that must be *culturally* promoted and controlled. Both male and female rites of passage are believed to do more than just socially acknowledge and celebrate physiological changes; they are cultural means for regulating them. Following Marilyn Strathern's line of thought (1987b, 1988), I suggest that these rites are also concerned with promoting the transition of boys and girls from an androgynous state of childhood to the genderized, hence sexually differentiated, state of masculine or feminine adulthood (see Lutkehaus's introduction).

Boys and girls are categorized as social beings by the same term, *nimoalala* (naked), referring to the fact that, in the past, children often wore no clothes until the age of nine or so. Gender differentiation began when a girl was given her first short skirt and a boy his first bark-cloth belt. To mark the occasion, their parents might hold a small feast, a rite that separated the child from her or his former "androgynous" state. Until their breasts began to appear, girls would be referred to as *aine baligo eke teke* (one-skirt female).

For both males and females, the transition to adulthood involves various stages. For a girl, the process of becoming socially recognized as a sexually active female begins with the imoaziri, continues with the rite of marriage, but is not fully achieved until she has borne at least one child. Special rites mark the birth of her first and second child, and separate terms distinguish her from women who have given birth to three or more children and from postmenopausal women. The imoaziri period is literally transitional between the phases of asexuality and sexuality, a time when a girl is no longer a child but not yet socially recognized as a sexually active adult woman.

AINE SARESARE 'O'O'O: THE CULTURAL MEANING OF MENSTRUATION

The Manam consider the moon to be the cause of a woman's monthly menstrual flow. They say, "*Kalea ngasereki be aine saresare daoko*"; since *saresare daoko* literally means "they put on banana-leaf skirts," the phrase means, "When a new moon appears, women will put on their banana-leaf skirts" or, figuratively, "With each new moon, women will menstruate." The Manam also metaphorically describe menstruation as caused by the moon "striking" (*iundi*) women (i.e., "*kalea iundi be saresare dioko* [Böhm 1983:94]).

Women had—and still have—to refrain from certain activities, such as planting taro and cooking food, because in this powerful state they would pollute the food, causing the taro to shrivel and die and bringing illness to those who ate what they had cooked. For the Manam, pollution is a central concept associated with menstruation and a key to understanding the meaning of many of the ritual activities conducted during the imoaziri rites. But the notion of pollution and the danger associated with it does not simply have a negative valence. Menstrual blood is considered to be powerful, and thus when a woman is experiencing menstruation she must treat herself with care lest any harm come to herself or others. Hence, too, the frequent washing of the girl, which is performed to counteract the potentially dangerous effects of menstrual blood. The use of leaves from the paru tree to wash her face has supernatural significance. In Zogari village, there is a paru tree near the women's section of the beach that is normally "off-limits," forbidden to women because of the powerful spirit (*nanaranga*) named Paru that inhabits it. Paru affects the health and well-being of women, causing problems with menstruation, conception, and childbirth. Imoaziri rites are the only occasion I know of when the leaves of the paru tree are ritually used by women. By washing the girl's face with the leaves each day during the rites, it was believed that she would be protected from the ill-effects of Paru.

Since a girl's first menstruation is the physiological basis for the celebration of her imoaziri rites—whether the two events coincide temporally or not—she and her followers wear saresare, the requisite apparel for all menstruating women, throughout the rites. When the rites end, the girl abandons her banana-leaf skirts and appears publicly for the first time dressed in a baligo, the type of skirt traditionally worn by adult women. Significantly, although men borrow their wives' and sisters' baligo when they perform certain dances, there is never an occasion when it is appropriate for a man to put on a saresare.

MALE "MENSTRUATION" IN MANAM

Men, however, do "menstruate"; or, more accurately, they did so in the past. Although Wedgwood did not mention the practice in her published articles (thus, Allen cannot be criticized for stating that Manam men did not perform this practice), Manam men in their fifties and sixties told me that they used to perform a type of ritual blood-letting, which they describe as the male equivalent of female menstruation.[10] Like their male counterparts on the neighboring island of Wogeo (Hogbin 1970), male elders taught Manam youths during their initiatory seclusion how and when to "menstruate" ritually by incising their penes.

The blood (*dara*) expelled in female and male menstruation is considered to be a dangerous and polluting substance—both to the individual and to others. Thus, although women menstruate "naturally," while men had to learn to menstruate "culturally," individuals of *both* sexes had to be taught how to act during these vulnerable states. Both men and women must observe special taboos, such as the prohibition against touching themselves or any food, tobacco, and so on with their hands when in the polluted condition associated with menstruation. These same prohibitions are observed in conjunction with several other events—such as childbirth and death—in which dangerous bodily substances are considered to contaminate the individuals involved and the self.

The rite necessary to remove the ill effects of contact with dangerous and powerful substances is bathing. Thus, some form of washing is an essential part of any Manam ritual in which it is necessary to purify an individual who has come into contact with some form of bodily pollution, as through childbirth, the burial of the dead, or sexual intercourse. Usually, there are special leaves with which to wash, and sometimes special incantations to be said, particular to each type of event and its associated form of pollution. The cultural significance of these bathings becomes even more apparent when we consider other ritual activities in Manam.

Like female rites, Manam male initiation rites also had a symbolic dimension that emphasized the physical attractiveness and sexuality of the youths. As with feminine adulthood, masculine adulthood was not achieved at one specific point but was a gradual process extending over a period of years. As for women, this process recognized the birth of a young man's first child as an indication of his transition to a more complete stage of masculine adulthood.

The meanings of menstruation and sexuality expressed in Manam initiation rites do not refer solely to individual human physiology; they also symbolize processes the Manam believe to be associated with supernatural powers that people attempt to control through ritual in order to ensure their communal welfare. Thus, the female body and the process of human reproduction is a symbol of, and metaphor for, the social body (be it lineage, clan, community, or some other group that constitutes a "body politic") and for social reproduction.

Specifically, in Manam culture, there is a complementarity between men's and women's roles in production and reproduction that is expressed symbolically in the processes of menstruation and childbirth. On the one hand, women, once they have begun to menstruate, are able biologically to reproduce children and to produce food both for their families and for exchange. On the other, Manam men traditionally "reproduced" their large seagoing canoes in order to produce valuables through overseas trade. In a secret ritual, men dressed in women's skirts and pantomimed the "birth" of a canoe—metonymically represented by the halyard (*moaboa*), a phallus-shaped piece of wood attached to the mast. They would dance around the newly carved canoe holding the moaboa, which they called their "child," before ritually attaching it to the mast. Finally, they sailed to the mainland with the primary purpose of visiting their exchange partners (*taoa*) to obtain valuables such as dog's teeth, shells, and pig's tusks that, back home, produced power and prestige for themselves and their clans. The ability to attract many valuables was expressed in terms of seduction (i.e., *repeki*, "to pull")—a sexual metaphor also used to describe this economic and political process.

The differences in men's and women's productive and reproductive roles relates to the question of why male initiation rites were conducted for *groups* of youths, while female rites were primarily held for *individuals*. As Allen (1967) states, one of the primary purposes of *male* initiation in Melanesia was to separate the sexes and to incorporate initiates into an exclusive group, one which had its own ritual secrets. I have written elsewhere about the political and economic functions of the men's embeki cult in Manam (Lutkehaus 1982, 1984, 1995). Male initiation was the locus in which the true identity of the embeki spirit was revealed to youths and they were instructed in how to perform the embeki flutes. The very fact of exclusivity served to create and perpetuate the politically dominant position of men and the patrilineal authority of males. Women, on the other hand, traditionally had no collectivity similar to the men's house and the activities associated with the embeki. Although a woman could inherit property from both her father and her mother, she was considered a member of her father's clan until she married, at which time, after the exchange of bridewealth, she gradually became incorporated into her husband's lineage. Should she divorce and return to her parents' home, her children were considered members of her husband's lineage and were expected to remain with him. Thus, from a structural perspective, there was no parallel function to be performed by a solidary group of women, and hence no social need for collective, first menstruation rites for women. Rather, women's social relations were the networks of kinship relations they maintained with their consanguineal and affinal kin, most clearly represented by the exchange of food, both raw and cooked, that they entered into individually and as members of their husbands' and fathers' clans. It was these relationships that were symbolized by the women who bathed and fed an initiate during her imoaziri rites.

BARASI DIRUKUI:
FEMALE GENDER SYMBOLISM AND
SOCIAL REPRODUCTION

Each village on Manam celebrates an annual "New Year's" ceremony, which marks a time toward the beginning of the dry season in May and June when new gardens are planted. This ritual is called *barasi dirukui* (they wash the barasi) or simply "barasi." As I have already mentioned, the term "barasi" describes a woman of childbearing age, the usual connotation being a young sexually mature woman. However, it also refers to the cluster of stars we call the Pleiades.[11]

The barasi celebration, the third meaning of the term, is directly related to the second because its date is determined each year by the day when the Pleiades first appear at dawn over Manam's volcanic crater. As part of the barasi celebration, boys and girls are beaten ritually, and a set of stones, known as the barasi stones, are ceremonially washed. These activities exemplify cultural themes that occur also in female first menstruation rites and male initiation. At the crack of dawn on the first day of the barasi celebrations, every boy and girl who has yet to be initiated (i.e., all prepubescent children) are sent down to the ceremonial grounds outside the men's house, where slit drums have been set up on the ceremonial grounds outside. One by one, each child lays across the drum and is beaten by a man wielding a baton made from the stalk of a banana plant. This beating and the ritual singing that accompanies it are said to ensure the child's growth and strength in the coming year. Immediately afterwards, the child is supposed to go down to the beach and swim in the sea.

If we consider this aspect of the barasi rites in conjunction with the imoaziri rites, we see that both are concerned with insuring the health and well-being of the ritual subjects, the important difference being that the barasi rites are *not* segregated by sex. According to Manam belief, the barasi beatings imply that supernatural aid must be invoked to ensure the growth of children. Gender distinctions have not yet become culturally significant because, as explained earlier, sexuality has not yet become an issue of importance.

A second significant activity during the barasi celebration is the ritual washing of the barasi stones (in those few villages, such as Zogari, that have them). The distinctive features of the Zogari barasi stones are naturally formed holes in some of them. For this reason they are said to be female and are believed to be imbued with special power (*marou*). The stones are first washed by sprinkling them with water. They are then smeared with the red pigment known as taro, an act symbolically analogous to washing and painting a young girl for her imoaziri rites and marriage. It is important, I was told, to wash the stones each year in order to renew their power and insure that they will continue to safeguard the good health and prosperity of the village. The fact that this annual ritual is expressed in the idiom of "washing," and associated primarily with images of female sexuality and procreation symbolized by the stones and their washing, suggests that the Manam use the metaphors of menstruation, human reproduction, and growth to express other dimensions of fertility and social reproduction (see Hauser-Schäublin, this volume, for a similar equation of a newly menstrual girl and fertility stones among the Abelam).

CONTEMPORARY CHANGES IN THE IMOAZIRI
RITES: RANK IN MANAM SOCIETY

The main changes European contact has wrought in Manam initiation rites concern male initiation, which has all but disappeared, except in a very attenuated form. Similarly, imoaziri rites are no longer performed for most girls. They are now said to be held primarily for moaede, the daughters of tanepoa, as was true of three of the four cases I observed. The fourth was sponsored by a commoner father who lived part of the time on the mainland and had come back to the village during the Christmas holiday specifically to hold the public portion of his daughter's imoaziri rites. This man was clearly proud of his financial success and status as a government functionary. His sponsorship of the event was as much a means of publicly demonstrating his own success as it was a display of his adherence to custom. The gap between the actual onset of menarche and its celebration, moreover, may have widened: in only one of the four cases I observed did the imoaziri celebration coincide with the girl's actual first menstruation. Finally, scarification is no longer performed.

Apart from these changes in timing and universality, imoaziri rites seem also to have become more "secularized" in their performance. Their focus now is more on the final public celebration than on the preliminary private activity of the ritual bathing associated with menstrual pollution. Böhm's descriptions of Manam attitudes toward a menstruating woman and the behavior expected of her indicate that, in the past, menstruation was regarded with more fear and proscriptions than it is today. According to Böhm's (1983:91) descriptions, menstruating women had to leave through a separate exit built especially for them in their houses. Women told me that, while menstruating, they had to circumnavigate the village by separate paths to avoid running into men and youths on their way to the beach, where they would remain during the day. The Manam no longer construct these separate openings in their houses and, while they do not work in their gardens or cook while menstruating, they no longer have to use special paths to circumvent public areas or remain hidden from others—especially men—in the village.

In discussing the effect of social change on female initiation rites in Africa, Richards (1956:114) notes that sometimes initiation ceremonies were reintroduced into societies where they had lapsed because the individuals responsible for their organization saw a chance to earn money or prestige for themselves through sponsoring the rites. Although initiation rituals never completely disappeared in Manam society, this statement reflects the nature of their transformation. At present the imoaziri rites that are performed have as much to do with enhancing the status and prestige of the individuals who sponsor them as with traditional ideas about individual sexuality, social potency, and reproduction. This statement is underscored by the fact that the few cases of male initiation I heard of were held for the firstborn sons of Manam *tanepoa labalaba* (village chiefs). These rites included only the public ceremonies (although the embeki flutes were performed in private), the final stage of what had once been an elaborate and extended series of rites. The main change in the rites now performed is their "secularization" and, thus, a reduction in the complexity of the meaning both male and female "initiation" rites once had in Manam culture. Ironically, although it should now be clear why Allen was mistaken in his interpretation of the nature of traditional Manam initiation rites, his comments do describe the transformed and attenuated nature of the rites as performed on Manam today.

NOTES

1. Grateful acknowledgment is made to the University of Sydney for permission to quote from the Camilla H. Wedgwood Archives.

2. I thank Terrence Hays, Paul Roscoe, and an anonymous reviewer for their helpful comments on earlier drafts of this essay.

3. A further difficulty with such a distinction is that apparently several girls occasionally celebrated their imoaziri rites at the same time, even though the physiological act of menarche may have occurred at different times prior to the staging of the imoaziri rites themselves. For example, I was told about a collective set of imoaziri rites held in Zogari for the eldest daughter of the eldest son of the current village *tanepoa labalaba* (village chief) and a number of other young women who were members of her clan. These girls had already had their first menses, but their imoaziri rites were held for them at the same time as those for the chief's granddaughter.

4. During the period of my own research on Manam (1978–79, 1983, 1987), no complete female puberty ceremonies were celebrated in Zogari village, where I conducted my primary research. I was able, however, to observe the final public portions of ceremonies held for three girls in three other villages on the island, and in 1983 the final stage of an imoaziri celebration held in Zogari. The rites I observed included the last two days of the traditional rites—the weaving of rattan bands, the oiling and painting of the initiate, her decoration with dog's-teeth and shell valuables, the singing of mourning songs, and the feasting.

5. Wedgwood said she did not actually see this happen; due perhaps to the rough terrain, the girls were led up to the arch and then into the sea by the most convenient path. Böhm mentions another (or alternative?) ritual activity performed at this point:

> For a girl's first menstruation a young leaf of a coconut frond which is not yet open is taken and pulled apart. This separated leaf is then bound by the women between two trees, a little bit above the ground. Another frond is bound a bit above that in the same manner. The girl then has to jump over these two fronds and run quickly to the sea. (Böhm 1983:89)

6. It is unclear from Böhm's description whether he meant that the moaede actually saw the embeki flutes or not. Statements I gathered from both men and women claimed that even moaede were forbidden to see the flutes.

7. The number of days is determined in part by the number of clans in the village and by the status of the girl. If she is a moaede, women from all the clans in her village, as well as women from neighboring villages, will invite her to eat at their homes. If a girl is a commoner, she is less likely to be feted by women from all of the clans in her village.

8. Two of the four girls whose imoaziri rites Wedgwood witnessed, and one of three that I observed, were betrothed.

9. On the nearby island of Wogeo, the mourning of the "death" of a girl's childhood self is even more explicitly expressed in her initiation ritual. At one stage, women take the skirt she wore as an adolescent and, pretending that the skirt represents the girl herself, perform a mock burial with it (Hogbin 1970).

10. Due in large part to pressure from SVD missionaries, who felt the practice encouraged masturbation, Manam men gradually abandoned the ritual performance of penis incision (K. Böhm, pers. comm.).

11. Although the stars comprising this group are anthropomorphized, they are not all considered female.

9

MARRIAGE AS THE MODEL
FOR A NEW INITIATION RITUAL

Lorraine Sexton

In the early 1960s, a grassroots woman's movement known as *Kafaina* sprang up in the Chuave area of the Simbu Province of Papua New Guinea (Warry 1986).[1] Within ten years, it had spread to Goroka in the Eastern Highlands, where it became known as the *wok-meri* (women's work/enterprise) movement. In the mid-1960s, the wok-meri movement reached the Daulo people who live on the eastern slopes of the Daulo Pass in the Asaro Mountain Range, Eastern Highlands Province.[2] Here, it comprises today a network of small women's groups that save and invest money and engage one another in ceremonial exchanges. Elsewhere (Sexton 1986), I have interpreted the movement as a collective effort by women to bring about changes in their socioeconomic status and in the cultural definitions of gender roles. Through the politics of the movement, women endeavor to enhance their rights to control money earned through their labor in coffee production. Through its rituals, they conduct a symbolic discourse about changing gender roles, and they assume prestigious statuses, including that of ceremonial transactor (Strathern 1972), which previously were monopolized by men.[3]

The creation of ritual forms is a subject fascinating to anthropologists, but what is of particular interest about wok meri is the initiation ritual that developed to incorporate new groups of women into the movement. In this essay, I attempt to show how the structure and symbols of these rites enable us to address important questions about the nature of female initiation in the Pacific and the comparability of female and male initiation rituals.

The guiding metaphor of wok-meri initiations is marriage, both as the institutional context for social and biological reproduction and as an alliance between social groups. The rites also recapitulate other major transitions in a woman's life, including birth, menarche, courting, betrothal, and, in particular, parturition. What is intriguing is that betrothal and parturition should be striking foci of ritual attention, while menarche, which in "real" life is marked with elaborate ceremony, is not. Although it may appear contrary to focus on the less conspicuous elements of a ritual form, this relative lack of emphasis on menarche in wok-meri initiation leads me to two interesting conclusions. First, it suggests that a girl's menarche celebration should be interpreted not as a discrete ritual event but rather as one of a series of rituals, including courting parties and the betrothal ceremony, that gradually transform a girl into a married woman. This analysis suggests a second important conclusion: "initiation" rituals for adolescent males and females have different goals and are not functionally equivalent rites of passage.

DAULO MENARCHE RITES

Traditionally, the Daulo people held rites of passage for both adolescent males and females.[4] Informants' accounts indicate that male rites were quite similar to the collective rites of the Gahuku Gama, described by Read (1952, 1965, 1984). They were discontinued following missionization in the 1950s, but menarche rites continue to the present. These days, some men say that these, too, should be abandoned as un-Christian, but most people seem to regard them as a joyous event.[5] In fact, modified menarche rites were held during a school holiday for female students who were likely to be at boarding school when they began to menstruate.

Traditional Daulo menarche rites follow a pattern familiar in the ethnographic literature: they are similar to rituals described for the neighboring Gururumba (Newman 1965), Gahuku Gama (Read 1965), and Simbu (Ross 1965; Whiteman 1965). When a girl begins to menstruate for the first time, she enters a house in which she will reside for several weeks. Unless she is a first child, she usually will be secluded inside her parents' house (traditionally her mother's house). Perhaps because a first child is more polluting than later offspring (see Meigs 1984), however, a daughter who is a first-born will be secluded in the house of a lineage member. Her parents cannot visit her during her confinement, and she delays her return home for a couple of months after the completion of the rites.

Informants' estimates of the length of a girl's seclusion ranged up to three weeks: in the two cases I was able to document, one girl was secluded for ten days, the other for seven. Within the seclusion house, a compartment is built out of woven strips of reed, cloth, and/or newspapers, and except for trips to the latrine, the girl remains in this room for the whole period. She is placed under a number of restrictions familiar from the literature on the dangers of liminal states (e.g., Turner 1969; Van Gennep 1960[1908]). Whenever she leaves the house, for example, she must move slowly and cover herself so that no one will see her. If she looks at the sun or the sky, she is warned, she will die. She may not wash and, because she may not touch food, it is served to her impaled on sticks. To absorb her menstrual flow, she must sit on a bed of leaves. When her period is finished, these leaves are burned by an older woman, and the direction in which the smoke travels is said to indicate the community of her future husband.

The girl is accompanied through the ritual by a few friends who have already reached menarche. In the evening, many visitors bearing food also come and are likely to spend the night. It is my impression that different relatives are invited each evening—her matrilateral relatives, for example, or patrilineal relatives from different clans in the phratry. Except in the case of a firstborn initiate, the only people forbidden to enter the house are youths and girls approaching menarche, the latter lest the odor of menstrual blood hasten their first menses. With the single exception of the girl's father, any visitor may enter the compartment to greet her. The format of each night's activities is the same as for male initiation, the eve of betrothal, and, as we shall see, intergroup wok-meri meetings. People spend the night alternating between periods of song and discussion. The girl is instructed in her responsibilities in gardening and pig husbandry. She is urged to be responsible and cooperative. And because the Daulo associate heat with learning, the hearth fire in the house is kept hot throughout the night.

On the day her confinement ends, the girl is allowed to wash, and then she and her attendants dress in traditional ceremonial garb. Before she leaves the house, she pauses at the threshold, preparing herself to walk down a wooden plank placed in the doorway. A lineage brother of her father holds her hand aloft and makes a brief speech about her newly ascribed status as a marriageable young woman and her kinspeople's pleasurable anticipation of her betrothal. The girl then walks down the plank and steps onto a trail strewn with several kinds of red flowers. My informants denied that the color or type of flower have any particular significance, but Newman

(1965:77–78) interprets similar flowers used in an identical manner in Gururumba menarche rituals as symbolic of menstrual blood. In the Chuave menarche rite, Warry (1986) reports an interesting variation on the same theme: netbags, money, and leaves, sometimes from coffee trees, are scattered on the girl's path. According to Warry, these items are "associated with productivity, wealth and fertility" (1986:5). "This act reverses the prohibition that women must not walk over material items or food for fear of contaminating them and stresses the girl's fertility and her ability to bring wealth to the clan in exchanges that will revolve around her marriage" (ibid.).

The girl follows the trail of flowers and then walks around an earth oven to a seat facing the house. Next, a man from her lineage hands her festive food items, such as bananas and taro. He holds up a large piece of pork, on which she and her attendants are urged to bite, and then hands the meat to the girl, who proffers it to her guests in the same manner. This act is described as a sign that she can now assume the womanly duty of providing food.

Although clan agnates, phratry members, and the girl's uterine kin participate in the rituals associated with her menarche, the conduct of these rituals is essentially the responsibility of her lineage. Her parents play an important role in organizing the events and providing some of the pigs, but it is the father's lineage brothers, not the parents, who make the speeches and orchestrate the feast. By doing so, they emphasize their rights to be involved in decisions about the girl's future marriage, and some lineage mates are given highly prized cuts of pork to signify that they will contribute also to its costs.

The active role of lineage mates and the relatively passive roles of the girl's parents illustrate Fortes's (1958:10–11) statement about the function of "initiation, puberty and nubility ceremonies":

> In these ceremonies the domestic group's task of social reproduction is terminated. Having bred, reared and educated the child, it hands over the finished product to the total society. It is a transaction in which the power and authority of the politico-jural order as the final arbiter over the human and social capital of society are asserted. (Ibid.)

Of course, kinspeople beyond the household have had implicit rights in relation to the girl since birth but, as she now approaches marriage, their rights are publicly affirmed and activated.

As these data suggest, Daulo menarche rites do not stand on their own but rather are the first steps toward marriage, the beginning of a ritual process that reaches fruition in a betrothal ceremony held upon a bride's arrival at her groom's village. Although the groom himself is absent from this ceremony, his immediate family and members of his lineage and clan ceremonially welcome the girl, and, in traditional times, she then would embark on a long period of residence with her mother-in-law before the marriage was consummated.

Several similarities between menarche and betrothal rituals underscore the former's role as part of a complex of rituals that transform a girl into a wife. Upon arrival at the groom's village, for example, the bride walks over a flower-strewn path to be received by her husband's kin, an act I interpret as completing the journey she began when she trod a similar, flower-bedecked path at her menarche. Another commonality involves a symbolic display of sexual unity. Staked outside the house on the day the girl emerges from her menstrual seclusion is a spear from which is suspended a woman's netbag or miniature string apron. Similar displays are presented as she dresses in her village for her betrothal and at the end of the flower path that she traverses on her arrival in her groom's community. Just as the spear is a common symbol of maleness, so the netbag and apron are symbols of womanhood, and their conjunction in these displays is described as a metaphor for the union of male and female.[6] Finally, as she did at her menarcheal ceremony, the bride feeds people pork at her betrothal. In this case, as a sign of her incorporation as a wife into her husband's community, she feeds it to her husband's relatives: this act of food-giving signifies that the food-giver stands in a nonthreatening social relationship to the receiver and that the receiver trusts in the giver's good will. Some time later, the bride and groom publicly will share a meal she has prepared to mark the beginning of their conjugal life.

WOK-MERI INITIATION RITUALS

Wok-meri groups are autonomous savings clubs led by one or more "big women" (*vena namba*). Members begin by depositing their earnings from vegetable marketing and sales of freshly picked coffee cherry into individual accounts modeled after bank-passbook accounts. Over the next five to nine years, they increase their deposits by including larger sums of money from their households' parchment coffee income. Elsewhere (Sexton 1986), I have discussed internal group structure and the investments made by wok-meri groups after they complete this savings phase of activities.

Wok-meri groups are comprised of the mature wives of lineage mates (see also Warry 1986). They grow as a network through the establishment of dyadic links between groups of mentors and protegees who call each other "my mother" and "my daughter." An established wok-meri group seeks out

potential initiates to whom they teach the principles and rituals of the movement and with whom they then engage in a series of monetary exchanges.
This mentoring process is described as "bearing a child" (*yahipa gendaiye*),
and the daughter group in turn is urged to "bear a child" of its own—in
other words, become mentors to a new protegee group. For the members of
each group, therefore, the process generates a wok-meri-group genealogy of
"my grandmothers" (*auneho*), "my mothers" (*oneho*), "my daughters"
(*aruneho*), and "my granddaughters" (*nakuneho*). The critical tie, however, is
between mother and daughter group; indeed, grandmother and granddaughter groups may not come into direct contact with one another or know the
names of each other's villages.

In addition to being mothers and daughters, mentor and protegee groups
are also bride-givers and bride-receivers respectively by virtue of a symbolic
"marriage" that initiates the novice group into the wok-meri network and its
activities. In this "marriage," the bride-giving mothers confer on their bride-
receiving daughters a symbolic "girl" (*noiri*)—a meshbag full of coins that
often also contains a rubber doll dressed as a bride. Like a real marriage, a
wok-meri "marriage" requires payment of bridewealth—although, in contrast
to real bridewealth, wok-meri bridewealth does not include pigs and is eventually repaid to the bride-receiving daughters by the bride-giving mothers.[7]

The ceremony in which this "marriage" occurs is intriguing because it
recapitulates all of the major rites of passage of a woman's life: besides the
marriage ceremony, it also encapsulates courting-party ritual, puberty rites,
the betrothal ceremony, and a postbetrothal, "mourning" ceremony. The
"marriage" takes place once the wok-meri protegees have paid the last
installment on the "bridewealth" and have compensated the "bride-givers"
for the money they will receive in the meshbag "bride." Like all mother-
daughter group meetings, the "marriage" is a private, all-night affair and is
held inside the house of the mother group's big woman.[8] The assembled
group clusters around a hot fire, and the night passes in periods of song
alternating with mentors' instruction of their new protegees, an interesting
innovation being the use of parliamentary procedure for the instructional
portions of the activities.

The actual transfer of the bride occurs following a dawn meal. As the
gathering becomes hushed, the "bride-receivers'" big woman and another
member of the mother group approach the compartment where the "bride"
is kept. This is the room in the big woman's house where her wok-meri
group keeps its savings under her lock and key—a safeguard, both men and
women say, against theft by men. The two women approach at a slow pace,
their bodies bent forward and a single length of cloth covering their heads.

Awaiting them, in front of the compartment doorway, stand the big woman of the "bride-giving" group and a female helper. When the "receivers" reach them, the two "bride-giving" women remove the cloth from the pair's heads and place the handle of the meshbag "bride" around both of their necks, resting it against their chests. They then replace the cloth over the "receivers'" heads and, as the latter turn to leave the house, the "bride-givers" begin to wail in sorrow. The two "receivers" now crawl out of the house under the outstretched arm of a "bride-giver," who obstructs the doorway. Outside the house, women from both mentor and protegee groups, and the few men allowed to attend, gather around the two "receivers" to shield them from view, some protecting them with an arm around the shoulders. As the "receivers" and their protectors walk away from the house, however, they encounter several "bride-givers" and/or their (actual) children sitting on the path in mourning posture: their faces and bodies are coated with mud, and their persons are decorated with dried banana leaves. These "mourners" are said to have slept on the ground because they are distraught at losing the "bride." Before the "bride" and her entourage are allowed to leave the village, they must compensate the "mourners" with coins.

Once the "betrothal" ritual is completed, the protegees become full-fledged members of the wok-meri movement, privileged to participate in its activities. They are now empowered to seek out their own daughter groups and they can "wash hands"—i.e., exchange small amounts of money—with their mentors and with other, unrelated wok-meri groups—transactions that force all participants to acquire more money for counterpayments, thus powering further savings. On the occasion of the first "washing hands," the "bride-receivers"/"daughters" make a second bridewealth payment and again receive the meshbag "girl" in marriage along the lines described above. Although this second payment is structurally similar to a childwealth payment, informants explicitly call it a bridewealth payment, offering no explanation for why a second "marriage" should occur.

WOK-MERI INITIATION, MARRIAGE, AND FEMALE RITES OF PASSAGE

Although informants discuss the ceremonial conferment of the netbag "girl" in terms of marriage, the associated ritual also aptly recalls other major female rites of passage. To begin with, the all-night gathering resembles a traditional courting party, at which young people "turned head" (i.e., flirted), sang, and wore the flower wreaths that since have become distinctive wok-meri regalia. The hot fire and the periods of song alternating with instruction also resemble female rituals at puberty as well as the night prior to a bride's betrothal. Pursuing the former theme, moreover, the compartment in which the "bride" is secluded has intriguing similarities to a girl's menarcheal confinement room, both in overall appearance and in the materials and building techniques used in its construction. And while informants made no mention of these similarities or of menarche in reference to the compartment, they nonetheless stressed the fact that it was a locked room to which the father of the house has no access. In other words, the one person barred from the menarcheal enclosure is the one person denied access to the symbolic girl's compartment. The all-night gathering also shares similarities with an actual bride's betrothal in that the "bride-givers" instruct the "bride" in her wifely duties and mourn their imminent loss with tears streaming down their faces. They exhort the "bride-receivers" to "look after" the "bride," who will miss her family.

The acts following the "bride's" conferment on the "bride-receivers" recall the parturition expected of marriage. In positioning the meshbag "girl" on the chests rather than the lower back of the "receivers," for example, the "bride-givers" evoke the way in which newborns are carried in real life. In crawling out of the door after spending the night in a womb-like house, the "recipients" also physically enact a birth. And, finally, the solicitous gestures of shielding and protecting the women carrying the "girl" suggest the serene atmosphere of a house in which a woman has recently given birth, not the hurly-burly of a village in which a betrothal is being celebrated. Birth/rebirth are common themes in life-transition rituals, but in this case they also draw attention to the fact that, by giving a "bride" in marriage to the protegees, the mentors in addition have given birth to wok-meri daughters.

The mourning behavior that follows conferment of the "bride" recalls people's sorrowful actions at death rather than their behavior at a marriage. In this instance, however, it also recalls the *gambo amo* (they come wearing mud) ritual, when a real bride's family makes a ritualized visit to her groom's village a few weeks after her marriage. The ceremony is named for the mourning mud that the bride's mother traditionally wore on her face during the visit. Today, although the mud is gone, a mother still keens for her daughter, marking her loss to her family and her incorporation into her husband's community. Wok-meri "bride-givers" also make formal visits to the "bride" at her new home, though, on the occasions I attended, there was no evident keening, mud-daubing, or other mourning behavior.

Perhaps the greatest symbolic significance of the ceremony, however, attaches to the meshbag "bride" itself. By associating a meshbag, money, and an iconic girl, the assemblage conveys a complex symbolic message about the value of women. The meshbag itself is the primary symbol of womanhood: its vernacular name, *owo*, is also the word for womb; and a netbag is part of a woman's everyday dress, characteristically dangling from her head down over her lower back. As an important means of carrying children, garden produce, and piglets, it is also pregnant with meaning about women's social value; in fact, in her later life, the discomfort that she has borne in carrying these items in her netbag is honored when her husband and/or sons make a "lower back" payment to her patrilineal kin.[9]

The placement of a doll and money inside this symbol of womanhood emphasizes the importance of women for both physical and social reproduction: not only do they bear children, they also produce money through their labor in coffee gardening. These images are charmingly replicated in the coffee leaves that often decorate the unstrung bows that recipients carry to "lower-back" payments. As informants explicitly state, coffee leaves are a postcontact symbol of womanhood; by decorating the recipients' bows, they signify that just as a coffee tree's production of berries earns income for its owner, so a woman's reproduction of children results in childwealth and "lower-back" payments to her agnates.

Money being a necessary component of bridewealth payments, marriages could not be concluded and children's clan membership would not be secure without women's labor. By combining the bride doll, the meshbag, and money in the wok-meri initiation ritual, then, women call attention to men's dependence on them for reproducing society. In everyday conversation, women state their dissatisfaction with their lack of control over the production of their labor, and it is this message they symbolically reinforce and expand in the ritual.

CONCLUSION

Marriage is an appropriate template for wok-meri initiation because both rites of passage establish links between social groups. By transferring rights over a bride's sexuality, reproduction, and labor from her own to her groom's agnates in return for bridewealth and the promise of a series of future payments, real marriage sets up (or reaffirms) a tie between two independent sociopolitical entities. And by transferring rights to a symbolic bride's reproductive potential—the power to "give birth" to a new group of protegees—in return for the payment of bridewealth, wok-meri initiation sets up a link between two groups that autonomously save and invest capital. This parallel is extended in the metaphor used to talk of a protegee group's industriousness: the symbolic bride is said to tend her garden carefully.[10]

While the highlight of initiation is the betrothal, the ritual also encapsulates all the stages of a woman's life. I can only speculate on why this is the case, but by recapitulating the female life cycle, the rite seems to call attention to women's critical importance to culture and society. We have seen how the symbolic combination of "bride" doll, money, and netbag dramatizes the irreplaceable contribution that women make to physical and social reproduction. But I suspect, in addition, that through the wok-meri rites women ritually promote the growth and strength of the human population as men did formerly in male cult activities. Moreover, women ritually claim control over their own lives by reenacting them as if men were peripheral: no fathers are involved in generating wok-meri offspring, and these offspring are all daughters.

The presence, but lack of prominence, of menarche in wok-meri initiation also raises the possibility that we should reevaluate the meaning of menarche rites among the Daulo people. The ritual elements shared by menarche and betrothal rites suggest that the former does not stand on its own as a discrete rite of passage. Rather, menarche rites are part of a larger complex of ritual activities that culminate in the betrothal ceremony, just one in a series of steps by which a girl is transformed into a wife.

This altered perspective on menarche suggests that we not consider adolescent female and male initiation among the Daulo as functionally equivalent rites of passage. A detailed analysis of Daulo male rites are beyond the scope of this paper, but certain critical differences deserve highlighting. The male rituals were concerned with forging relations among male agnatic kin. They were intragroup, centripetal events that drew initiates away from their scattered, individualized attachments to mothers and pulled them together into the communal life of the men's house, opposing them to women and to men outside the clan or phratry. In contrast, menarche rites are part of a centrifugal process that eventually propels the girl into a new community to forge new ties. The lineage as a corporate group publicly affirms its rights in the girl's marriage, and the speeches made by her lineage elders explicitly celebrate her nubility and the role of her future marriage in linking her clan to beyond the phratry.

These contrasting aspects of adolescent rites of passage for females and males also may bear on their historical fortunes. The male rites shared essential, male political concerns that were also expressed in other male cult activities and in warfare. As these concerns have faded in the historical era, however, male initiation has passed from the scene. By contrast, marriage continues to thrive as the institution that connects sociopolitical groups. Concomitantly, menarche rites, which are integral to the process of creating marriageable young women, also endure with few challenges.[11]

NOTES

1. I thank the National Institute of Mental Health for supporting fieldwork in 1976–78 through a predoctoral fellowship and grant, and the Institute for Applied Social and Economic Research and the Programme Division, UNICEF, for funding my research in 1980–81. As always, I am grateful to Daulo people for their gracious and good-humored participation in the research. I would also like to thank Dan Franz Bauer, Terence Hays, and Marilyn Strathern for their helpful comments on earlier drafts of this paper.

2. In addition to data I gathered among the Daulo, I was able to extend my research on wok meri eastward into Goroka and westward to Watabung. I also exchanged research visits with Wayne Warry and Leeanne Greenwood, who were working in Chuave.

3. In the Kafaina movement of Chuave, extending women's political participation is also an objective (Warry 1986).

4. For present purposes, I include rites held for adolescent males, adolescent females, and wok-meri protegees under the rubric of initiation rituals. For a wide range of definitions of initiation see, for example, Allen (1967), Brown (1963), La Fontaine (1985), and Schlegel and Barry (1980); for a discussion of these definitions, see Roscoe's conclusion (this volume).

5. This positive attitude toward menarche rites among most Daulo men and women contrasts sharply with the resentment expressed by Chuave women who, according to Warry (1986:12), "regard [menarche rites] as antiquated, unjust and perpetuated at the insistence of men."

6. At one menarche ritual I observed, a one kina coin also was displayed with the spear and netbag to connote the anticipated bridewealth.

7. The economic importance of this "marriage" lies in the benefits that both groups receive from the bridewealth obligations: this capital can be invested; and, because the same banknotes and coins making up a wok-meri loan may not be used to repay it, the bride-givers have an incentive to earn and save "new" money.

8. The only daytime, public wok-meri event is the ceremony known as *aneno kuiyono*, "we wash hands," at which several groups from the same village

jointly conclude their years of capital accumulation and announce the amounts they have saved.

9. This concatenation of meshbag and coins, and the Daulo use of coffee leaves to symbolize women's production of wealth, recall Warry's (1986:5) description of the path along which the Chuave girl emerges from seclusion at menarche. Among the Chuave, however, the netbag is an ambivalent symbol of womanhood: unlike the Daulo, they have separate words for "netbag" and "womb"; and female witches are said to endow unsuspecting women with the power of witchcraft either by touching their skin or giving them netbags (Warry 1986:6).

10. The obligations to pay the second bridewealth and to take part in smaller, less formal exchanges with their mentors are powerful incentives for the protegees to earn and save money.

11. My analysis of this point owes a large intellectual debt to Marilyn Strathern (pers. comm.).

Part V

CONCLUSION

10

"INITIATION" IN CROSS-CULTURAL PERSPECTIVE

Paul B. Roscoe

Initiation has fascinated anthropology from the discipline's earliest days.[1] Among the details of English burial mounds and African skulls that regaled readers of the *Journal of the Ethnological Society of London* in its very first year, for example, was an account of the exotica of Guianan male and female initiation (Schomburgk 1844:269). Few volumes of other early anthropologica were without similar accounts of how, among "rude tribes," boys were relieved of eye-teeth or girls paraded through villages after their circumcisions. Not until the 1860s, however, did *initiation* become the common term by which anthropology recognized such practices. Since then, the phenomenon has come under increasing scrutiny, generating numerous theories concerning its form, content, and variable emergence among the societies of the world.

These theoretical musings are distinctive in two ways. First, initiation has attracted considerable attention from comparative anthropologists, and, consequently, to a degree exceeded by few other human institutions, initiation theory has been shaped by cross-cultural comparisons, be they informal surveys of a few regional neighbors or formal statistical analyses of worldwide samples. The attraction of initiation for comparativists lies in its variability. Initiation appears here but not there; it is elaborate in some places yet almost perfunctory in others; it involves circumcision in some communities but other ordeals, or none at all, elsewhere; and so on. Relative to rites that seem more universal and uniform, such as those attending birth, marriage, and death, therefore, initiation holds forth greater promise that comparison will illuminate antecedent explanatory conditions.

If initiatory theory has been powerfully shaped by cross-cultural comparison, its second distinctive characteristic is its male focus. Debates about initiation have been primarily debates about male initiation. With too few exceptions, female initiation is either ignored or treated as an analytical afterthought, something to be fitted into theoretical molds forged from studies of male initiation. Young's (1965) analysis of female initiation fits effortlessly alongside his analysis of male rites, for example, but he frankly admits (1965:1) that the study began as a reinterpretation of male initiation and was later extended to encompass female initiation. Likewise, although Bettelheim's (1962[1954]) well-known work on the psychoanalytic significance of initiation purports to embrace both male and female rites, less than 10 percent of its pages are devoted to "girls' rites," and their treatment is clearly an extension of his analysis of male rites. What, then, emerges when the focus of attention is shifted to female initiation? In this concluding essay, I explore some implications for initiatory theory in general and the comparative study of initiation in particular.

INITIATORY THEORY AND FEMALE INITIATION

Theories of initiation have varied with the times. To borrow Young's (1965) useful terminology, most early theorizing on the subject can be conveniently divided into sociogenic and psychogenic approaches. The sociogenic approach, heralded in Van Gennep's (1960[1908]:13) *Les rites de passage*, casts initiation rites as responses to social imperatives, in particular those provoked by integrational, demographic, or subsistence exigencies. In Radcliffe-Brown's (1948:276) view, for example, they were the means by which society recognized and legitimated a child's change of status to an adult. For Read (1952), to give a Melanesian example, the *nama* initiation cult affirmed and expressed the enduring order of male relationships, portrayed as absolutes the social values underlying them, and indexed and maintained male dominance over females. More recently, La Fontaine (1985) has argued that initiation demonstrates the power of traditional knowledge and legitimizes a continuing social order.

Psychogenic arguments, by contrast, portray initiation rites as functional or expressive responses to psychodynamic tendencies within human minds.

Sociogenic arguments also saw links between initiation and psychology. Radcliffe-Brown (1948:276, 1956:146), for example, believed that the taboos, ordeals, and solemnity of initiation taught initiates self-control and communicated the seriousness of life and its duties. The difference between the two views is in the causal arrows. In the sociogenic view, social imperatives are the "cause" of initiation, and its psychological entailments are simply consequences of these imperatives. In the psychogenic view, however, psychology is cause as well as consequence. Thus, initiatory practices are warnings against psychodynamic inclinations to parricide and Oedipal incest (Bonaparte 1953; Daly 1950; Reik 1946; Róheim 1969[1945]); means of actually or symbolically mastering conflicts generated by the conjunction of pre-Oedipal cross-sex envy and the role society expects of the individual (Bettelheim 1962[1954]); or symbolic reactions by males to their envy of female procreative ability and the mother-son bond (Hiatt 1971).

Perhaps the most influential critical response to these approaches was a protest that initiation could not be reduced to a "single set of circumstances," be these social-structural, material, psychodynamic, or whatever (Norbeck, et al. 1962:482; see also Kennedy 1970:189–190). Some scholars therefore suggested that both sociogenic and psychogenic causes are implicated in initiation. In Murphy's (1959:97) view, "the stuff of the unconscious tends to be expressed in cultural symbols where it serves some function in terms of social structure" (for a Melanesian example, see Allen 1967). But the more lasting legacy was a willingness to grant a more complex, multicausal nature to initiation—to allow that a particular initiatory sequence may "do" several things at once, or that superficially similar rites in different communities may "do" different things (e.g., Keesing 1982; Lincoln 1981). One senses in this development some despair at the theoretical intransigence of the phenomenon, but it cleared the way for less ambitious probings of selected aspects of initiation. Many have been hermeneutic—for example, Boddy's (1982, 1989) detailed analysis of how Nubians view the womb as a house of childbirth and female circumcision and infibulation as symbolic acts that emphasize and embody the essence of femininity: uncontaminated, morally appropriate fertility (see also Talle 1993). In Melanesian studies, Lindenbaum (1972) has examined how initiation regulates population; Poole (1982) has analyzed how it transforms person, self, and body; and Gelber (1986:35–39) has argued that it buttresses and justifies male domination and undermines female feelings of efficacy. A few, ambitious treatments have explored initiation complexes along several dimensions simultaneously (e.g., Herdt 1981, 1987; Keesing 1982; Tuzin 1980).

As noted earlier, both the ethnographic and theoretical literature on initiation is tilted significantly toward male initiation. As the essays in this volume help demonstrate, this has masked some serious theoretical problems. The common assertion that initiation is a kind of socialization, for example, can be comfortably sustained when the focus is solely on male rites, but it becomes problematic when extended to female initiation. As Strathern pointed out at one of the sessions from which this volume emerged, there are many societies in Highland New Guinea where males are initiated but not females. Thus, "if we regard initiation ritual as having a socializing function, then we are faced with the fact that Highlands boys need to be socialized where girls do not, or at the least that what takes place for girls is of a very different order" (1987b:7).

This criticism is not necessarily relevant to psychogenic arguments. If, for example, initiation serves to "sever" males psychologically from the realm of women and children (e.g., Whiting, et al. 1958), then there is no reason to expect the presence of female initiation. But psychogenic arguments run afoul of other difficulties. On the one hand, if initiation "breaks" young men out of the domestic sphere, how are we to explain the presence in many societies, including some represented in this volume, of female rites that can be just as plausibly dubbed "initiation"? On the other hand, if initiation rituals are functional or expressive responses to universal psychodynamic tendencies like cross-sex envy, why do we find only male initiation in some societies, male and female initiation in others, and only female initiation in yet others (Schlegel and Barry 1980:699)?

A second drawback to focusing on male initiation is that it peripheralizes the social significance of female ritual life, and this is surely a mistake. Among many peoples of the world, it is common for ritual actions in male initiation to be compared with women's bodily accomplishments (Strathern 1987b:2). Initiates and initiators often are said metaphorically to menstruate and/or give birth to new "men"—a theme that can spill over into other cult activity, as in Manam and Murik where men secretly "give birth" to canoes (Barlow, Lutkehaus, this volume). In the past, such activities have been interpreted as products of cross-sex envy (Bettelheim 1962[1954]), homeopathically based attempts to control female resources (Langness 1974), and the like. But, as Strathern (1987b) points out, it seems rather that the female body and the processes of human reproduction are symbols of, and metaphors for, the social body and social reproduction. If this is so, then in all probability what is done to the female body in female initiation is at least as important, if not more so, than what is done to males in male initiation.

This seems to be the case with the Rauto (Maschio, this volume). Although Melanesian male initiation frequently is viewed as the expressive focus of a people's worldview or of their existential and ontological questioning (e.g., Leenhardt 1979[1947]; Newman and Boyd 1982; Tuzin 1980), the Rauto express these themes instead in female initiation. Like many Melanesian societies, they present pictures of their world in the category of the person, but what is of theoretical and ethnographic note is that they see this world in the person not of a man but of a big woman and articulate this idea during the course of female puberty ritual. As Brigitta Hauser-Schäublin (this volume) demonstrates in her comparison of Abelam and Iatmul ritual life, female initiation also can be the key that unlocks other aspects of male cult activity. Abelam male cult life centers on two complexes: male initiation and the long-yam cult. In the past, analysts of Abelam life have construed the long-yam cult as phallic but, in a subversive analysis, Hauser-Schäublin makes the case that the cult's core symbols are female, not male. Moreover, she implies, it is the yam cult rather than male initiation that forms the real male counterpoint to female initiation.

To judge by other essays in this collection, for example, shifting the focus toward female initiation also reveals a striking ritual theme centered on gender complementarity. Among the Yangoru Boiken (Roscoe, this volume), a series of ritual *wala* displays and performances in the course of female initiation appear symbolically to integrate male and female in a way that reflects a politico-ritual emphasis in this society on gender complementarity. Rauto female puberty ritual similarly symbolically conflates male and female realms to espouse the amalgam of male and female powers as an ideal of humanity (Maschio, this volume). These themes are in striking contrast to the misogynist streak commonly reported of male initiation, and they raise questions about whether themes of gender complementarity are limited to female initiation—a means, perhaps, of mystifying or disguising male dominance—or whether they have been overlooked or misinterpreted in studies of male initiation (see Herdt 1987).

Finally, when female rites are given the sort of attention they deserve, they tend to be fitted into analytical frames developed primarily to explain male initiation. The essays in this collection, though, tend to corroborate Schlegel and Barry's (1979, 1980) cross-cultural findings: female initiation does *not* always do for females what male initiation does for males (see also Sexton, this volume). Not only do female rites tend to have different structures and contents, they also can have different ostensible goals (Hays n.d.:18). The further problem is that, by casting female initiation as merely a sex-specific equivalent or reflex of male initiation, the possibility is excluded, a priori, that the two are interrelated and that analysis should focus as much on this complex whole as on its constituent parts. Such a focus might reveal that, far from doing for males what female initiation does for females, male initiation instead does for females what female initiation does for males.

Alternatively, male and female initiation may achieve some of their ends together, not separately. It has been remarked, for instance, that the putative products of initiation ritual—fully empowered young men and women—are frequently exemplars of male and female. What is less often noted is that the conjunction of these products may create an equally powerful construction of gender relations. Among the Yangoru Boiken (Roscoe, this volume), as noted above, gender complementarity was thematically stressed in female initiation. But the same theme was apotheosized in the conjunction of qualities supposedly instilled by male and female initiation: not only did the rites produce exemplars of masculinity and femininity, they presented these exemplars as complementary in a marital pair's achievement of renown. Among the Murik (Barlow, this volume), male and female cult initiations "do not merely define and focus separately the means to power for each gender. Ultimately, they portray a dynamic interdependence among men and women, premised on personhood as a unitary concept."

INITIATION AND COMPARISON

As different as theoretical approaches to initiation have been, all share a common, core assumption: initiation has some kind of transcultural existence in the sense that locally variable, "surface" manifestations share a fundamental identity at some "deeper" level. This assumption is seldom ever explicit, but it occasionally surfaces in Linnaean metaphors. Keesing (1982:5), for example, describes New Guinea male initiation rites as comprising "species of a genus distinctive in important ways from those in other parts of Melanesia and other regions of the tribal world." In Levinson's and Malone's (1980:11) terms, cross-cultural analysis of initiation assumes that we are dealing with limes, oranges, grapefruits, and tangerines, and properly calling them all citrus fruits. Without this sort of assumption, of course, the comparative study of initiation would be moot. Just as biologists compare different species to illuminate organic function, specie morphology, even the processes of biological evolution, so comparativists presume, at least implicitly, that comparing the types of a social institution such as initiation will illuminate the structures and processes of the social world.

As Holy (1987b) notes, however, in an extremely useful summary of developments in comparative anthropology, this analytical strategy is increasingly at odds with the general direction of modern cultural anthropology. Comparative anthropology, especially holocultural (i.e., global) comparison, Holy argues, has usually taken its data to be "social facts," variables such as descent type, political structure, and initiatory form that are considered "objective" and hence unproblematic. The problematic issues are the generalizations generated and tested with these data. But to modern "interpretative anthropology," as Holy dubs it, this puts the cart before the horse. Unlike the phenomena of the natural world—oranges, grapefruits, and the like—social phenomena are not "objective facts": they are constituted by meaning; meaning is culturally relative; therefore social phenomena are incomparable. Where comparativism sees data as unproblematic and generalization as problematic, interpretative anthropology sees description of the data—actors' meanings, experiences, and views of reality (1987b:7–10)—as problematic and the comparative exercise as moot. Consequently, modern anthropology has become "an interpretative humanity concerned with cultural specificity and cultural diversity, rather than . . . a generalizing science" (1987b:8).

Holy perhaps overstates the degree to which modern anthropology has repudiated comparison. Cultural ecologists and Marxist and feminist anthropologists, to name just some subfields, continue to use comparative surveys to try and illuminate their arguments. Still, as the label "interpretative anthropology" implies, Holy aptly summarizes mainstream anthropology to the extent that it is underwritten by symbolic and semiotic viewpoints. To these schools, cross-cultural comparison is premature at best and misplaced at worst because it may think it is taking limes, oranges, and tangerines and calling them all citrus fruits when, in fact, it is taking apples, oranges, and melons and calling them all apples. Instead of fitting analytical categories to phenomena, it takes phenomena and tries to fit them to analytical categories. It takes what *we* mean by *family*, *initiation*, or whatever and artificially maps them onto the features of other cultures in a sort of anthropological Rorschach test.

This sort of critique has been launched with particular effect against anthropological notions such as "kinship," "marriage," "descent," and "incest." Such terms are "very handy in all sorts of descriptive sentences, but worse than misleading in comparison and of no real use at all in analysis" (Needham 1971:7–8; see also Schneider 1976:4, 1984). Similar critiques have been offered of ritual institutions, including witchcraft (Crick 1976:109–129), totemism (Lévi-Strauss 1963), and cargo cults (Lindstrom

1993; McDowell 1988). Thus far, initiation has escaped this deconstruction-ist attention, but the findings presented in this volume reveal that indeed theoretical preconceptions about initiation have been imposed on the data in the course of comparative analysis. In particular, assertions that initiation is an institution distinguishable from puberty or menarcheal rites, and that it marks a transition from childhood to adolescence or adulthood, emerge as highly suspect.

A QUESTION OF DEFINITIONS

"If one wanted to be provocative," Magee (1975:50–51) observes, "one might assert that the amount of worthwhile knowledge that comes out of any field of enquiry ... tends to be in inverse proportion to the amount of discussion about the meanings of words that goes on in it." The point is a favorite with natural scientists, who can smugly compare the successes of their own disciplines, in which definitions are seldom controversial, to the limited progress of the social sciences, with their famously unproductive wranglings over terms like *magic, religion, ethnicity, caste,* and *class.* Surprisingly, students of *initiation, puberty rites, menarcheal rites,* and the like have managed largely to avoid such squabbles; they have done so, though, not because their terms are unproblematic but because they have largely avoided probing their definitions in the first place.

Historically, anthropological definitions of initiation have been entwined with Van Gennep's (1960[1908]) concept of rites of passage. Contrary to common assumption, Van Gennep never offered a formal definition of such rites. Instead, he characterized them rather loosely in terms of what he perceived to be their goal ("to insure a change of condition or a passage from one magicoreligious or secular group to another" [ibid.:11]), their function (reducing the "harmful effects" of such changes on the society and individual [ibid.:13]), and their structure ("the ceremonial patterns which accompany a passage from one situation to another or from one cosmic world to another" [ibid.:10]).

Thus delineated, of course, rites of passage cover an enormous range of activities, from frontier-crossing ceremonies, through harvest rites, to mortuary rituals. As British anthropology began to develop the structural functionalism incipient in Van Gennep's analysis, however, rites of passage gradually came to be subdivided on the basis of social functions attributed to their effects. One important change, La Fontaine (1985:27–30) points out, was to reclassify as *calendrical* those rites concerned with changes in the natural world, reserving the term *rites of passage* for those associated with human or social changes—"rites at the so-called 'life crises': birth, initiation, marriage, and death" (Gluckman 1962:3).

The more important legacy, however, was to smuggle into the classificatory exercise the Durkheimian, structural-functional thesis that ritual reflects and/or maintains the social constitution. This functional heritage has had two unfortunate consequences. The first was to dictate that rites only qualify as initiation if they are mandatory for all members of a sex (e.g., Brown 1963:838; Cohen 1964:102; Levinson and Malone 1980:207). Unfortunately, as the essays in this volume illustrate, such an assertion provokes a host of arbitrary conclusions. Among the Iatmul, for example, a few women occasionally were inducted in male initiation rites (Hauser-Schäublin, this volume). If, then, we accept that initiation is only initiation if it is mandatory for all members of a sex, we must conclude that these young women were not initiated even though the males accompanying them were. Or take the *imoaziri* rites of Manam Island (Lutkehaus, this volume). Nowadays, they are no longer celebrated for every girl, but only a few decades ago they were; do we therefore conclude that they once were initiation rites but are no longer? And what are we to make of the Rauto case (Maschio, this volume), where initiation *ideally* is mandatory but in practice some girls go uninitiated for lack of a solvent sponsor?

The second structural-functional legacy is the convention of assigning the term *initiation* to rituals involving *groups* of initiates and differentiating rites for *individuals* as *puberty rites, menarcheal rites, nubility rites,* and so on (e.g., Allen 1967:5; Cohen 1964:102–103; La Fontaine 1985:12; Wedgwood 1933:132).[2] It is this standard that makes female initiation seem so rare, since about three times as many societies practice group rites for males as practice them for females. Yet, again, an individual/group distinction leads to highly artificial conclusions. The Rauto (Maschio, this volume) initiate girls individually, in pairs, or in groups; conversely, among the Saniyo-Hiyowe (Townsend, this volume) and Mountain Arapesh (Mead 1940:422), boys can be initiated individually or as part of a group. Thus, to proponents of group-based definitions of initiation—but not apparently to the Rauto, Saniyo, and Mountain Arapesh—some boys and girls in these societies are initiated but others, of the same sex and subject to much the same ritual experience, are not. Supposedly, they are instead the subjects of qualitatively different rites—puberty rites, menarcheal rites, or whatever.

A group-based definition of initiation also artificially separates what, indigenously, may not be separate at all. Among the Yangoru Boiken (Roscoe, this volume) girls pass at menarche through individual *narandauwa* rites that, by a group-based criterion, would not constitute initiation. Yet the Yangoru Boiken draw an explicit parallel between these and the collective, *hworumbo* initiation rites once practiced for groups of adolescent boys. Later in their life, females went on to experience collective rites, also described as hworumbo rites, that by a group-based standard would be differentiated as "initiation" from their narandauwa "puberty" rites. Yet this analytical distinction was not reflected in indigenous perception: the later rites were viewed as processual sequels to the narandauwa rites, the total sequence being intended to advance females through successive stages of purity, sagacity, and capability just as were their male counterparts.

To complicate matters further, some scholars have added rather different meanings to the terms *puberty rite* and *initiation*. Allen (1967), for example, followed convention in reserving *puberty rite* for individual rites that emphasize puberty as an important event in the life cycle, and *initiation* for group-based rites. But initiation rites, he added, were also secret rites of entry into ritual or secular "associations." At the time, to make "initiation" turn on cult membership rather than life-cycle transition was to flout accepted usage, and it is debatable whether the reconfiguration was worthwhile.

The problem was his (1967:7) definition of *association* as "a discrete group of individuals who co-operate in certain activities, share common property and are conscious of their existence as an organized body." There are, of course, well-known difficulties in defining *group*, which Allen only compounded by using the term interchangeably with *category* (e.g., 1967:7). Applied to female rites, however, the definition becomes more problematic (cf. Keesing 1982:5). Among the Eastern Abelam, Manam, Rauto, and Yangoru Boiken (Hauser-Schäublin, Lutkehaus, Maschio, and Roscoe, this volume), some newly pubescent girls are differentiated from children of either sex by possession of secret knowledge (Rauto, Yangoru Boiken) or exposure to *sacra* or secret ritual acts (Eastern Abelam, Manam, Rauto, Yangoru Boiken)—acts that Allen (1967:6) sees as indicative of *initiation*, not puberty rites. In some of these societies, it is unclear whether postpubescent girls "co-operate in certain activities" or have any "consciousness of their existence as an organized body"—but Allen had no more precise information about many of the Melanesian rites he classified as "male initiation." In the case of the Yangoru Boiken, at least, there were no significant cooperative activities among women who had passed through the narandauwa rites, and it is doubtful that they were conscious of being part of an organized group as Allen construes it. But much the same would have to be said of initiated *males*. In formulating these questionable distinctions, Allen apparently intended to draw analytical attention to the importance of cultism in life-cycle transitions; his mistake was to use the terms *initiation* and *puberty ritual* to isolate this object of analysis.

Rigby (1967) and Richards (1956) add a different twist to the distinction between initiation and puberty rites. Whether or not rites occur at the physical event of puberty,

> Puberty can only become a "social fact" when the physiological fact is recognized socially, either at the time of its occurrence or at some later period. If the *rites de passage*, whenever they occur, do not refer to the physiological fact, then they are not puberty rituals but something else, such as initiation or circumcision rituals, although they often include both elements. (Rigby 1967:434; see also Richards 1956:52)

For Rigby, apparently, the primary "physiological fact" of puberty is first menstruation in females and first nocturnal emission in males. Thus, rites that make reference to these events—and only those rites—are puberty rites. All others, whether or not they occur at puberty, are something else—initiation rites, circumcision rites, or whatever. Since male rites refer to nocturnal emission far less often than do female rites to first menstruation, female puberty rites become much more common than male puberty rites and female initiation much rarer than male initiation.

Unfortunately, these stipulations are more complicated than they seem. They fail to specify what constitutes reference to, or social recognition of, the "physiological fact" of puberty. Must it be explicit informant statements that the rites are practiced *because* of, and are focused exclusively on, the physiological event? Or is it enough that some exegesis or symbolism seems to refer, no matter how incidentally, to the event? What should we make, moreover, of the many instances in which males are made to "menstruate" in their initiation (e.g., Lutkehaus, this volume)? To be sure, in Western terms, these practices hardly constitute a physiological fact of puberty but, in indigenous terms, "induced" penile or nose bleeding, not "natural" nocturnal emissions, may be precisely what signifies the physical event of puberty. Finally, it is difficult to see what grounds motivate Richards's and Rigby's definitional distinctions, for they provide neither empirical grounds nor clear theoretical justification to buttress it. Rigby suggests that female "puberty rites" announce the availability of marriageable girls to the local community, but this formulation encounters many of the same problems as the common definition that initiation marks a transition to adolescence or adulthood, to which I shall momentarily turn.

In sum, attempts to distinguish puberty rites, practiced mainly on females, from initiation rites, practiced mainly on males, offer no compelling empirical or theoretical reasons to justify the effort. This is not to deny that a sound distinction might be found, especially if more attention is paid to the emic significance of these rites. Sexton's finding (this volume)— that Daulo adolescent female and male initiations are not comparable because the former seem "centrifugal," designed to propel a young woman into a new community, whereas the latter are "centripetal," aiming to forge relations among male agnatic kin—may have much broader applicability (see also Townsend, this volume). Efforts to date, however, have produced no more than the kind of artificial constructs that deconstructionists take justifiable delight in exploding. At present, therefore, there seems little point in disenfranchising female rites from analysis as initiation rites by differentiating them as puberty or menarcheal rites. It is to draw attention to my use of the term in this broad sense that I have enclosed *initiation* in quotation marks in the title of this essay.

SHORN OF CONTEXT: INITIATION AND THE TRANSITION TO ADULTHOOD

Initiation is perhaps an unfortunate term for the rites commonly intended by this term because it presumes an initiation *into* something. This semantic gloss may be connected to initiation into freemasonry, for early observers frequently noted the similarity of these indigenous rituals to freemason rites, some even concluding they *were* freemason rites (e.g., Bonwick 1886:209; Daniell 1846:216; Miles 1854:26; Walker 1876:120). Whatever the case, it is now commonly assumed—to the point of being definitional—that what these rites initiate individuals into is adulthood. They mark and/or effect a transition from childhood to adolescence or adulthood (e.g., Benedict 1959[1934]:25; Levinson and Malone 1980:207; Morinis 1985:163; Schlegel and Barry 1980:698). A critical issue here is whether "the transition from childhood to adolescence or adulthood" is meant to apply emically or etically. Are the terms *childhood*, *adolescence*, and *adulthood* to be construed in indigenous or Western terms? And is a rite an initiation rite if it marks the transition from adolescence to adulthood for the *ethnographer* or only if it marks this passage for (at least some of) the people practicing it?

To my knowledge, no authority has addressed these questions explicitly, but it seems clear that the concepts were intended etically.[3] Van Gennep, as noted earlier, characterized rites of passage like initiation in terms not of indigenous statements or understandings but of analytical perceptions of

"ceremonial patterns," "activities," and "function" (1960[1908]:10, 11, 13).
Subsequently, structural functionalists subclassified these rites in terms of
analytically discerned social functions, while sociogenic, psychogenic, and
other approaches implicitly presume etic notions of adulthood and what is
involved in becoming an adult.

By incorporating etic ideas of childhood, adolescence, and adulthood,
ideas about initiation fall victim to the polysemic imprecision of these
terms: in Western perceptions, a young person can attain physiological, psychological, social, jural, and political adulthood at different ages. The usual
strategy, it seems, has been to assume a physiological definition, but this
runs afoul of two problems. The first becomes vividly apparent in those few
analyses that operationalize their terms, explicitly defining initiation rites as
certain types of rite occurring between specific ages, such as eight and
twenty (e.g., Brown 1963:838; Schlegel and Barry 1980:698). This device is
immediately vulnerable to the question: Why eight and twenty? Why should
identical rites conducted, say, at the age of seven or twenty-one be
excluded? The second problem lies in theories that use this definition to
explain initiation. Though the transition is defined in physiological terms,
these theories invariably assume also that it marks—indeed produces—
social, politico-jural, or psychological maturity. To be sure, in non-Western
contexts these dimensions conveniently might coincide; but this issue needs
to be established empirically, not assumed a priori.

What this implies, of course, is that etic definitions cannot help but presume certain emic interpretations. And to modern interpretative anthropology—especially deconstructionism—the problem with the etic approach is
precisely this act of presumption. It pays little if any heed to the actual
perceptions indigenes have of what initiation is and does, thereby assigning
a subsidiary status to meaning—a relegation that may or may not be justified in light of the evidence but cannot be resolved by presumptive fiat.
Unfortunately, once we begin to consider the emic frame, the idea of initiation rites as making adults or marking adulthood begins to dissolve. As
often as not, these rites are found to be deeply entwined with other rites
celebrated at other stages of life—so much so, in fact, that analytically
shearing them from this context becomes a highly artificial exercise.

Many societies, for example, practice "initiation" rites that involve entry
into multiple grades. Among the Murik (Barlow, this volume) and Yangoru
Boiken (Roscoe, this volume), rites for pubescent females and males are
indigenously recognized as but the first in a sequence that continues long
after the achievement of adolescence and adulthood, emically and etically
defined. In the past, scholars motivated by an etic perspective have dealt

with these later rites either by ignoring them (e.g., Whiting, et al. 1958), by defining as initiation only those rites practiced before age twenty-one (e.g., Brown 1963), or by distinguishing "adolescent initiation rites" from later rites and disregarding the latter (e.g., Schlegel and Barry 1980). Were they to confront the issue, however, as Strathern (1987b:12) points out, they would have to argue either that the later ceremonies are "boosters" for the first, or that the adult-making or adult-marking process in these societies continues throughout much of a person's life.

Nor is it just later ritual grades to which adolescent "initiation" rites may be emically linked: marriage ceremonies also can be implicated. Among the Saniyo-Hiyowe (Townsend, this volume), rites at menarche are viewed as important precursors to marriage, opening up negotiations on the bride's side by identifying who will be claimants to her bridewealth. Among the Yangoru Boiken (Roscoe, this volume), wealth exchanges at a girl's first menstruation are important precursors for the wealth exchanges at her marriage. Among the Daulo (Sexton, this volume), rites accompanying menarche begin a ritual process that only reaches fruition when a young woman undergoes a betrothal ceremony at her future husband's home. Manam islanders (Lutkehaus, this volume) perceive the rites practiced at a girl's puberty as, at most, a necessary condition for the transition to adult-hood; the sufficient—and apparently more important—conditions are rites practiced at marriage and first birth.[4]

Nor do marriage and birth rites exhaust "initiation's" emic ritual context. Among the Saniyo-Hiyowe, Townsend (this volume) argues, puberty ritual is mirrored antithetically in widowhood rituals that deconstruct, so to speak, the nubility and femininity constructed by puberty rituals. Among the Yangoru Boiken (Roscoe, this volume), the female initiatory sequence was ritually integrated not only with a woman's first intercourse and birth but also with the initiations of her children as part of a total process of matura-tion and ritual purification. Among the Babae (Fergie, this volume), public ritual is composed of three sequences: the *vevene* rites, which celebrate a woman's first childbearing experience and correspond most closely to tradi-tional notions of female initiation; mortuary rites; and *lukara* rituals, which transform the deceased's spirit from a named to a generalized ancestral spirit. As Fergie points out, each of these sequences is a rite of passage. But the total ritual corpus—the sequence of sequences—is also a kind of rite of passage, moving the individual through all of the culturally important dimensions and states of human existence.

These broader ritual connections are seldom reported of male initiation, and it is tempting to suppose that here, at least, is a fundamental difference between male and female initiation rites. Alternatively, however, male initiation may be surrounded by just as many connections, but these have been overlooked. Herdt's (1987:101–169) detailed description of Sambia male initiation, for example, makes clear that the fourth stage also constitutes the formal marriage rite, while the birth of a man's first child heralds the final stage, marking "the attainment of full manhood: fatherhood" (1987:167). Among the Yangoru Boiken (Roscoe, this volume), the male as well as the female initiation sequence is integrated with first intercourse, parturition, and the initiation of children. Among the Rauto (Maschio 1988), both male and female initiation are but part of a cycle of ceremonies through which notice is served that children are being readied to invest themselves forcefully in the social relationships and the spiritual and physical tasks of the adult world.

A focus on female initiation, then, renders visible what perhaps should hardly surprise us. As a life-cycle rite, initiation is frequently inseparable from other life-cycle rites, and divorcing it analytically from this extended ritual context may be an exercise in artificiality. Consequently, comparative work on "initiation" might be better served if it becomes comparative work on life-cycle rites as complexes. Given the attention devoted to male initiation, it is puzzling that this finding should emerge from a survey of female initiation. The reason may be the very feature that for so long has kept female initiation in the analytical shadows. So much more grand and dazzling than other rituals of the life cycle, male initiation rites may have seemed to exist in ritual isolation—set apart, and separable from, other more "mundane" rites of passage. So much dimmer by contrast, female initiation rites are more on a scale with other life-cycle rites, rendering their ritual interconnections more visible.

IN DEFENSE OF INITIATION
AS A TRANSCULTURAL CATEGORY

With respect to initiation, in sum, it seems that interpretative anthropology is correct: analytical categories have been imposed on the data and in inappropriate ways. But it does not necessarily follow that "initiation" has no validity as a transcultural category. Just as citrus fruit is a transspecies category with oranges, grapefruits, tangerines, and so on as its variable local manifestations, it remains a possibility that a valid transcultural category, "initiation," can be pinpointed underlying particular ritual manifestations. Because anthropological categories are incapable of fully characterizing a phenomenon in terms of necessary and sufficient features, moreover, does not thereby mean they are less valid than "natural" categories such as *bird*, *game*, or *citrus fruit*. As Mahmood and Armstrong (1992) note, findings in cognitive science now suggest that these "natural-kind" categories are equally incapable of completely defining their reference in terms of necessary and sufficient features. Rather, they appear to operate through "prototype features," features that "are not necessarily shared by all the members [to which the category is applied] but are shared by a substantial number of them, and weighed in virtue of how much they are shared" (1992:5).

Certainly, in comparing initiation, comparativists need to examine more rigorously the bases of, and motives behind, their classifications and subclassifications, and their schema need to take more account of cultural context, of the situated meanings and stated purposes of these rites. If anything, we should be comparing sequences of life-cycle rites. Rather than gender-specific sequences, moreover, it may be useful to consider a community's male and female gender rituals as together forming a complex, and compare these complexes to one another.

To say that such exercises are arbitrary mappings of Western categories onto other cultures, though, is, at one level, to state the unavoidable and the trivially obvious and, at another level, to assert the operation of multiple-end-point reasoning (Diaconis and Mosteller 1989) without demonstrating it. It states the unavoidable and trivially obvious insofar as all our understandings of the Other must be through Western categories. And it asserts but does not demonstrate that the apparent frequency and similarity with which youths around the world are secluded, hazed, scarified, exposed to sacra, taught secret knowledge, and so on is a perceptual artifact, the same sort of apparent coincidence as the fact that, given enough time, twenty-five people in a room can always find something they all have in common. This *might* be the case for initiation, but asserting it does not make it so; interpretivists need to consult the mathematics of multiple end points, if they are to make a convincing case (ibid.).

In any case, the interpretative assertion that social phenomena are culturally relative and that therefore the proper endeavor of anthropology is not comparison and generalization but "the non-comparative analytical description" (Holy 1987b:8) of the meanings, experiences, and views of reality that characterize a culture leaves a number of fundamental questions unanswered. Most critically, it sets aside the question of why particular cultures are as they are. No matter how adequate is the description of a particular culture, it tells us nothing about *why* that culture is as it is, the question that comparativists are interested in. Apparently, interpretative anthropologists find this question uninteresting because they presume that the determining processes that might impose the cross-cultural regularity necessary to make it interesting do not exist. "Underlying the anthropologists' current preoccupation with the culturally specific meaning," Holy (1987b:7) tells us, "is the awareness . . . that the people they are studying are not 'living among various unconscious systems of determining forces of which they have no clue' (Rabinow 1977:152), and to which only the anthropologists holds the key" (see also Hammersley and Atkinson 1983:7; Murphy 1971:85, 101; Schulz and Lavenda 1990:52). But if humans are *not* living among determining forces, what *are* they living among?

The interpretative answer is cultural logic. "Cultures of course would not be different," Holy (1987b:11) asserts, "if they were not built on different cultural logics." Unfortunately, the notion of cultural logic is radically underdetermined. Although it darts ubiquitously in and out of interpretative discourse, it is one of many anthropological closets—positivism, adaptation, and structure are perhaps others—into which crucially important but highly complex matters are dumped, away from the mind's eye. This intellectual closeting is useful—indeed, anthropology could hardly proceed without it—but too often the intellectual laundry these closets contain goes unaired.

To be convincing, the interpretative alternative to comparativism has to be more forthcoming about several questions concerning cultural logic. First, how do nonideational conditions and contingencies—material phenomena, demographic circumstances, genes, and the like—articulate with cultural logic? Are they reducible to it? Do they have no influence on it? Or are they, to some degree, "exogenous" to it and therefore capable of some autonomy in influencing it? By design or default, the interpretative emphasis on meaning, and meaning alone, as the focus of inquiry leaves the impression that cultural logic is some kind of disembodied calculus that produces change epigenetically as it were, uninfluenced by—indeed, completely dominating—nonideational conditions and contingencies. Even human neurobiology sometimes seems to be cast as irrelevant to the operation of culture, those who would invoke it being peripheralized as unreflective ethnocentrics. If, on the other hand, it is allowed that cultural logic operates within, and adjusts itself to, "exogenous" constraints and enablements, then in principle these operations and adjustments constitute points of departure for comparative analysis. If, for instance, it is granted that cultural logic alone does not dictate the use of bows or spreadnets in hunting—that environment, say, shapes human logic as well as being shaped by it—then it becomes permissible to compare hunting societies and propose processes by which vegetational structure influences the technologies deployed (Roscoe 1990b). If the material universe is indeed under no obligation to conform to the dictates of cultural logic (Sahlins 1981:67), though, many interpretivists seem uninterested in, or unaware of, the fact.

A second issue deserving further clarification is the extent to which cultural logic is localized. Does every society have a different cultural logic? Do neighboring societies in regular contact with one another share a general cultural logic or paradigm that is manifest in localized transformations? Is there a single, human cultural logic that in different contexts and conditions produces different cultural forms? Or is the situation a combination of these possibilities: some aspects of human culture are the product of a common cultural logic shaped by local conditions and contingencies; some are local transformations of a cultural paradigm shared by neighboring societies; yet others are produced by logics unique to particular cultures; and so on? The interpretativist view is unclear, but to judge from the frequency of references to cultural logics, plural, the idea of every culture as the product of a unique logic seems the most popular working hypothesis (Holy 1987b:11). This is the position most hostile to the idea of cross-cultural comparison, but it is also the least defensible for it presumes a kind of cultural essentialism. In asserting that each culture has its own unique logic, it implies that societies bearing these cultures are somehow separated off from one another, as though they were hermetically sealed units. In fact, what we loosely call societies are not separated—geographically, socially, or temporally: over time they fission and coalesce. At any one point in time, there is constant interaction among them to the geographic limits of social interaction; and it is therefore impossible to pinpoint unique cultural logics within these interactional spheres. To the extent that interpretivists must concede this diffusion of cultural logic, they must also concede the possibility that comparison may be fruitful.

A third issue, related to the foregoing, concerns the extent to which interpretivists see cultural logic as determining human affairs—in the sense of bringing spatial and temporal regularity to human belief and behavior. Clearly, they must assume this logic produces regularity *within* a particular "society," for without it social life would be impossible. But what about regularity—and regularized differences—across cultures, the very stuff of cross-cultural generalization? Although cultural logic must to some degree extend beyond the boundaries of what we commonly take to be particular "societies," it is still conceivable that within these limits cultural trajectories (however defined) follow entirely contingent paths through time, robbing them of the transcultural regularities that would permit comparison and generalization. This is the position that interpretivists apparently favor. Contrasting themselves to "positivists," they argue that humans have certain unique characteristics—self-awareness, reflexivity, creativity, intentionality, purposiveness, and so on—that confer on them freedom to dictate their action (e.g., Giddens 1977:80–90; Hammersly and Atkinson 1983:7; Schulz and Lavenda 1990:52). In consequence, the argument seems to go, human action continually undermines the sorts of regularity out of which comparativists seek to construct cross-cultural generalizations. The behavior of the natural world may follow laws, but humans, unlike atoms, can reflect on the conditions of their actions and therefore change them.

What seems to get overlooked in these appeals to human freedom of action, however, is that this freedom is not, and cannot be, unconstrained; it injects no more than a *degree* of irregularity into human thought and behavior. Thus, when Rabinow claims that humans do not live among various unconscious systems of determining forces, he is right to reject the seemingly total determinism envisaged, say, by early structural functionalism. But if he is implying that human ideas and behavior are completely undetermined, then he is mistaken. As Giddens (1984:343–347) notes in some detail, agents are never wholly autonomous; their actions are never completely under their control. They are always subject to social and material constraints that they are unable to change; they are enmeshed in the dialectic of control—their asymmetric access to resources; and there are limits on the range of practices they are capable of competently performing. In addition, although they can in principle reflect upon and undermine regularities in their actions, there are whole sets of circumstances under which this ability has no transformational consequences—not least when the empirical referent is to past events; when reflexive knowledge is used to sustain rather than undermine existing circumstances; and when those who might seek to apply reflexive knowledge are in no situation to be able to do so effectively (ibid.:341–343).

In sum, if interpretivists really do believe there can be no interesting and useful answers to the question of why cultures or cultural complexes like initiation are as they are—why they differ (and, the converse: why they are also the same)—then they do so by fiat. Whether and to what extent this question will lead to interesting and useful answers cannot, of course, be determined ahead of time. Assuredly, if valid transcultural generalizations— about initiation or any other aspect of humanity—are possible, they will turn out to be far more complex and embedded in many more contingencies than comparative anthropology currently envisages. For the present, as Holy (1987b:17) rightly observes, we can only make proposals, and leave it to members of the anthropological community to decide for themselves to what extent they are justified by the results. To assert, however, on the basis of the arguments that interpretivists have thus far advanced, that the endeavor is futile seems premature at best, indefensible at worst.

NOTES

1. For comments on an earlier draft of this chapter, I am deeply grateful to Terry Hays, Nancy Lutkehaus, and an anonymous reviewer.

2. Van Gennep (1960[1908]:66–67) was the first to distinguish initiation from puberty rites, but he did so on the basis that *puberty rites* was a misnomer for *initiation rites* since the latter frequently failed to correspond with puberty.

3. There are a few exceptions: Benedict (1959[1934]:25) adopted a more emic measure—but, significantly, was attacked for it (Rigby 1967).

4. La Fontaine (1985:102) admits much the same of marriage rites but then ignores the implications of her remark.

REFERENCES

Abrams, M. H., 1971. The Mirror and the Lamp. London: Oxford University Press.

Allen, Bryant, 1986. Some Environmental Considerations in Sepik Culture History. Paper presented at the Wenner-Gren Symposium, Sepik Culture History: Variation, Innovation and Synthesis. Mijas, Spain.

Allen, M. R., 1967. Male Cults and Secret Initiations in Melanesia. Victoria: Melbourne University Press.

Ardener, Edwin, 1975. Belief and the Problem of Women. *In* Perceiving Women. Shirley Ardener, ed. pp.1–17. London: Malaby.

Auerbach, E., 1991. Mimesis. Willard Trask, trans. Princeton: Princeton University Press.

Aufenanger, Henry, n.d. The Passing Scene in North-East New–Guinea. Collectanea Instituti Anthropos, vol. 2. St. Augustin, Germany: Anthropos Institute.

Barker, John and Anne Marie Tietjen, 1990. Women's Facial Tattooing among the Maisin of Oro Province, Papua New Guinea: The Changing Significance of an Ancient Custom. Oceania 60:217–234.

Barlow, Kathleen, 1985a. The Role of Women in Intertribal Trade among the Murik of Papua New Guinea. Research in Economic Anthropology 7:95–122.

———, 1985b. The Social Context of Infant Feeding in the Murik Lakes of Papua New Guinea. *In* Infant Care and Feeding in the South Pacific. Leslie B. Marshall, ed. pp.137–154. New York: Gordon and Breach.

———, 1988. Achieving Womanhood and the Achievements of Women: Puberty Rites, Cult Initiation, and the Cultural Construction of Gender. Paper presented at the Annual Meetings of the Association for Social Anthropology in Oceania,. Savannah Ga.

———, 1992. "Dance When I Die!": Context and Role in the Clowning Behavior of Murik Women. *In* Clowning as Critical Practice: Performance Humor in the South Pacific. William E. Mitchell, ed. pp.58–87. Pittsburgh: University of Pittsburgh Press.

Barlow, K., L. Bolton, and D. Lipset, 1987. Trade and Society in Transition along the Sepik Coast. Unpublished Report. Sydney: Australian Museum.

Barlow, Kathleen and David Lipset, 1989. The Construction of Meaning in Ethnography and Culture: The Fabrication of Canoes in the Murik Lakes. Paper presented at the symposium, Objects Inform, Object in Forms: The Ethnography of Oceanic Art. Baltimore: Baltimore Museum of Art.

Barthes, Roland, 1990. Image, Music, Text. New York: The Noonday Press.

Bateson, Gregory, 1958[1936]. Naven. Stanford: Stanford University Press.

————, 1973. Steps to an Ecology of Mind. St. Albans, UK: Paladin.

Battaglia, Debbora, 1985. "We Feed our Father": Paternal Nurture among the Sabarl of Papua New Guinea. American Ethnologist 12:427–441.

————, 1990. On the Bones of the Serpent: Person, Memory, and Mortality in Sabarl Island Society. Chicago: University of Chicago Press.

Benedict, Ruth, 1959[1934]. Patterns of Culture. Boston: Houghton Mifflin.

Bettelheim, Bruno, 1962[1954]. Symbolic Wounds. Glencoe: The Free Press.

Biersack, Aletta, 1982. Ginger Gardens for the Ginger Woman: Rites and Passages in a Melanesian Society. Man (N.S.) 17:239–258.

————, 1991. Thinking Difference: A Review of Marilyn Strathern's The Gender of the Gift. Oceania 62:147–154.

Boddy, Janice, 1982. Womb as Oasis: The Symbolic Context of Pharaonic Circumcision in Rural Northern Sudan. American Ethnologist 9:682–698.

————, 1989. Wombs and Alien Spirits: Women, Men, and the Zār Cult in Northern Sudan. Madison: University of Wisconsin Press.

Böhm, Karl, 1983. The Life of Some Island People of New Guinea. Collectanea Instituti Anthropos, vol. 29. Berlin: Dietrich Reimer.

Bonaparte, Marie, 1953. Female Sexuality. John Rodker, trans. New York: International Universities Press.

Bonwick, J., 1886. The Australian Natives. Journal of the Anthropological Institute 16:201–210.

Brandes, Stanley, 1981. Like Wounded Stags: Male Sexual Ideology in an Andalusian Town. In Sexual Meanings: The Cultural Construction of Gender and Sexuality. Sherry B. Ortner and Harriet Whitehead, eds. pp.216–239. Cambridge: Cambridge University Press.

Brod, Harry, ed., 1987. The Making of Masculinities: The New Men's Studies. Boston: Allen and Unwin.

Brown, Judith K., 1963. A Cross-Cultural Study of Female Initiation Rites. American Anthropologist 65:837–853.

Brown, Paula and Georgeda Buchbinder, 1976. Man and Woman in the New Guinea Highlands. Washington, D.C.: American Anthropological Association.

Buckley, Thomas and Alma Gottlieb, 1988. Blood Magic: The Anthropology of Menstruation. Berkeley: University of California Press.

Camp, Cheryl, 1979. A Female Initiation Rite in the Neigrie Area. In Powers, Plumes, and Piglets. Norman C. Habel, ed. pp.68–83. Bedford Park, South Australia: Australian Association for the Study of Religions.

Caplan, Patricia, ed., 1987. The Cultural Construction of Sexuality. London: Tavistock.

Clay, Brenda Johnson, 1977. Pinikindu: Maternal Nurture, Paternal Substance. Chicago: University of Chicago Press.

————, 1986. Mandak Realities: Person and Power in Central New Ireland. New Brunswick: Rutgers University Press.

Clifford, James, 1982. Person and Myth: Maurice Leenhardt in the Melanesian World. Berkeley: University of California Press.

Cohen, Yehudi A., 1964. The Transition from Childhood to Adolescence: Cross-Cultural Studies of Initiation Ceremonies, Legal Systems, and Incest Taboos. Chicago: Aldine.

Collier, Jane F. and Michelle Z. Rosaldo, 1981. Politics and Gender in Simple Societies. In Sexual Meanings: The Cultural Construction of Gender and Sexuality. Sherry B. Ortner and Harriet Whitehead, eds. pp.275–328. Cambridge: Cambridge University Press.

Collier, Jane Fishburne and Sylvia Junko Yanagisako, 1987. Introduction. In Gender and Kinship: Essays Toward a Unified Analysis. Jane Fishburne Collier and Sylvia Junko Yanagisako, eds. pp.1–13. Stanford: Stanford University Press.

————, 1989. Theory in Anthropology Since Feminist Practice. Critique of Anthropology 9(2):27–37.

Comaroff, Jean, 1985. Body of Power, Spirit of Resistance: The Culture and History of a South African People. Chicago: University of Chicago Press.

Crick, Malcolm, 1976. Explorations in Language and Meaning: Towards a Semantic Anthropology. Malaby: London.

Daly, C. D., 1950. The Psycho-Biological Origins of Circumcision. International Journal of Psychoanalysis 31:217–236.

Daniell, W. F., 1846. On the Natives of Old Callebar, West Coast of Africa. Journal of the Ethnological Society of London 1:210–224.

Deacon, A. B., 1925. The Kakihan Society of Ceram and New Guinea Initiation Cults. Folk-lore 36: 332–361.

————, 1934. Malekula: A Vanishing People in the New Hebrides. London: Routledge.

Diaconis, Persi, and Frederick Mosteller, 1989. Methods for Studying Coincidences. Journal of the American Statistical Association 84:853–861.

Diamond, Irene and Lee Quinby, eds., 1988. Feminism and Foucault: Reflections on Resistance. Boston: Northeastern University Press.

Douglas, Mary, 1966. Purity and Danger: An Analysis of Concepts of Pollution and Taboo. London: Routledge and Kegan Paul.

————, 1970. Natural Symbols: Explorations in Cosmology. New York: Vintage Books.

————, 1975. Implicit Meanings: Essays in Anthropology. London: Routledge and Kegan Paul.

Dye, T. Wayne, 1974. An Experiment in Indigeneity. Unpublished manuscript.

————, 1990. Economic Development at the Grass Roots: Wagu Village 1963–1983. In Sepik Heritage: Tradition and Change in Papua New Guinea. Nancy Lutkehaus, Christian Kaufmann, William E. Mitchell, Douglas Newton, Lita Osmundsen, and Meinhard Schuster, eds. pp.221–231. Durham: Carolina Academic Press.

Dye, W., P. Townsend, and W. Townsend, 1968. The Sepik Hill Languages: A Preliminary Report. Oceania 39:146–156.

Edholm, F., O. Harris, K. Young, 1977. Conceptualizing Women. Critique of Anthropology 9–10:101–30.

Eggan, Fred, 1954. Social Anthropology and the Method of Controlled Comparison. American Anthropologist 56:743–763.

Eliade, Mircea, 1958. Rites and Symbols of Initiation: The Mysteries of Birth and Rebirth. New York: Harper and Row.

Elkin, A. P., 1964[1938]. The Australian Aborigines. New York: Doubleday.

Errington, Frederick and Deborah Gewertz, 1987. Cultural Alternatives and a Feminist Anthropology. Cambridge: Cambridge University Press.

Etienne, Mona and Eleanor Burke Leacock, eds., 1980. Women and Colonization: Anthropological Perspectives. New York: Praeger Publishers, CBS Educational and Professional Publishing.

Evans-Pritchard, E. E., 1965. The Comparative Method in Social Anthropology. *In* The Position of Women in Primitive Societies and Other Essays in Social Anthropology. E. E. Evans-Pritchard. pp.13–36. New York: Free Press.

Faithorn, Elizabeth, 1976. Women as Persons: Aspects of Female Life and Male-Female Relations among the Kafe. *In* Man and Woman in the New Guinea Highlands. Paula Brown and Georgeda Buchbinder, eds. pp.86–95. Washington, D.C.: American Anthropological Association.

Fardon, Richard, 1984–1985. Sisters, Wives, Wards and Daughters: A Transformational Analysis of the Political Organization of the Tiv and their Neighbours. Africa 54(4):2–21; 55:77–91.

Feil, D. K., 1978. Women and Men in the Enga Tee. American Ethnologist 5:263–279.

———, 1987. The Evolution of Highland Papua New Guinea Societies. Cambridge: Cambridge University Press.

Forge, Anthony, 1966. Art and Environment in the Sepik. Proceedings of the Royal Anthropological Institute of Great Britain and Ireland, 1965:23–31.

———, 1970a. Learning to See in New Guinea. *In* Socialisation: The Approach from Social Anthropology. Philip Mayer, ed. pp.269–291. London: Tavistock.

———, 1970b. Prestige, Influence, and Sorcery: A New Guinea Example. *In* Witchcraft, Confessions and Accusations. M. Douglas, ed. pp.257–275. Tavistock: London.

———, 1979. The Problem of Meaning in Art. *In* Exploring the Visual Arts of Oceania. Sidney M. Mead, ed. pp.278–286. Honolulu: University Press of Hawaii.

Fortes, Meyer, 1958. Introduction. *In* The Developmental Cycle in Domestic Groups. Jack Goody, ed. pp.1–14. Cambridge: Cambridge University Press.

———, 1969. Kinship and the Social Order: The Legacy of Lewis Henry Morgan. Chicago: Aldine.

Foucault, Michel, 1978. The History of Sexuality, Vol. 1: An Introduction. New York: Pantheon.

———, 1979. Discipline and Punish: The Birth of the Prison. New York: Vintage Books.

Frayser, Suzanne G., 1985. Varieties of Sexual Experience: An Anthropological Perspective on Human Sexuality. New Haven: HRAF Press.

Friedl, Ernestine, 1978. Society and Sex Roles. *In* Conformity and Conflict: Readings in Cultural Anthropology. James P. Spradley and David W. McCurdy, eds. pp.229–238. Glenview: Scott, Foresman and Little Brown Higher Education.

Geertz, Clifford, 1973. Ethos, World View, and the Analysis of Sacred Symbols. *In* The Interpretation of Cultures. pp. 126–141. New York: Basic Books.

Gelber, Marilyn G., 1986. Gender and Society in the New Guinea Highlands. Boulder: Westview.

Gesch, Patrick F., 1985. Initiative and Initiation. Studia Instituti Anthropos, vol. 33. St. Augustin, Germany: Anthropos Institut.

Gewertz, Deborah B., 1977. From Sago Suppliers to Entrepreneurs: Marketing and Migration in the Middle Sepik. Oceania 48:126–140.

————, 1983. Sepik River Societies: A Historical Ethnography of the Chambri and their Neighbors. New Haven: Yale University Press.

————, 1984. The Tchambuli View of Persons: A Critique of Individualism in the Works of Mead and Chodorow. American Anthropologist 86:615–629.

Giddens, Anthony, 1977. Studies in Social and Political Theory. New York: Basic Books.

————, 1984. The Constitution of Society: Outline of the Theory of Structuration. Berkeley: University of California Press.

Gilmore, David D., 1990. Manhood in the Making: Cultural Concepts of Masculinity. New Haven: Yale University Press.

Ginsburg, Faye and Rayna Rapp, 1991. The Politics of Reproduction. Annual Review of Anthropology 20:311–343.

Gluckman, Max, 1962. Les Rites de Passage. In Essays on the Ritual of Social Relations. Max Gluckman, ed. pp.1–52. Manchester: Manchester University Press.

————, 1963. Rituals of Rebellion in South-East Africa. In Order and Rebellion in Tribal Africa. Max Gluckman, ed. pp.110–136. New York: Free Press of Glencoe.

Godelier, Maurice, 1986. The Making of Great Men: Male Domination and Power Among the New Guinea Baruya. Rupert Swyer, trans. Cambridge: Cambridge University Press.

Gordon, Daniel, 1991. Female Circumcision and Genital Operations in Egypt and the Sudan: A Dilemma for Medical Anthropology. Medical Anthropology Quarterly 5:3–14.

Gough, Kathleen, 1955. Female Initiation Rites on the Malabar Coast. Journal of the Royal Anthropological Institute 85:45–80.

Gregory, James R., 1984. The Myth of the Male Ethnographer and the Woman's World. American Anthropologist 86:316–327.

Haberland, Eike and Siegfried Seyfarth, 1974. Die Yimar am Oberen Korowori (Neuguinea). Wiesbaden: Franz Steiner.

Hammersley, Martyn and Paul Atkinson, 1983. Ethnography: Principles in Practice. New York: Tavistock.

Handelman, Don, 1979. Is Naven Ludic? Paradox and the Communication of Identity. Social Analysis 1:177–191.

Harding, Sandra G., 1987. Feminism and Methodology: Social Science Issues. Bloomington: Indiana University Press.

Harding, Sandra G. and Merrill B. Hintikka, eds., 1983. Discovering Reality: Feminist Perspectives on Epistemology, Metaphysics, Methodology and Philosophy of Science. Boston: Reidel.

Harris, Olivia and Kate Young, 1981. Engendered Structures: Some Problems in the Analysis of Reproduction. In The Anthropology of Pre-Capitalist Societies. Joel S. Kahn and Joseph R. Llobera, eds., pp. 109–147. London: MacMillan.

Harrison, Simon, 1982. Yams and the Symbolic Representation of Time in a Sepik River Village. Oceania 53:141–162.

———, 1985. Concepts of the Person in Avatip Religious Thought. Man (N.S.) 20:115–130.

Hauser-Schäublin, Brigitta, 1977. Frauen in Kararau. Zur Rolle der Frau bei den Iatmul am Mittelsepik, Papua New Guinea. Basler Beiträge zur Ethnologie, vol. 18. Basel: Wepf.

———, 1983. Abelam. In Menschenbilder früher Gesellschaften. Klaus E. Müller, ed. pp.178–203. Frankfurt: Campus.

———, 1988. Ritueller Wettstreit mit Feldfrüchten: Yamsfeste im Sepik-Gebiet, Papua-Neuguinea. Verhandlungen der Naturforschenden Gesellschaft Basel 97:87–102.

———, 1989a. The Fallacy of "Real" and "Pseudo" Procreation. Zeitschrift für Ethnologie 114:179–194.

———, 1989b. Kulthäuser in Nordneuguinea. Abhandlungen und Berichte des Staatlichen Museums für Völkerkunde, vol. 43. Dresden: Akademie.

Hays, Terence E., n.d. A Cross-Cultural Background for the Study of Female-Centered Rites in New Guinea. Paper presented at the Meetings of the Association for Social Anthropology in Oceania, 1988. Savannah Ga.

Hays, Terence E. and Patricia H. Hays, 1982. Opposition and Complementarity of the Sexes in Ndumba Initiation. In Rituals of Manhood: Male Initiation in Papua New Guinea. Gilbert H. Herdt, ed. pp.201–238. Berkeley: University of California Press.

Herdt, Gilbert H., 1981. Guardians of the Flutes: Idioms of Masculinity. New York: McGraw-Hill.

———, ed., 1982a. Rituals of Manhood: Male Initiation in Papua New Guinea. Berkeley: University of California Press.

———, 1982b. Fetish and Fantasy in Sambia Initiation. In Rituals of Manhood: Male Initiation in Papua New Guinea. Gilbert H. Herdt, ed. pp.44–98. Berkeley: University of California Press.

———, 1984. Ritualized Homosexuality in Melanesia. Berkeley: University of California Press.

———, 1987. The Sambia: Ritual and Gender in New Guinea. New York: Holt, Rinehart and Winston.

———, ed., 1994. Third Sex, Third Gender: Beyond Sexual Dimorphism in Culture and History. New York: Zone Books.

Herdt, Gilbert H. and Fitz John P. Poole, 1982. "Sexual Antagonism": The Intellectual History of a Concept in New Guinea Anthropology. Social Analysis 12:3–28.

Herdt, Gilbert and Robert Stoller, 1990. Intimate Communications: Erotics and the Study of Culture. New York: Columbia University Press.

Hermann, Anne and Abigail Stewart, 1994. Theorizing Feminism: Parallel Developments in the Humanities and Social Sciences. Boulder: Westview.

Heusch, L. de, 1982[1972]. The Drunken King, or the Origin of the State. Bloomington: Indiana University Press.

———, 1985. Sacrifice in Africa: A Structuralist Approach. Manchester: Manchester University Press.

Hiatt, L. R., 1971. Secret Pseudo-Procreation Rites among the Australian Aborigines. *In* Anthropology in Oceania: Essays Presented to Ian Hogbin. L. R. Hiatt and C. Jayawardena, eds. pp.77–88. San Francisco: Chandler.

Hieb, Louis A., 1972. Meaning and Mismeaning: Toward an Understanding of the Ritual Clown. *In* New Perspectives on the Pueblos. Alfonso Ortiz, ed. pp. 163–195. Albuquerque: University of New Mexico Press.

Hogbin, Herbert Ian, 1935. Trading Expeditions in Northern New Guinea. Oceania 5:375–411.

———, 1970. The Island of Menstruating Men: Religion in Wogeo, New Guinea. Scranton: Chandler.

Holy, Ladislav, ed., 1987a. Comparative Anthropology. Oxford: Basil Blackwell.

———, 1987b. Introduction: Description, Generalization and Comparison: Two Paradigms. *In* Comparative Anthropology. Ladislav Holy, ed. pp.1–21. Oxford: Basil Blackwell.

Hoskins, Janet, 1989. Why Do Ladies Sing the Blues? Indigo Dyeing, Cloth Production and Gender Symbolism in Kodi. *In* Cloth and Human Experience. Jane Schneider and Annette B. Weiner, eds. pp.141–173. Washington, D.C.: Smithsonian Institution Press.

Jacobs, Jane M., 1989. "Women Talking Up Big": Aboriginal Women as Cultural Custodians, A South Australia Example. *In* Women, Rites and Sites: Aboriginal Women's Cultural Knowledge. Peggy Brock, ed. pp.76–98. Winchester: Unwin Hyman.

Jacobus, Mary, Evelyn Fox Keller, and Sally Shuttleworth, eds., 1990. Body/Politics: Women and the Discourses of Science. New York: Routledge.

Jaggar, Alison M. and Susan Bordo, eds., 1989. Gender/Body/Knowledge: Feminist Reconstructions of Being and Knowing. New Brunswick: Rutgers University Press.

James, Wendy, 1993. Matrifocus on Women. *In* Defining Females: The Nature of Women in Society. Shirley Ardener, ed. pp.123–145. Providence: Berg.

Jolly, Margaret, 1991. Soaring Hawks and Grounded Persons: The Politics of Rank and Gender in North Vanuatu. *In* Big Men and Great Men: Personifications of Power in Melanesia. Maurice Godelier and Marilyn Strathern, eds. pp.48–80. Cambridge: Cambridge University Press.

———, 1992. Banana Leaf Bundles and Skirts: A Pacific Penelope's Web? *In* History and Tradition in Melanesian Anthropology. James Carrier, ed. pp.38–63. Berkeley: University of California Press.

Jolly, Margaret and Martha Macintyre, eds., 1989. Family and Gender in the Pacific: Domestic Contradictions and the Colonial Impact. Cambridge: Cambridge University Press.

Jorgensen, Dan, 1983. The Facts of Life, Papua New Guinea Style. Mankind 14:1–12.

Josephides, Lisette, 1985. The Production of Inequality: Gender and Exchange among the Kewa. London: Tavistock.

Kaberry, Phyllis, 1941. The Abelam Tribe, Sepik District, New Guinea: A Preliminary Report. Oceania 11:233–258, 345–367.

———, 1973. Political Organization among the Northern Abelam. *In* Politics in New Guinea: Traditional and in the Context of Change: Some Anthropological Perspectives. Ronald M. Berndt and Peter Lawrence, eds. pp.35–73. Seattle: University of Washington Press.

Kapferer, Bruce, 1983. A Celebration of Demons: Exorcism and the Aesthetics of Healing in Sri Lanka. Bloomington: Indiana University Press.

Keesing, Roger M., 1982. Introduction. *In* Rituals of Manhood: Male Initiation in Papua New Guinea. Gilbert H. Herdt, ed. pp.1–43. Berkeley: University of California Press.

———, 1985. Kwaio Women Speak: The Micropolitics of Autobiography in a Solomon Islands Society. American Anthropologist 87:27–39.

Kelly, Raymond C., 1993. Constructing Inequality: The Fabrication of a Hierarchy of Virtue among the Etoro. Ann Arbor: University of Michigan Press.

Kennedy, John G., 1970. Circumcision and Excision in Egyptian Nubia. Man (N.S.) 5:175–191.

Kimmel, Michael S. and Michael A. Messner, eds., 1989. Men's Lives. New York: Macmillan.

Kirby, V., 1989. Capitalising Difference: Feminism and Anthropology. Australian Feminist Studies 9:1–24.

Knauft, Bruce M., 1993. South Coast New Guinea Cultures: History, Comparison, Dialectic. Cambridge: Cambridge University Press.

Kolodny, Annette, 1992. Letting Go Our Grand Obsessions: Notes Toward a New Literary History of the American Frontiers. American Literature 64:1–18.

Kuper, Adam, 1982. Wives for Cattle. London: Routledge and Kegan Paul.

La Fontaine, J. S., 1972. Ritualisation of Women's Life-Crises in Bugisu. *In* The Interpretation of Ritual. J. S. La Fontaine, ed. pp.159–186. London: Tavistock.

———, 1982. Introduction. Chisungu: A Girls' Initiation Ceremony among the Bemba of Zambia. Audrey Isabel Richards. London: Tavistock.

———, 1985. Initiation: Ritual Drama and Secret Knowledge across the World. Harmondsworth: Penguin Books.

Lamphere, Louise, 1993. The Domestic Sphere of Women and the Public World of Men: The Strengths and Limitations of an Anthropological Dichotomy. *In* Gender in Cross-Cultural Perspective. Caroline B. Brettell and Carolyn F. Sargent, eds., pp. 67–76. Englewood Cliffs: Prentice Hall.

Langness, L. L., 1967. Sexual Antagonism in the New Guinea Highlands: A Bena Bena Example. Oceania 37:161–177.

———, 1974. Ritual, Power, and Male Dominance. Ethos 2:189–212.

Lattas, Andrew, 1989. Trickery and Sacrifice: Tambarans and the Appropriation of Female Reproductive Powers in Male Initiation Ceremonies in West New Britain. Man (N.S.) 24:451–69.

Lawrence, P. and M. J. Meggitt, 1965. Introduction. *In* Gods Ghosts and Men in Melanesia. P. Lawrence and M. J. Meggitt, eds. pp.1–26. Melbourne: Oxford University Press.

Layard, John W., 1942. Stone Men of Malekula. London: Chatto and Windus.

Laycock, D. C., 1965. The Ndu Language Family (Sepik District, New Guinea). Series C, No.1. Canberra: Linguistic Circle of Canberra.

Leacock, Eleanor Burke, 1972. Introduction. *In* The Origin of the Family, Private Property and the State, by Frederick Engels. Eleanor Leacock, ed. pp.7–67. New York: International Publishers.

———, 1981. Myths of Male Dominance: Collected Articles on Women Cross-Culturally. New York: Monthly Review Press.

Lederman, Rena, 1980. Who Speaks Here? Formality and the Politics of Gender in Mendi, Highland Papua New Guinea. Journal of the Polynesian Society 89(4):477–498.

———, 1986. What Gifts Engender: Social Relations and Politics in Mendi, Highland Papua New Guinea. Cambridge: Cambridge University Press.

———, 1990. Contested Order: Gender and Society in the Southern New Guinea Highlands. In Beyond the Second Sex: New Directions in the Anthropology of Gender. Peggy Reeves Sanday and Ruth Gallagher Goodenough, eds. pp.51–73. Philadelphia: University of Pennsylvania Press.

Ledoux, Louis Pierre, 1936. Unpublished Field Notes. New York: American Museum of Natural History.

Leenhardt, M., 1948. L'Arts de l'Oceanie. Paris: Musée de l'Homme.

———, 1979[1947]. Do Kamo: Person and Myth in the Melanesian World. Chicago: University of Chicago Press.

Le Guin, Ursula K., 1989. Dancing at the Edge of the World: Thoughts on Words, Women, Places. New York: Grove Press.

Leonardo, Micaela di, 1991. Gender at the Cross-roads of Knowledge: Feminist Anthropology in the Postmodern Era. Berkeley: University of California Press.

Lepowsky, Maria Alexandra, 1993. Fruit of the Motherland: Gender in an Egalitarian Society. New York: Columbia University Press.

Levinson, David and Martin J. Malone, 1980. Toward Explaining Human Culture. New Haven: HRAF Press.

Lévi-Strauss, Claude, 1963. Totemism. Boston: Beacon.

Lidz, Theodore, 1989. Oedipus in the Stone Age: A Psychoanalytic Study of Masculinization in Papua New Guinea. Madison: International Universities Press.

Lincoln, Bruce, 1981. Emerging from the Chrysalis: Studies in Rituals of Women's Initiation. Cambridge: Harvard University Press.

Lindenbaum, Shirley, 1972. Sorcerors, Ghosts, and Polluting Women: An Analysis of Religious Belief and Population Control. Ethnology 11:241–253.

———, 1984. Variations on a Sociosexual Theme in Melanesia. In Ritualized Homosexuality in Melanesia. Gilbert H. Herdt, ed. pp.337–361. Berkeley: University of California Press.

———, 1987. The Mystification of Female Labors. In Gender and Kinship: Essays Toward a Unified Analysis. Jane Fishburne Collier and Sylvia Junko Yanagisako, eds. pp.221–243. Stanford: Stanford University Press.

Lindstrom, Lamont, 1993. Cargo Cult: Strange Stories of Desire from Melanesia and Beyond. Honolulu: University of Hawaii Press.

Linnekin, Jocelyn and Lin Poyer, eds., 1990. Cultural Identity and Ethnicity in the Pacific. Honolulu: University of Hawaii Press.

Lipset, David M., 1984. Authority and the Maternal Presence: An Interpretive Ethnography of Murik Lakes Society, East Sepik Province, Papua New Guinea. Ph.D. Dissertation. University of California, San Diego.

———, n.d. Mangrove Man: The Maternal Body in the Poetics of Moral Order, Masculinity and Social Context. Unpublished manuscript.

Lipset, David and Kathleen Barlow, 1987. The Value of Culture: Regional Exchange in the Lower Sepik. Australian Natural History 23:156–168.

LiPuma, Edward, 1988. The Gift of Kinship: Structure and Practice in Maring Social Organization. Cambridge: Cambridge University Press.

Losche, Diane Sara Brady, 1982. Male and Female in Abelam Society: Opposition and Complementarity. Ph.D. Dissertation. Columbia University, New York.

Lutkehaus, Nancy C., 1982. Ambivalence, Ambiguity and the Reproduction of Gender Hierarchy in Manam Society. Social Analysis 12:36–51.

———, 1984. The Flutes of the *Tanepoa*: The Dynamics of Hierarchy and Equivalence in Manam Society. Ph.D. Dissertation. Columbia University, New York.

———, 1995. Zaria's Fire: Engendered Moments in Manam Ethnography. Durham: Carolina Academic Press.

Lutkehaus, Nancy and Paul Roscoe, 1987. Sepik Culture History: Variation, Innovation, and Synthesis. Current Anthropology 28:577–581.

MacCormack, Carol P. and Marilyn Strathern, eds., 1980. Nature, Culture, and Gender. Cambridge: Cambridge University Press.

MacLennan, Wendy, n.d. Menstruation, Pregnancy and Childbirth among the Abelam, Maprik, New Guinea, 1962–1963. Papua and New Guinea: Medical Research Division, Department of Public Health.

MacLennan, Wendy and Robert MacLennan, n.d. Abelam Menstruation, Pregnancy and Childbirth. Unpublished manuscript.

Magee, Bryan, 1975. Popper. Glasgow: Fontana/Collins.

Mahmood, Cynthia K. and Sharon L. Armstrong, 1992. Do Ethnic Groups Exist?: A Cognitive Perspective on the Concept of Cultures. Ethnology 31:1–14.

Malinowski, Bronislaw, 1922. Argonauts of the Western Pacific. New York: Dutton.

———, 1927. Sex and Repression in Savage Society. London: International Library of Psychology, Philosophy and Scientific Method.

———, 1929. The Sexual Life of Savages in North-Western Melanesia. London: Routledge and Kegan Paul.

Maschio, Thomas, 1988. Sacred Symbols and the Making of a Big Woman in Rauto Female Initiation. Paper Presented at the Annual Meetings of the Association for Social Anthropology in Oceania, 1988. Savannah Ga.

———, 1994. To Remember the Faces of the Dead: The Plenitude of Memory in Southwestern New Britain. Madison: University of Wisconsin Press.

Mauss, Marcel, 1967. The Gift: Forms and Functions of Exchange in Archaic Societies. New York: Norton.

McDowell, Nancy, 1984. Complementarity: The Relationship between Female and Male in the East Sepik Village of Bun, Papua New Guinea. *In* Rethinking Women's Roles: Perspectives from the Pacific. Denise O'Brien and Sharon W. Tiffany, eds. pp.32–52. Berkeley: University of California Press.

———, 1988. A Note on Cargo Cults and Cultural Constructions of Change. Pacific Studies 11(2):121–134.

Mead, Margaret, 1928. Coming of Age in Samoa. New York: Morrow.

———, 1930. Growing Up in New Guinea. New York: Morrow.

———, 1935. Sex and Temperament in Three Primitive Societies. New York: Morrow.

———, 1940. The Mountain Arapesh II. Supernaturalism. Anthropological Papers of the American Museum of Natural History 37:317–451.

————, 1949. Male and Female: A Study of the Sexes in a Changing World. New York: Morrow.

Meggitt, Mervyn, 1964. Male-Female Relationships in the Highlands of Australian New Guinea. American Anthropologist 66(4):204–224.

Meigs, Anna S., 1976. Male Pregnancy and the Reduction of Sexual Opposition in a New Guinea Highlands Society. Ethnology 15:393–407.

————, 1984. Food, Sex, and Pollution: A New Guinea Religion. New Brunswick: Rutgers University Press.

Metraux, Rhoda, 1978. Aristocracy and Meritocracy: Leadership among the Eastern Iatmul. Anthropological Quarterly 51:47–58.

Miles, W. Augustus, 1854. How Did the Natives of Australia Become Acquainted with the Demigods and Daemonia, and with the Superstitions of the Ancient Races? Journal of the Ethnological Society of London 3:4–50.

Miller, Barbara D., ed., 1993. Sex and Gender Hierarchies. Cambridge: Cambridge University Press.

Modjeska, Nicholas, 1982. Production and Inequality: Perspectives from Central New Guinea. In Inequality in New Guinea Highlands Societies. Andrew Strathern, ed. pp.50–108. Cambridge: Cambridge University Press.

Moore, Henrietta L., 1988. Feminism and Anthropology. Minneapolis: University of Minnesota Press.

Morinis, Alan, 1985. The Ritual Experience: Pain and the Transformation of Consciousness in Ordeals of Initiation. Ethos 13:150–174.

Mosko, Mark S., 1983. Conception, Deconception and Social Structure in Bush Mekeo Culture. Mankind 14:24–32.

————, 1985. Quadripartite Structures: Categories, Relations, and Homologies in Bush Mekeo Culture. Cambridge: Cambridge University Press.

————, 1989. The Developmental Cycle among Public Groups. Man (N.S.) 24:470–484.

Murphy, Robert F., 1959. Social Structure and Sex Antagonism. Southwestern Journal of Anthropology 15:89–98.

————, 1971. The Dialectics of Social Life: Alarms and Excursions in Anthropological Theory. New York: Basic Books.

Nanda, Serena, 1990. Neither Man Nor Woman: The Hijras of India. Belmont, Ca.: Wadsworth.

Needham, Rodney, 1971. Remarks on the Analysis of Kinship and Marriage. In Rethinking Kinship and Marriage. Rodney Needham, ed. pp.1–34. London: Tavistock.

Newman, Philip L., 1965. Knowing the Gururumba. New York: Holt, Rinehart and Winston.

Newman, Philip L. and David J. Boyd, 1982. The Making of Men: Ritual and Meaning in Awa Male Initiation. In Rituals of Manhood: Male Initiation in Papua New Guinea. Gilbert H. Herdt, ed. pp.239–285. Berkeley: University of California Press.

Newton, D., 1972. Art. In Encyclopaedia of Papua and New Guinea. Peter Ryan, ed. pp.29–50. Melbourne: Melbourne University Press and the University of Papua New Guinea.

Nilles, Johann, 1939. Mädchen-Reifefeierbei den Östlichen Waugla im Bismarck-gebirge Neuguineas. Anthropos 34:402–406.

Norbeck, Edward, Donald E. Walker, and Mimi Cohen, 1962. The Interpretation of Data: Puberty Rites. American Anthropologist 64:463–485.

O'Brien, Denise and Sharon W. Tiffany, eds., 1984. Rethinking Women's Roles: Perspectives from the Pacific. Berkeley: University of California Press.

Ortiz, Alfonso, 1972. Ritual Drama and the Pueblo World View. *In* New Perspectives on the Pueblos. Alfonso Ortiz, ed. pp.135–161. Albuquerque: University of New Mexico Press.

Ortner, Sherry B., 1974. Is Female to Male as Nature Is to Culture? *In* Woman, Culture, and Society. Michelle Zimbalist Rosaldo and Louise Lamphere, eds. pp.67–87. Stanford: Stanford University Press.

———, 1981. Gender and Sexuality in Hierarchical Societies: The Case of Polynesia and Some Comparative Implications. *In* Sexual Meanings: The Cultural Construction of Gender and Sexuality. Sherry B. Ortner and Harriet Whitehead, eds. pp.359–409. Cambridge: Cambridge University Press.

———, 1990. Gender Hegemonies. Cultural Critique 4:35–80.

Ortner, Sherry B. and Harriet Whitehead, 1981. Introduction: Accounting for Sexual Meanings. *In* Sexual Meanings: The Cultural Construction of Gender and Sexuality. Sherry B. Ortner and Harriet Whitehead, eds., pp.1–27. Cambridge: Cambridge University Press.

Paige, Karen and Jeffrey M. Paige, 1981. The Politics of Reproductive Ritual. Berkeley: University of California Press.

Poole, Fitz John Porter, 1982. The Ritual Forging of Identity: Aspects of Person and Self in Bimin-Kuskusmin Male Initiation. *In* Rituals of Manhood: Male Initiation in Papua New Guinea. Gilbert H. Herdt, ed. pp.99–154. Berkeley: University of California Press.

Rabinow, Paul, 1977. Reflections on Fieldwork in Morocco. Berkeley: University of California Press.

Radcliffe-Brown, A. R., 1948. The Andaman Islanders. Glencoe: Free Press.

———, 1956. Structure and Function in Primitive Society. Glencoe: Free Press.

Rappaport, Roy A., 1971. Ritual, Sanctity, and Cybernetics. American Anthropologist 73:59–76.

Read, K. E., 1952. Nama Cult of the Central Highlands, New Guinea. Oceania 23:1–25.

———, 1965. The High Valley. New York: Charles Scribner's Sons.

———, 1984. The *Nama* Cult Recalled. *In* Ritualized Homosexuality in Melanesia. Gilbert H. Herdt, ed. pp.211–247. Berkeley: University of California Press.

Redfield, James M., 1975. Nature and Culture in the Iliad: The Tragedy of Hector. Chicago: University of Chicago Press.

Reik, Theodor, 1946. Ritual: Four Psycho-Analytic Studies. New York: Farrar, Strauss and Co.

Reiter, Rayna R., ed., 1975a. Towards an Anthropology of Women. New York: Monthly Review Press.

———, 1975b. Introduction. *In* Toward an Anthropology of Women. Rayna R. Reiter, ed. pp.11–19. New York: Monthly Review Press.

Richards, Audrey Isabel, 1956. Chisungu: A Girls' Initiation Ceremony among the Bemba of Zambia. London: Tavistock.

Rigby, Peter, 1967. The Structural Context of Girls' Puberty Rites. Man (N.S.) 2:434–444.

Rivière, Peter, 1984. Individual and Society in Guiana. Cambridge: Cambridge University Press.

Rodman, M. C., 1981. A Boundary and a Bridge: Women's Pig-Killing as a Border-Crossing between Spheres of Exchange in East Aoba. In Vanuatu: Politics, Economics and Ritual in Island Melanesia. M. R. Allen, ed. pp.85–104. Sydney: Academic Press.

Róheim, Gèza, 1969[1945]. The Eternal Ones of the Dream. New York: International Universities Press.

Rosaldo, Michelle Zimbalist, 1974. Woman, Culture, and Society: A Theoretical Overview. In Woman, Culture, and Society. Michelle Zimbalist Rosaldo and Louise Lamphere, eds. pp.17–42. Stanford: Stanford University Press.

———, 1980. The Use and Abuse of Anthropology: Reflections on Feminism and Cross-Cultural Understanding. Signs 5:389–417.

Rosaldo, Michelle Zimbalist and Louise Lamphere, eds., 1974. Woman, Culture, and Society. Stanford: Stanford University Press.

Roscoe, Paul B., 1994 Who are the Ndu?: Ecology, Migration, and Linguistic and Cultural Change in the Sepik Basin. In Migration and Transformations: Regional Perspectives on New Guinea. Andrew J. Strathern and Gabriele Stürzenhofecker, eds. pp.49–84. Pittsburgh: University of Pittsburgh Press.

———, 1988. Images of Women: Female-Centred Rites and Local Polity among the Yangoru Boiken. Paper Presented at the Annual Meetings of the Association for Social Anthropology in Oceania, 1988. Savannah Ga.

———, 1989. The Flight from the Fen: The Prehistoric Migrations of the Boiken of the East Sepik Province, Papua New Guinea. Oceania 60:139–154.

———, 1990a. Male Initiation Among the Yangoru Boiken. In Sepik Heritage: Tradition and Change in Papua New Guinea. Nancy Lutkehaus Christian Kaufmann, William E. Mitchell, Douglas Newton, Lita Osmundsen, and Meinhard Schuster, eds. pp.402–413. Durham: Carolina Academic Press.

———, 1990b. The Bow and Spreadnet: Ecological Origins of Hunting Technology. American Anthropologist 92:691–701.

———, 1991. The Yangoru Boiken. In Encyclopedia of World Cultures, vol. 2: Oceania. Terence E. Hays, ed. pp.388–391. Boston: G. K. Hall.

———, 1994. Amity and Aggression: A Symbolic Theory of Incest. Man (N.S.) 29:49–76.

———, 1995. Of Power and Menace: Sepik Art as an Affecting Presence. The Journal of the Royal Anthropological Institute 1:1–21.

Ross, John Alan, 1965. The Puberty Ceremony of the Chimbu Girl in the Eastern Highlands of New Guinea. Anthropos 60:423–432.

Rubel, Paula G. and Abraham Rosman, 1978. Your Own Pigs You May Not Eat: A Comparative Study of New Guinea Societies. Chicago: University of Chicago Press.

Rubin, Gayle, 1975. The Traffic in Women: Notes on the "Political Economy" of Sex. *In* Toward an Anthropology of Women. Rayna R. Reiter, ed. pp.157–210. New York: Monthly Review Press.

Sacks, Karen, 1979. Sisters and Wives: The Past and Future of Sexual Equality. Westport: Greenwood.

Sahlins, Marshall, 1981. Historical Metaphors and Mythical Realities: Structure in the Early History of the Sandwich Islands Kingdom. Ann Arbor: University of Michigan Press.

———, 1983. Raw Women, Cooked Men and Other "Great Things" of the Fiji-Islands. *In* The Ethnography of Cannibalism. Paula Brown and Donald Tuzin, eds. pp.72–93. Washington: Society for Psychological Anthropology.

Sanday, Peggy R., 1974. Female Status in the Public Domain. *In* Woman, Culture, and Society. Michelle Zimbalist Rosaldo and Louise Lamphere, eds. pp.189–206. Stanford: Stanford University Press.

Scaglion, Richard, 1978. Seasonal Births in a Western Abelam Village, Papua New Guinea. Human Biology 50:313–323.

———, 1986. Sexual Segregation and Ritual Pollution in Abelam Society. *In* Self, Sex, and Gender in Cross-Cultural Fieldwork. Tony Larry Whitehead and Mary Ellen Conaway, eds. pp.151–163. Urbana: University of Illinois Press.

Schapera, I., 1953. Some Comments on Comparative Method in Social Anthropology. American Anthropologist 55:353–362.

Schindlbeck, Markus, 1980. Sago bei den Sawos (Mittelsepik, Papua New Guinea). Basler Beiträge zur Ethnologie, vol. 19. Basel: Wepf.

———, 1981. Sawos: Einbrennen von Mustern in die Haut. Göttingen: Publikationen zu Wissenschaftlichen Filmen.

Schlegel, Alice and Herbert Barry, III, 1979. Adolescent Initiation Ceremonies: A Cross-Cultural Code. Ethnology 18:199–210.

———, 1980. The Evolutionary Significance of Adolescent Initiation Ceremonies. American Ethnologist 7:696–715.

Schmid, Jürg and Christin Kocher-Schmid, 1992. Söhne des Krokodils. Männerhausrituale und Initiation in Yensan, Zentral-Iatmul, East Sepik Province, Papua New Guinea. Basler Beiträge zur Ethnologie, vol. 36. Basel: Wepf.

Schmidt, P. Joseph, 1923–24. Die Ethnographie der Nor-Papua (Murik-Kaup-Karau) bei Dallmannhafen, New Guinea. Anthropos 18–19:700–732.

———, 1926. Die Ethnographie der Nor-Papua (Murik-Kaup-Karau) bei Dallmannhafen, New Guinea. Anthropos 21:33–71.

———, 1933. Neue Beiträge zur Ethnographie der Nor-Papua (Neuguinea). Anthropos 28:321–354; 29:663–682.

Schneider, David M., 1976. The Meaning of Incest. Journal of the Polynesian Society 85:149–169.

———, 1984. A Critique of the Study of Kinship. Ann Arbor: University of Michigan Press.

Schomburgk, Robert, 1844. On the Natives of Guiana. Journal of the Ethnological Society of London 1:253–276.

Schulz, Emily and Robert H. Lavenda, 1990. Cultural Anthropology: A Perspective on the Human Condition. St. Paul: West.

Scoditti, Giancarlo M. G., 1990. Kitawa: A Linguistic and Aesthetic Analysis of Visual Art in Melanesia. New York: Mouton de Gruyter.

Sexton, Lorraine Dusak, 1982. Wok Meri: A Women's Savings and Exchange System in Highland Papua New Guinea. Oceania 52:167–198.

———, 1986. Mothers of Money, Daughters of Coffee: The Wok Meri Movement. Ann Arbor: UMI Research Press.

Shore, Bradd, 1981. Sexuality and Gender in Samoa: Conceptions and Missed Conceptions. In Sexual Meanings: The Cultural Construction of Gender and Sexuality. Sherry B. Ortner and Harriet Whitehead, eds. pp.192–215. Cambridge: Cambridge University Press.

Silverman, Eric K., 1993. Tambunum: New Perspectives on Eastern Iatmul (Sepik River, Papua New Guinea) Kinship, Marriage, and Society. Ph.D. Dissertation, University of Minnesota.

Snitow, Ann Barr, Christine Stansell, and Sharon Thompson, eds., 1983. Powers of Desire: The Politics of Sexuality. New York: Monthly Review Press.

Spiro, Melvin, 1982. Oedipus in the Trobriands. Chicago: University of Chicago Press.

Stoler, Ann L., 1989. Making Empire Respectable: The Politics of Race and Sexual Morality in 20th-Century Colonial Cultures. American Ethnologist 16:634–660.

———, 1991. Carnal Knowledge and Imperial Power: Gender, Race, and Morality in Colonial Asia. In Gender at the Crossroads of Knowledge: Feminist Anthropology in the Postmodern Era. Micaela di Leonardo, ed. pp.51–101. Berkeley: University of California Press.

Strathern, Marilyn, 1972. Women in Between: Female Roles in a Male World. New York: Seminar Press.

———, 1976. An Anthropological Perspective. In Exploring Sex Differences. Barbara Lloyd and John Archer, eds. pp.49–70. London: Academic Press.

———, 1978. The Achievement of Sex: Paradoxes in Hagen Gender-Thinking. In Yearbook of Symbolic Anthropology. E. Schwimmer, ed. pp.171–202. London: Hurst.

———, 1980. No Nature, No Culture: The Hagen Case. In Nature, Culture and Gender. Carol P. MacCormack and Marilyn Strathern, eds. pp.174–222. Cambridge: Cambridge University Press.

———, 1981a. Culture in a Netbag: The Manufacture of a Subdiscipline in Anthropology. Man (N.S.) 16:665–688.

———, 1981b. Self-interest and the Social Good: Some Implications of Hagen Gender Imagery. In Sexual Meanings: The Cultural Construction of Gender and Sexuality. Sherry B. Ortner and Harriet Whitehead, eds. pp.166–191. Cambridge: Cambridge University Press.

———, 1984. Domesticity and the Denigration of Women. In Rethinking Women's Roles: Perspectives from the Pacific. Denise O'Brien and Sharon W. Tiffany, eds. pp.13–31. Berkeley: University of California Press.

———, 1986a. Dual Models and Multiple Persons: Gender in Melanesia. Notes Presented at the Annual Meetings of the American Anthropological Association, 1986.

————, 1986b. An Awkward Relationship: The Case of Feminism and Anthropology. Signs 12:276–292.

————, 1987a. Introduction. *In* Dealing with Inequality: Analysing Gender Relations in Melanesia and Beyond. Marilyn Strathern, ed. pp.1–32. Cambridge: Cambridge University Press.

————, 1987b. Making Incomplete: A Comment on Female Initiation in Melanesia. Paper presented at the Annual Meetings of the Association for Social Anthropology in Oceania, 1988.

————, 1988. The Gender of the Gift. Berkeley: University of California Press.

————, 1992. Reproducing the Future: Anthropology, Kinship and the New Reproductive Technologies. New York: Routledge.

————, 1993. Making Incomplete. *In* Carved Flesh/Cast Selves: Gendered Symbols and Social Practices. Vigdis Broch-Due, Ingrid Rudie, and Tone Bleie, eds. pp.41–51. Providence: Berg.

Talle, Aud, 1993. Transforming Women into "Pure" Agnates: Aspects of Female Infibulation in Somalia. *In* Carved Flesh/Cast Selves: Gendered Symbols and Social Practices. Vigdis Broch-Due, Ingrid Rudie, and Tone Bleie, eds. pp.83–106. Providence: Berg.

Terrell, John, 1986. Prehistory of the Pacific Islands: A Story of Variation in Language, Customs, and Human Biology. New York: Cambridge University Press.

Thomas, Nicholas, 1989. The Force of Ethnology: Origins and Significance of the Melanesia/Polynesia Division. Current Anthropology 30: 27–41.

————, 1991. Entangled Objects: Exchange, Material Culture and Colonialism in the Pacific. Cambridge: Harvard University Press.

Tiffany, Sharon W., 1984. Introduction: Feminist Perceptions in Anthropology. *In* Rethinking Women's Roles: Perspectives from the Pacific. Denise O'Brien and Sharon W. Tiffany, eds. pp.1–11. Berkeley: University of California Press.

Townsend, Patricia K., 1969. Subsistence and Social Organization in a New Guinea Society. Ph.D. Dissertation. University of Michigan.

————, 1971. New Guinea Sago Gatherers: A Study of Demography in Relation to Subsistence. Ecology of Food and Nutrition 1:19–24.

————, 1974. Sago Production in a New Guinea Economy. Human Ecology 2:217–236.

————, 1978. The Politics of Mobility among the Sanio-Hiowe. Anthropological Quarterly 51:27–35.

————, 1985. Infant Mortality in the Saniyo-Hiyowe Population, Ambunti District, East Sepik Province. Papua New Guinea Medical Journal 28:177–182.

————, 1990. *Our* Women Are Okay: Aspects of Hiyewe Women's Status. *In* Sepik Heritage: Tradition and Change in Papua New Guinea. Nancy Lutkehaus, Christian Kaufmann, William E. Mitchell, Douglas Newton, Lita Osmundsen, and Meinhard Schuster, eds. pp.374–379. Durham: Carolina Academic Press.

Turner, Victor, 1969. The Ritual Process: Structure and Anti-Structure. Ithaca: Cornell University Press.

Tuzin, Donald, 1972. Yam Symbolism in the Sepik: An Interpretative Account. Southwestern Journal of Anthropology 28:230–254.

————, 1980. The Voice of the Tambaran: Truth and Illusion in Ilahita Arapesh Religion. Berkeley: University of California Press.

van Baal, Jan, 1966. Dema: Description and Analysis of Marind-Anim Culture (South New Guinea). The Hague: Martinus Nijhoff.

Van Gennep, Arnold, 1960[1908]. The Rites of Passage. Monika B. Vizedom and Gabrielle L. Caffee, trans. Chicago: University of Chicago Press.

Vance, Carole, ed., 1984. Pleasure and Danger: Exploring Female Sexuality. Boston: Routledge.

Vorman, P., 1915. Initiationsfeiern der Jünglinge und Mädchen bei den Monumbo-Papua. Anthropos 10:159–179.

Wagner, Roy, 1991. The Fractal Person. In Big Men and Great Men: Personifications of Power in Melanesia. Maurice Godelier and Marilyn Strathern, eds. pp.159–173. Cambridge: Cambridge University Press.

Walker, Alice and Pratibha Parmar, 1993. Warrior Marks. New York: Harcourt and Brace.

Walker, James Broom, 1876. Notes on the Politics, Religion, and Commerce of Old Calabar. Journal of the Anthropological Institute 6:119–124.

Warry, Wayne, 1986. Kafaina: Female Wealth and Power in Chuave, Papua New Guinea. Oceania 57:4–21.

Wedgwood, Camilla, n.d. The Camilla H. Wedgwood Archives. University of Sydney.

————, 1933. Girls' Puberty Rites in Manam Island, New Guinea. Oceania 4:132–155.

————, 1934. Report on Research in Manam Island, Mandated Territory of New Guinea. Oceania 4:373–403.

————, 1937. Women in Manam. Oceania 7:401–428; 8:170–192.

————, 1938. The Life of Children in Manam. Oceania 9:1–29.

Weiner, Annette B., 1976. Women of Value, Men of Renown: New Perspectives in Trobriand Exchange. Austin: University of Texas Press.

————, 1978. The Reproductive Model in Trobriand Society. Mankind 11:175–186.

————, 1979. Trobriand Kinship from Another View: The Reproductive Power of Women and Men. Man (N.S.) 14:328–348.

————, 1980. Reproduction: A Replacement for Reciprocity. American Ethnologist 7:71–85.

————, 1987. Introduction. In B. Malinowski, The Sexual Life of Savages in North-Western Melanesia. pp.xiii–xlix. Boston: Beacon Press.

————, 1988. The Trobrianders of Papua New Guinea. New York: Holt, Rinehart and Winston.

————, 1992. Inalienable Possessions: The Paradox of Keeping-While-Giving. Berkeley: University of California Press.

Weiss, Florence, 1994. Die Unterdrückung der Fraueninitiation. Zum Wandel des Ritualsystems bei den Iatmul. In Geschichte und mündliche Überlieferung in Ozeanien. Brigitta Hauser-Schäublin, ed. pp.237–259. Basler Beiträge zur Ethnologie, vol. 37. Basel: Wepf.

White, Geoffrey M. and John Kirkpatrick, eds., 1985. Person, Self, and Experience: Exploring Pacific Ethnopsychologies. Berkeley: University of California Press.

Whitehead, Harriet, 1981. The Bow and the Burden Strap: A New Look at Institutionalized Homosexuality in Native North America. *In* Sexual Meanings: The Cultural Construction of Gender and Sexuality. Sherry B. Ortner and Harriet Whitehead, eds. pp.80–115. Cambridge: Cambridge University Press.

———, 1986. The Varieties of Fertility Cultism in New Guinea. American Ethnologist 13:80–99, 271–289.

———, 1987. Fertility and Exchange in New Guinea. *In* Gender and Kinship: Essays Toward a Unified Analysis. Jane Fishburne Collier and Sylvia Junko Yanagisako, eds. pp.244–267. Stanford: Stanford University Press.

Whiteman, J. 1965. Girls' Puberty Ceremonies amongst the Chimbu. Anthropos 60:410–422.

Whiting, John W. M., 1941. Becoming a Kwoma: Teaching and Learning in a New Guinea Tribe. New Haven: Yale University Press.

Whiting, John W. M., Richard Kluckhohn, and Albert Anthony, 1958. The Function of Male Initiation Ceremonies at Puberty. *In* Readings in Social Psychology. Eleanor E. Maccoby, Theodore M. Newcomb, and Eugene L. Hartley, eds. pp.359–370. New York: Holt.

Whyte, Martin King, 1978. The Status of Women in Preindustrial Societies. Princeton: Princeton University Press.

Williams, Walter L., 1986. The Spirit and the Flesh: Sexual Diversity in American Indian Culture. Boston: Beacon Press.

Williamson, Margaret Holmes, 1979. Cicatrisation of Women among the Kwoma. Mankind 12:35–41.

———, 1987. Women's Coming of Age in Kwoma Culture. Paper presented at the Annual Meetings of the Association for Social Anthropology in Oceania, Monterey Ca.

Yanagisako, Sylvia Junko and Jane Fishburne Collier, 1987. Toward a Unified Analysis of Gender and Kinship. *In* Gender and Kinship: Essays Toward a Unified Analysis. Jane Fishburne Collier and Sylvia Junko Yanagisako, eds. pp.14–50. Stanford: Stanford University Press.

Young, Frank W., 1965. Initiation Ceremonies: A Cross-Cultural Study of Status Dramatization. Indianapolis: Bobbs-Merrill.

INDEX